Please, Don't Send Me Flowers

Lianne Saffer

Cover design by Bethany Bauman
Cover photo by Gia Goodrich
Author photo by Mera Eischell
Edited by Valerie Cervarich Writing Help KC
Interior layout by Debbie Lum

To request permission, contact the author at www.liannesaffer.com

ISBN: 978-1-7359266-0-5 (paperback)
        978-1-7359266-1-2 (hardcover)
        978-1-7359266-2-9 (ebook)

I'm the type of girl that puts my keys in the fridge when I get home and searches for my phone while I'm talking on it. I don't remember what my most embarrassing moment was or what I ate for dinner last night—but I do remember these stories. These stories are told truthfully to the best of my ability, although others may remember them differently. All that to say, while my memory can be shit sometimes—my integrity is not. Some conversations in this book are recollections and have been told in such a way to evoke the feeling and meaning of what was said or felt in the particular instance; what it felt like to be in my body as the one absorbing it all. I am not here to vilify anyone as I believe that people can change and we all have our moments when we are not, in fact, perfect. In an effort to keep identities private and maintain anonymity, I have changed or removed some identifying details and names. The truth is, the names don't matter anyway. This story is about things that happened to me and how I felt about them. My name is Lianne, and I don't like flowers.

"So often in life, things that you regard as an impediment turn out to be great, good fortune."

—Ruth Bader Ginsburg

Contents

Prologue

It's interesting when you have a lot to say but you don't know how to say it without offending someone. I mean, I guess I'm less of a people pleaser than I used to be, but exploiting facts can be harmful to people.

I went back and forth over writing this book for years. Then the last segment woke me up. I realize that people will react the way they want to react. And that's based on their own emotion about a situation, not mine. The facts are facts. The world doesn't speak enough about real struggles, or real joys for that matter.

Everything that has happened in my life has happened to other people. I'm not that special. I'm not reinventing the shit-wheel. However, I AM talking about it—the good, the bad, the ugly, the joyful, and the what the fuck! Communication is helpful. And I often wonder how things would have played out differently for me if I'd had exposure to more people going through similar situations.

I've gotten quite used to ruffling feathers in the last few years. Chalk it up to life lessons and finding my voice along the way. Well, and the humbling realization that shit you didn't think could happen to you does, and will in fact, happen to you...without warning. And sometimes it keeps happening to you. And then, once you feel like you might be shit out of luck, life dumps a teeny bit more on you just to see what you are made of.

In the early years of said shit happening, I was living a boring and miserable existence. Now don't get me wrong, it was lively enough on paper. I was what they call *happy*. My life kept me on my toes, but it wasn't the life I wanted. It was the one that my mom, dad, religion, husband, and society wanted for me:

> You should follow the rules. Find a man who can provide for you and wait to have sex until you are married. Go to church and pray for the gays and their lifestyle. Have babies and raise them the same as you, with the same beliefs and so on. Because that's what makes good people— playing it safe and being the same.

So in that case, I deserved a miserable existence. My world was small, and my mind was small. But I also didn't realize that I had a choice. I was lacking the emotional skills needed to break free. I always knew I wanted a big life, I just didn't know what it would look like or how it would feel.

Sometimes life can feel like a roller coaster that you aren't tall enough to ride yet. Or maybe you aren't old enough, your parents won't let you, or you can't keep your limbs inside of the cart that goes 150 miles per hour. It's like when you finally make it to the top of the roller coaster where there is simultaneous fear and excitement, and it's too late to back out. Yet, you don't know if you are going to smile and scream the whole way down or barf off the side. It can feel like you're teetering on the edge between triumph and struggle. There's adrenaline on both sides.

I'm not sure where or who I would be without the last fifteen years of my life. Sometimes I'm not sure where or who I am now. But what I can tell you is I am SO insanely thankful for all of the shit that life threw at me, and that I was thrust down the steepest part of the roller coaster when I was too short and not at all ready.

At times, I completely fell off the roller coaster. It woke me up. It shook me to my core. It made me proud, compassionate, and vulnerable. I learned strength, resilience, and a love I didn't believe in. I learned how to look on the bright side even when my world felt shattered. It gave me perspective, it made me fall head over heels for my life, and it all felt like freedom in the end. Darkness and uncertainty brought the gift of transformation, even if I struggled to see my way out of it.

If you are in the thick of the shit, I encourage you to press on and read how this all went down for me. If you aren't, know that at some point you will be, or someone close to you will be...and read on. We can all learn from each other.

PART I

The Big D

1: Small town roots

I've flirted with emotional and physical death and decided neither were for me. I spent years suffocating in my own thoughts and traditional values. I was born whole but was reprogrammed to think that I was less than and never could be. I've replayed and accepted my experiences for what they were as I planned my own funeral from a hospital bed.

People have never really known what to do with me. As it turns out, my life hasn't really known what to do with me either. I am blunt and opinionated, yet well-spoken and tactful when needed. I could scare the shit out of someone or make them feel completely at home, depending on what the situation called for. I could be set off like a loose cannon or stay dormant like a volcano that was never meant to blow, yet there is always heat inside of me. I've been told I can be intimidating, but I think it's just because I know what I want and don't tolerate bullshit. I'm not a tomboy, but I'm not a girly girl either. I want to wear heels and lashes, but I also want to set things on fire and cut things down with my chainsaw. I embrace being unpredictable. In fact, I prefer myself that way.

I am someone who has spent my whole life waiting for shit to hit the fan. I don't necessarily live in fear, but I used to always wonder when something bad would happen in my life because I seemed to have it pretty good. Growing up I felt like someone always had an addict sibling, or a parent who had died, or a sister who got knocked up in high school, or a brother who was having an affair, or a grandpa with cancer. You get the idea. I always felt like it was only a matter of time before shit would hit the fan for my family. I just didn't realize that all the shit raining down would all be my own.

Thankfully during my childhood, nobody in my immediate family had died, gotten sick, or was an addict. We were a picture-perfect all-American family of four. We were established in the 80s, went to private school, ate stroganoff for dinner, and watched TGIF on Fridays—or at least the first two shows because I had a bedtime, and *Step by Step* was a bit risky with the split family and all. We went to church on Sunday mornings, and we all got along. And if we didn't, we sure as hell didn't say anything about it. All that to say, life was good. It was safe and comfortable. Yet, I was always uncomfortable, like I didn't fit the family mold.

I'd like to think that I had a seemingly normal childhood, besides the fact that my parents never bought me a Big Wheel. Something about not having enough money or some garbage excuse like that. (Just kidding, now that I am a parent, I realize how valid this excuse is.) But as it turns out, Big Wheels were a rich kid toy, and we ate canned chili for dinner— you do the math. They decided a Skip-It would do just fine. There is nothing quite like tripping over a neon pink plastic rope that attaches to your own foot, just for entertainment. Despite all that, I had a great childhood. Apparently, a Big Wheel wasn't necessary. I had what I needed, I played outside, and I was spoiled enough without having all the excess. Good work, Mom and Dad.

My parents loved me completely...like number-one-fan kind of love. I grew up in a home where my mom didn't work. I mean, she did. She drove me everywhere, cleaned, and cooked for our family. I guess they'd call her a stay-at-home mom. I'm calling it being a saint. My dad owned his own company and worked Monday through Friday for the most part, coming home as early as possible to be with the family. I remember on Fridays he would come home for the day around lunch. We would ride our bikes down the mile-long hill to the end of the road, past the fields and the cows, and a few houses, to where the hill hit the main road. We'd wait for him to pick us up. He would load my brother and me and our bikes in the back of the truck, and drive us back up the hill, past the cows and the vineyards, to our house.

My childhood was fun. I didn't suffer any major trauma, and we lived in the middle of nowhere so I got to learn how to be a little bit of a hick and have pet cows and journal by the creek after eating shit falling off my go-kart on the way down to the water. My brother and I picked mistletoe from the trees around the holidays and sold it to our neighbors. In the summers, we got paid five cents per weed to pull thistles from the fields. The air always smelled like grass, and I fell asleep to the sound of irrigation sprinklers outside my windows at night.

My teenage years weren't so pretty. I liked my parents, but only in the way that teenagers like their parents. Basically my like came out as hate when I was told I had a curfew, or I couldn't go out with a friend. It was feeling embarrassed of every single breath that left their body. And when I was on my period, well, they just absolutely sucked and couldn't do anything right. In my mind, they knew nothing and couldn't relate to me in the slightest. But we had good snacks, so I had to play it cool because my friends came over a lot. A typical teen. I was a dick and self-absorbed. Sorry about that, Mom and Dad. But I'm sure the payback clock is ticking away as I type this.

I kept my circle tight and my priorities straight. I had the opportunity to graduate early because my grades were so high. But I chose to take one class my senior year so I could graduate with my friends. I held down three jobs that year to save money, going to school two mornings a week and working the rest of the time.

I loved working. I loved being good at things, feeling valued, and getting paid. It was a rush, and it also made me fiercely independent, almost to a fault. I was the only kid I knew who paid for most of my first car, gas, and so on by myself. I didn't want to rely on anybody, not even my parents. Looking back, I wish I would have been a little more relaxed about it. What kid wants the stress of their own bills for as long as possible? Yes, I had massive saving skills, but I missed out on so much of just being a teen by working so much. My friends were always hanging out, and I would have to meet them after work. I worked like I was caring for a family of four and had to make a mortgage payment.

And then I grew up and got married. I wasn't technically a grown up though—I was barely twenty-two years old. It was more like the after-teen phase, or the childhood afterlife. It was too young. We should have an infant, toddler, kid, pre-teen, teen, POST-TEEN, and then young adult, adult, post-adult, middle-aged, etc.

Anyway, THEN CAME THE BIG D...

Now get your head out of the gutter, we are talking about divorce here, people. That's when shit first hit the fan.

* * *

I was once married to someone who made me feel like I was the size of a flea. Someone who hired a private investigator to follow me around town and told me the only way to fix a grumpy man was to have sex with him. I married someone who made me question every word that left my mouth. Someone who told me I was crazy when I tried to express my feelings. I married a man who could charm any living thing and manipulate it all the same without them knowing. I married someone who kept my finances from me and chose a soccer game over his wife's thirtieth birthday party. I married a man who made me feel like I was too much of this or not enough of that. I married someone who wrote down a strategy that was merely "drag my feet" when I asked for a divorce. I married someone that gave me eleven years of lessons, quite a few laughs, more heartaches, and two beautiful children.

This someone also happened to be my first kiss.

I was in the eighth grade when he kissed me. He was wearing wide white skater shoes, a band tee, a silver ball necklace, and had frosted piss-yellow spiky tips on his gel-lacquered hair. He had a bad boy/good boy vibe and was what we called "fine" in 1999. I was smitten.

He had taken me to see the movie *Never Been Kissed* and then kissed me outside of the movie theater after the show. And by kiss, I mean he wrapped his scrawny, white, freckled fifteen-year-old arms around my waist, and leaned in for the world's shortest, driest peck. It almost felt like his lips were wrapped inward as we awkwardly tilted our heads to the right and the left until we found the angle that wasn't going to bang our foreheads together.

Then we finally landed *the kiss*. I got butterflies and instantly fell in love and wanted to run away at the same time.

I think these are all normal feelings for a fourteen-year-old girl. It's a confusing time in life. Everything makes you cry. At any moment, a word from a friend, boy, or parent can completely shatter your world. Any guy that gives you the time of day is somehow the love of your life, and every break up is a volcano of emotions where the ashes don't settle for at least three weeks, or twenty-four hours, depending on when the next boy passes you a note asking you to check yes or no.

The reality is, I got home, freaked the fuck out, and broke it off. I claimed it was a "God thing" because that was the easiest way out without having to explain myself. If he wanted an explanation, he could take it up with the man upstairs. *You can't argue with the Lord, right?* I mean, there is no way he could be in the same conversation that me and the big man were having.

But the truth is, I didn't even ask the Lord. I was never quite sure if I could hear him answering, so I just trusted my gut. Therefore, in this case, my gut is god. I wish I would have realized this sooner. When people say trust your gut, just know that your gut is god.

I did date a bit here and there in the years following, but he's the only one that made it more than one day to two months. (My wife likes to tell me that it's because I was gay, but I disagree, even though that would be a much easier way to explain it all.) The truth is, I just got bored, and my expectations were high. None of those guys could level up.

We reconnected in 2004 after I had moved home from a short stint in Santa Barbara, California, attending photography school. Yes, I dropped out. I had been swallowed in an art school full of trust funds, drug addicts, and skinny blondes. There was (un)fortunately no way I was going to make myself into any of those to fit in.

I was eighteen years old when we reconnected. I ran into him one night, and I thought he was cute. The next day, I looked him up in the yellow pages, left a voicemail on his home phone, and we started dating very shortly after. I guess I was forward.

* * *

But I should have known he wasn't the right fit a few months after we started dating the second time around. He said that he was uncomfortable with how close me and one of my guy friends were. I also should have seen the writing on the wall that said CONTROLLING in neon letters, or maybe it said,

RUN FAST. It must have been very blurry. I was young, and turns out I didn't have a backbone. So I started seeing my friend less and less to appease my boyfriend. I still regret losing that friendship. If anyone ever tells you to lose a friendship because they are jealous, lose them and keep the friendship.

We dated for almost four years before we got married. But ages eighteen to twenty-two are no ages to be in a serious relationship if you ask me. I was a child, and I didn't know that I could have a different life than the ones my parents had. It seemed like the easiest thing to do was to just stay with the guy who liked me enough, get married, and have some kids. *After all, isn't that what life is supposed to look like?*

It was the safe route. I'd wondered what would happen if I broke up with him and never found someone else. Being single in my early twenties? That would have been awesome! Yes, I missed out on so many drinks being purchased for me at the bars. But more importantly, I missed out on a lot of discovering who I was.

There were multiple breakups during the years we dated. I didn't like being broken up with. I was a winner, I was cute, and goddamnit, I was a catch.

Every time we got back together, he promised to change. Each break up was a bit more intense and completely necessary. I knew we were terrible for each other. I felt horrible about myself when I was around him. But I also wanted to prove to myself that I was lovable. It was a game. When he got me back, he would spend weeks making me feel like he couldn't live without me, like I was the best thing in the world. I thought that maybe he was good for me after all.

The relationship felt extremely manipulative. I said one thing, and he twisted it to mean something else. There were small jabs about me or my character. There was damage to my self-esteem, my self-worth, and who I was. There were the warnings of "you shouldn't eat that" and the small innuendos of where a woman belongs. He was also vocal about what a woman deserves, which turns out, wasn't much. Even as a joke it stung. There was the silent treatment.

I never felt smaller or like I had more to prove than when I was with him. I also never felt more disposable. It was a hamster wheel that I kept flying out of and climbing back in because it was all I knew.

He only wanted to hang out with me if his friends weren't available, and if they were, I was to basically cook food and fetch beers and be the butt of sarcastic jokes. I would clean up the kitchen after they left, while he passed out on the couch without helping me at all. I didn't even drink beer. My association with beer was a drunk guy that burps and farts a lot, so I really had no interest in it, yet I was always taking bottles from the table to the recycling bin.

When I was upset, I was "too emotional," and he was the "logical" one. But if you ask me, there is zero logic in not listening to your partner and shutting them down. He told me I was "acting crazy" or "sounded insane." When I was quiet he would ask, "What's wrong with you?" I would cook every night and then he would sit with his phone or watch TV as I cleaned up the mess. When I asked about his past girlfriend, he told me it was none of my business and would change the subject. When I told him what I wanted to do with my life I was met with a laugh, a "good luck," or "how do you think you are going to do that?"

At one point when my ex and I were dating, my roommate's boyfriend bought her flowers. He was always surprising her or leaving her notes. I asked my boyfriend why he never did anything like that. I was always trying to be a good enough girlfriend that he would notice and do something thoughtful. His response was that a guy only bought flowers when he wanted to get laid. Now, mind you, my roommate DID end up pregnant post-flowers, but that's beside the point. I wondered if maybe he would buy me flowers or leave me a note just because after we got married.

I later found out that he would never think of anyone but himself, and that also, I hated flowers. Looking back, I wonder if he's the reason why. Flowers = Assholes.

I started to shut down. I didn't know how to communicate when everything that came out of my mouth was so skillfully manipulated. I started to communicate with him via email. That way, I could make sure that it was in writing, and he couldn't interrupt me.

Writing saved me and my sanity. I saved every one of those conversations. I read them to my best friend as they were happening to make sure that I wasn't actually crazy. She always confirmed that I was calm, cool, collected, a catch, and in fact, not crazy.

* * *

One of the only sweet gestures that my boyfriend ever did, was to write me a song...to break up with me. Has anyone ever written you a breakup song? No? Weird. It was called "Goodbye." A brilliant name.

He recorded it at home and had burned it to a CD that said, "For Lianne," written in sharpie. Back in those days, if a guy handed you a burned CD, you knew it was the real deal. Those were YOUR songs as a couple.

He popped it into the stereo in the dash of his car so we could listen to it together. We had been hanging out all night, and this beautiful compact disc was about to be the most— okay, only—romantic thing he had ever done for me. I couldn't wait to hear it. *Maybe he was finally catching on to the whole romance thing.*

But as the words started playing, I realized I was being broken up with. Again. My body started to shake, and I avoided eye contact at all costs because I was absolutely mortified. Completely blindsided, I was stuck in the passenger seat of a two-door 1987 something or other with one working headlight, being broken up with via song, after dinner and making out. I was still buckled up for safety, for Christ's sake.

And that was that. I didn't know whether to laugh or to cry.

He was moving to Portland. "Long distance doesn't work," he blurted out, "I love you." But what I heard was *I don't love you enough* and *you aren't worth it*. If you want to be with someone, you fight for them. Another sign I shouldn't have ignored. I had to stay in our current town for another three months to finish beauty school.

I was completely thrown off by his gesture. He put more effort into the breakup than he did our whole relationship. I wasn't even that sad. I was mad and embarrassed.

I was hot (sometimes), I was funny and kind (most of the time), and I was smart (all of the time). *Why didn't he want me? Why wasn't I good enough?*

And that sentence—you aren't good enough—has forever haunted me because that's always how I felt with him. I hear it in one capacity or another in almost everything I do. It's a constant battle to shut it up.

* * *

A few months later, I graduated and moved to Portland as well. I had planned on moving there all along, my ex just beat me to it. It wasn't long before he wanted to hang out with me. I hesitated at first. I hadn't talked to him in three months, I had cut him off cold turkey, and it was wonderful. I felt free, I felt worthy, and I felt strong. I was making decisions for myself, not for him or what he would approve of. But, when you are twenty years old, in a new city, only know two people, and you don't have a job yet…well, let's just say my backbone was weak and it snapped.

And there we were again. In the vicious cycle of "I'm going to change," and then proceeding to do only what worked for him all the time. Twisting my words and saying no to everything. Somehow questioning every single breath that left my lungs, putting me down in front of his friends, and never asking about my heart or my soul. It was perfect, really.

2: My first wedding

We got married because I'm an idiot. I mean, after reading all of that, I wonder why anyone would think it would be a bad idea. Just kidding, it was a terrible idea.

I'll have you know that I am no longer an idiot, so let me rephrase that. I was, in my past life, an idiot. What twenty-two-year-old doesn't want to go out to the bars? Meet guys? Be free? Travel the world? Explore every societal barrier in their mind? Not do someone else's laundry? Apparently I thought I got that out of my system because in my teens, I somehow managed to kiss two-thirds of the guys in every high school in town and got blackout drunk a few times.

As it turns out, there are so many more things to do before you get married.

He was nice enough, interested enough, cute enough, had a family that cared about him, and he was smart...enough.

I was young enough, naive enough, raised in a church that basically married people off at nineteen, and insecure enough. You've seen it before. It was your typical small town movie.

* * *

A week before my wedding, my best friend of fifteen years pulled me aside and told me she thought I was making a mistake. She took me to coffee specifically to tell me it wasn't too late to back out. *But what did she know about it?* She hadn't had to back out of a wedding that was already paid for.

She sat me down over a white chocolate mocha, my diet of choice back then, and proceeded to tell me that she hated the way he treated me. She didn't like how I shriveled into nothingness when I was around him. I didn't want a toxic relationship. It was terrifying to me. She thought I deserved better.

I remember this conversation so clearly, even as the huge Starbucks I was sitting in started to blur, and the yellow walls closed in on me. Her words slowly slithered through my ears like tiny snakes that I wanted nothing to do with. She mentioned the patterns of him knocking me down, embarrassing me in front of my friends, then not letting me do anything without him. Breaking up with me, and then acting like a completely different person to win me back.

I knew she was right. However, I had spent years trying not to believe it. I knew it before I walked in, and I knew it in the way my jaw clenched, and my body stiffened when she spoke about her concerns. *But how could I back out now?* My stomach was in knots from the combination of the milk in my mocha and the truth in my stomach.

My parents had poured $12,000 into the wedding, and I wasn't about to disappoint them. Not to mention, problems like this in the church weren't really problems at all. The only problem in a church is when people questioned the Bible, or when they were gay, or didn't believe that some guy rose from the dead. For this, I would have been met with a lecture about going to counseling, submitting to my husband, or trusting the Lord. But not even baby Jesus was going to fix this. If He was real, He already knew what was going on. Not to mention, He created the guy this way, so He would have fixed him by then if he really cared.

Nobody had ever talked to me about how a successful and loving relationship should work or feel. The communication in my family was fine, but there was a lot of assuming going on. My parents just assumed I understood the mechanics of how a successful partnership should work. My dad is great with words and he did his best, but he was protective and kept my world safe. I was sheltered and this was how they pictured my life. And if I swayed from it at all, even if I was happy and doing great things, I felt guilt-like I wasn't doing it right, like I was disappointing them.

I learned to hide my feelings. It ate me up inside. If you don't feel understood in your own family, and you have different thought processes than them, why would you speak? But also, if you don't feel understood in your own family, you grow apart.

My mom and dad have been married since they were twenty, happily (as far as we knew), besides the occasional bump in the road. But nobody in my family ever talked about feelings, dreams, or desires. We talked more around them. We talked about the weather, we played games, and we went to church.

My parents didn't know my heart or my beliefs. Maybe they were afraid to ask and maybe I was afraid to say. It was simpler that way. Nobody had to talk about anything that would ruffle anyone else's feathers. You just get to talk about what's on the surface, and nobody gets hurt. Maybe they knew there would be confrontation, or maybe it was just the times we were in. I wonder how many relationships are alive because of sweeping things under the rug in avoidance of uncomfortable conversations. It seems much easier to avoid them, but in the long run, they can cause so much pain and misunderstanding.

I knew something inside of me didn't align with the life they lived. I respected it, but it wasn't mine. I was born to push the limits, to ask the hard questions, and to live out loud. To move to a bigger city and hear other opinions. To soak it all in.

But there was a lot of shame in saying what I really felt. Things were to go a certain way to be raised as a good person, a Christian. You were to stay between the lines that had been drawn for you. It was like a life checklist. But the boxes weren't mine to check, and it didn't feel right. I felt complacent.

* * *

My dad walked me down the aisle. I remember the whole thing being a bit surreal. Not because it was my wedding day, but because the guy at the end of the aisle didn't respect me.

My body was trembling as I walked toward him while everyone stared at me. I was thinking, *Wait...forever? Is this love?*

I wondered if my dad was thinking the same thing and just trusting that I knew what I was doing at twenty-two. I also wondered if we all were thinking the same thing. *Were the beliefs of the church, society, and how I was raised silencing us?*

For as many opinions my family had about marriage, I felt weird that they didn't know our relationship better. It all felt like a lie. I think part of me thought that maybe if they had genuinely known what our relationship was like, they would have stopped the whole thing, told me it was okay, and that I didn't have to go through with it. I think I wished that was happening for a split second that day. I knew there was a big love out there, and this wasn't it. I think I hoped it would change with vows.

The wedding was fun—your girl knows how to throw a party. I had a flower ball that I slingshot off the top of a barn as a flower toss. I should have seen the writing on the wall when nobody caught it. The flower ball hit the cement and broke into a pile, foreshadowing the trajectory of my marriage.

The wedding night was awkward to say the least. We left the reception and basically drove in silence for the next thirty minutes to get to our hotel. I was starving. The caterer had packed us food to take to the hotel, but my new husband had forgotten it because he had sex on the brain. He had surprised me and booked the bed and breakfast himself, which I will admit, was a very nice gesture. I had never been there, and the second I walked in, I knew I never wanted to come back.

I also realized that this guy didn't know me at all. It was the complete opposite of the type of room I would choose to spend money to sleep in, especially on my wedding night. It was incredibly dark and eerie, and the bed had a quilt. Anybody that knows me, knows that I refuse to sleep in a bed with any type of pattern or quilt. It grosses me out. I automatically assume that the bedding is sixty years old and rarely gets washed and therefore there are hundreds more germs from thousands more people in the fibers. I can't un-think it. There was no way I was getting naked in that bad boy.

When it came time to have the wedding-night sex that is so glamorized in movies, I looked for any and every exit in the room. I stalled by taking a bath. I was shaking from hunger, but also from my nerves. Inevitably, it came time to "do it."

And so, in "doing it," I did nothing. I just laid there. I had a pit in my stomach. I closed my eyes and let it happen to me, on an old, quilted four-post cherrywood bed. Taking breaths only to get me one step closer to the end. Making noise because I was supposed to, and I thought it would end the thing sooner.

Turns out sex was like this for me the majority of the time in the coming years. I wasn't asked what I wanted, how I felt, or even if I wanted it—he just did it. If I said no, I got the silent treatment, or he would leave for a whole day with his friends and leave me with the kids. If he was moody, he told me it's because men needed sex to be happy, and if I wanted him to be nice, sex would solve it. I was a doormat, a useful one, but I got walked on for eleven years. I'd eventually became numb to it all.

The next morning was similar. I had eggs benedict. I hate eggs benedict. The chairs were dark wood, in a dark restaurant, with dark green walls, and a white tablecloth. I hate dark wood, and dark walls, and especially tablecloths. They are basically giant napkins that you aren't supposed to use. *What are they hiding under there? Is the table dirty?*

We sat in silence across a table for two by the window. We had nothing to talk about. We had nothing in common, other than four years of ups and downs, and a wedding ring. This was my reality. Day one of marriage.

* * *

The honeymoon was more of the same. We had nine days of wedded non-bliss and bedbugs in Mexico. My husband couldn't make a damn decision about anything to do to save his life, and when I suggested something, it was too far or too expensive. He wanted to get our daily coffee at Starbucks instead of local cafes, and only eat the free food at the hotel for meals. You couldn't get through a meal without a mariachi band yelling "Hey, honeymooners" and serenading you until you gave them five bucks to go away. We had welts all over our bodies from bedbug bites. All I wanted was to go home...alone. I started to wonder if anyone had ever accidentally left their new groom in Mexico.

* * *

The next few years, my husband was finishing college. He was working an intern job during school and I was doing hair at a well-known salon downtown. Doing hair and laundry I should say. Doing hair, laundry, and cleaning.

WAIT.

I was doing hair, laundry, cleaning, cooking, grocery shopping, picking up the dry cleaning, bill paying, house hunting, car maintenancing, Costco-ing, staying home every weekend while he went on boys' trips, obligatory sexing, keeping a physique that would keep him attracted to me, not saying too much, not spending a penny that he could see, explaining myself but also keeping my mouth shut, and questioning myself.

We went on occasional dates, but we never had much to talk about. We were the couple that just sat there and looked awkward and left right after we ate because there was no reason to stay for another drink. I was constantly racking my brain for something to say that he would react to without making me feel stupid, something that could start a healthy conversation. Oftentimes I was too afraid to speak because I feared being shut down or made fun of. But there was a part of me that also wanted to stay out too late because then I would be too tired and wouldn't have to have sex when we got home.

This was a theme in our marriage. Our babysitters used to make fun of us for coming home so early, usually about two hours after we had left. We had nothing in common, and Lord knows he wouldn't stay out to go dancing with me. He also didn't want to spend more money hitting another bar for a drink, even if I wanted to. Sometimes he would meet up with his friends after, and I would go home to relieve the babysitter, but I was never allowed to do the same.

He was a finance major. So the budget conversation was real in our house. I was questioned for every dollar spent on our joint card.

"What's this twenty dollar charge from Victoria's Secret?"

Ummm...I needed some new underwear and they were having a five-for-twenty sale.

"Did you really need new underwear? Wow, that's expensive. We can't afford that right now."

But you can afford a day of golf and beers?

* * *

"Why did you spend sixty dollars at Safeway?"

Why did I marry you? But also—to make you dinner? To get groceries since you refuse to let me get takeout EVER, yet you eat lunch at Chipotle every day?

"We should start going to Winco instead of Safeway."

You mean I should start going to Winco to save an extra five bucks.

* * *

"What is this two-fifty charge from Starbucks?"

It's called caffeine. I worked an eleven-hour day on my feet and needed a pick-me-up. Also, the black coffee is the cheapest thing on the menu. You should feel lucky that I'm not a triple shot Caramel Frappuccino girl. Because I could be.

"Can't you just take coffee from home?"

Yes. We all can. But I make money and can spend it too if I want.

And then he would proceed to spend a full day of his wages golfing and drinking beer or a week's worth renting a house with his buddies for the weekend. He called it networking, but most of the time he was with his friends from high school. No networking needed, they all sold phones for a living.

I started putting things on my business debit card. I was making decent money for my age, and I deserved to buy a new shirt or a coffee here and there. I never went out with my girlfriends because it made him uncomfortable; it wasn't even up for discussion. He also didn't want me spending money or being looked at by other men. If he noticed anything new, which was rare, I had to lie and say a friend gave it to me. My friends sure were generous. I couldn't handle the questioning and the guilt. It got to the point where every single charge on our joint credit card was either a utility, gas, groceries, boys' nights, or his clothes. I felt like a robot.

3: Kids make things better, right?

I always say you lose a little bit of yourself when you have a baby. And the women that I tell this to are usually pregnant and look at me like I just stole their dreams right out of their head and shattered them with sledgehammer in front of their eyes.

Before they can cry, I help them pick their jaw up off the floor—they can't bend over that far because they are growing a life inside of them. And then I go on to explain that it is a beautiful loss. A tragic one, yes. But also one followed by immense growth and honor.

You see, parts of you literally leave your body as a baby is born. Nine months of worrying and caring and obsessing and nourishing and sharing blood and DNA, all in one seven-ish pound vessel that comes straight out of the vag with a lot of pain.

Years of making decisions solely based on yourself and what you want are out the window. Gone are the days of leaving the house whenever you want, going to bars on Friday nights, sleeping past five in the morning, eating a full meal, or taking a shower without interruption.

Over that first year, you become a servant to something that relies on you and only you to keep it alive. Nobody else can provide food and comfort the way you do. So, you sacrifice. You sacrifice sleep, sanity, relationships, meals, and friendships.

You stuff yourself in your home for hours and hours, rocking a baby to sleep and wake up in the middle of the night when you had just fallen asleep for two minutes. All to feed a baby that will just go back to sleep. Meanwhile, you lay there, hoping that the baby won't roll onto their belly and choke, while also hoping that they don't have a personality disorder or any of your husband's traits. Because at the moment you are mad at him for not waking up with said baby and also mad at him because he doesn't have a swollen vagina, so he just doesn't get it.

You start talking in a high-pitched voice because your baby is cute, and you think that they understand you better that way because that's how you always heard people talk to babies. In fact, you even tilt your head to the side while you do it, like it makes you more tender. You neglect all your relationships because they just don't get it either, and you are also tired.

When it comes time to make love, you just lay there and fake that you are enjoying yourself until it's over. And then you get up and make dinner because everyone needs to eat, and it doesn't make itself. All while the baby is in the front pack and you are holding a pacifier in its mouth while you stir with the other hand and hope the taco meat oil doesn't splatter and burn your baby. The baby also has a blow out all over your shirt after you had finally just showered. So then you make a cocktail with shit on your shirt.

You neglect yourself because, well, what is the point? Your boobs leak 24/7, your hair is falling out from hormones, you suddenly have acne, you're carrying an extra fifteen pounds that the world tells you need to lose, and you're wearing the same sweatpants you wore when you were pregnant because it's the only thing familiar anymore.

Mostly, though, you don't do a damn thing for yourself because you are a walking zombie. In some cases, you're probably a little bit drunk, trying to make sense of it all by numbing the pain and fear of losing what you once were and stepping into something that you have no fucking idea how to deal with. Oh, and you are lonely, because again, nobody gets it.

But then, about eight months later, when the baby starts smiling and your boobs start shrinking into a more normal and acceptable size (yet totally like a deflated pancake), something shifts. You get four hours of solid sleep for the first time. You realize that you grew this beautiful thing inside of you, and that you are more than just a milk cow in a woman's body. You see glimmers of hope that you have never experienced before in your child's eyes. You are excited for who they are becoming and who they are making you to be. If you choose, anyway.

You have a huge opportunity to look at the seventy-five percent of you that you have left and build the other twenty-five percent back from scratch, improved this time. Because you have something that is one hundred percent perfect in front of you.

You ask yourself, "Hey, where'd you go? This person needs you." You get to create your own strength, curate your dreams. You realize that your body is fucking amazing and that giving birth was such an honor because men will never get to experience it. You get to set an example for another human, so you level the fuck up and check yourself at the door. Because goddamnit, that baby is watching you.

My kids made me better. They made me stronger, and they made a huge impact on how I decided to change my life. They made me vulnerable, selfless, and authentic.

I will forever look at them when I am facing a tough situation and ask myself, *Would they be proud of me if I did this? If I reacted like that? Or showed up like this? If I spoke up like that or walked away like this?* I constantly want to make them proud.

And in a society where our children are taught that they need to please their parents, I think we all need to flip it and please our children once in a while. (And I'm not talking give them candy for breakfast. Okay, maybe sometimes when you just want to be a cool mom.)

Yes, I want to be proud of my kids, but more, I want them to be proud of me. To look up to me and say "I want to be a strong motherfucker like my mom. I want to be giving and compassionate and silly and funny and vulnerable and honest and loving and open." This is what I strive for. I think when I realized that, that's when I truly felt like I could put myself back together. And I was thankful for the twenty-five percent reduction in my former self.

Kids—they make us better if you let them, then you can be proud of them for that.

4: One-hit wonder

I had never been one to be super excited about babies. I knew I wanted a family because as you get older, your friends become a little fewer and further between. Everyone has kids and grandkids, so who do you hang out with? The answer is your kids.

Your kids become your friends, or at least you hope they do. But I never felt that maternal "I love babies and I can't wait to have them keep me up at night and wipe their asses and be spit up on and run on their schedule" desire. Call me selfish. But I knew I wanted to be young enough to be cool and able to hang out when they were older. So I did what any smart twenty-five-year-old would do. I got knocked up. I like to call my kids one-hit wonders because, well, it only took one try.

My husband was on a business trip when I peed on my first stick. It was five days before my missed period, but I had felt a twinge in my ovary. I just knew little Harper was hanging on to my insides.

I went to buy a test and the woman ringing me up was a bit overweight, her hair color needed to be touched up, and apparently so did her tact. She was in a pink shirt and her boobs were down to her belly button. She wore glasses on the tip of her nose and didn't make eye contact, or maybe that was me because I looked like I was thirteen at the time and I was buying a pregnancy test. To a stranger, it just looked like another episode of teen mom. She picked up the box and said "uh-oh" as she slid the Clearblue across the price scanner. I was thinking, *Girl, you aren't allowed to say that!*

I rushed home, sat on the toilet, and with a shaky hand, held the test between my legs as I aimed as best a woman can aim to hit the stick without peeing on my hand.

Sure enough, the plus sign appeared within seconds.

I didn't want to tell him while he was gone, it needed to be in person. To pass the time, I went to the dollar store and bought five more tests just to be sure. It was five bucks and five confirmations, and the charges were on my business debit, so no questions asked. For all he knew, it was a buy one get five sale. Surprise, surprise...they were all positive.

I don't know that I was excited. I was young and in shock. I had no idea what I was doing. I also bought a book called *What to Expect When Your Wife Is Expanding*. It was a parody and quite a perfect way to tell my husband I was pregnant, so I thought. I wrapped it up, put a cigar on top, and patiently waited until he got home from god knows where.

He wasn't too phased by the gifts. I was always gifting or going above and beyond because I was always seeking validation from him. Trying to get him to notice me, buy me flowers. It seemed easier at the time to continue to do this than to leave. There I was, again, with another gift. He didn't understand it.

"Huh," he said it like a statement, not a question.

I followed it with the cold hard truth. "I'm pregnant."

He started laughing.

I was not laughing. *What's happening?*

I said it again.

He asked if I was serious. Not like a "this is so great, you have got to be kidding me" kind of asking. It was more of a you're-an-idiot-and-there's-no-way tone.

Have a little more faith in yourself, buddy. I showed him the six tests that I had taken over the course of three days. I was finally excited and sure it was real and ready for him to be excited. Hell, I needed him to be.

I got nothing from him but questions—the kind that made me feel bad. In the back of my mind, I knew it could go down like this, but I was in denial and hopeful that he would be excited, that this could help us. After all, he was the one that knocked me up.

"Are you sure? That's probably false. You need to take more tests." He made me buy five more, at the dollar store of course, but then he questioned if those were even viable.

I took eleven tests. Every single one of them was positive. There was no amount of questioning that could make it negative. The guy wasn't going to believe I was pregnant until about two days after our daughter's first birthday.

* * *

She came out screaming and didn't stop. Like a black-haired troll with a set of bagpipes for lungs, only cuter.

I stopped working the Saturday before Harper was born. It was nine days before my due date and the earliest I could quit without a guilt trip from my husband. He didn't want me taking off any earlier than that and I was to go back two weeks after she was born. Not full time, but back to work two weeks later, nonetheless. I was thirty-five pounds heavier than normal at that point and standing on my feet all day doing hair. I was also working in heels like an amateur. The pressure on my bladder and pelvis was out of control and causing so much pain in my hips and sciatic nerve that it would take my breath away. I was happy to have a week off. I just wanted to be pregnant and chill for half a second.

The next morning, I woke up at an ungodly hour to horrible cramps. I went to the bathroom and felt something huge and slimy slip out of me, and I heard it plunk into the toilet. It was such a big plop that the water splashed up and hit my ass cheeks. *Oh shit.*

I looked down and saw, what I'm pretty sure from my research, was either my baby or the mucus plug. I had been unplugged. *Double oh shit.*

I went and laid back down, not waking the man from his precious sleep because I knew he would question my plug—like he knew what anything coming out of my vagina could be. I kept it to myself, just me and my baby girl knew what was up. But the cramps turned into contractions as my belly would tighten over her, and I knew my girl was ready to make her entrance. Punctual and awkwardly early, just like her mommy.

Just as suspected, when he woke up, he assured me that I wasn't having contractions. It was nuts because he doesn't have a uterus, and he definitely wasn't inside of my body. And he definitely didn't read any of the *What to Expect* books or watch any of the birthing videos I'd asked him to. Not to mention he had definitely never experienced a contraction. The only thing he had ever experienced was a stomach cramp when he was taking a shit, and he was sure that's all this was. God forbid that at 38.7 weeks, our baby would be making her debut on anything but her due date.

But he had plans that day. Neither I nor our baby girl was going to get in the way. It was boys' day—no bitches allowed. Golf with pizza, beer, and a Blazers game that night. There was no baby or wife in those plans.

So he left. I was told to call him if the contractions got closer together. I spent the first couple of hours wandering in circles around our house. What do you do when you are waiting for the inevitable? The one person that was supposed to be there wasn't. I felt like he didn't care, so why should I call anyone else and assume that they might?

This was before the smartphone, so I grabbed my iPad and downloaded a contraction timer app. It recorded how long each contraction was and how frequent. I knew the hospital didn't want me until they were five minutes apart. But I did the ten-minute apart thing for a solid twelve hours.

I finally called a friend when I felt like I might actually be going crazy. She took me for a pedicure. I held my breath and hit my iPad timer each time I had a contraction, trying not to let the Vietnamese women know I was in labor. I didn't need them to ask me if I wanted a flower on my nails or if I wanted to try to have a boy after having a girl. I just needed this one out of me.

After a few laps through Target, where I very nonchalantly (read: super aggressively) hung onto the end of an aisle with each wave of contractions, I went home to take a bath. My body was exhausted. I tried to cram my swollen limbs into the bathtub as I watched my baby kick and punch and felt what I can only describe as her trying to claw her way out. And as I looked past my bump, I saw pink water. There was blood everywhere. I called my husband to tell him it was go time/ask him for a ride to the hospital like he was some sort of Uber. I was met with a request to wait a little longer to go to the hospital as if I could just do a few casual Kegels and keep her in my uterus.

I had waited fifteen hours already. No.

When he finally came home, I was standing in the hallway with my overnight bag, exhausted. It was 11 p.m.

The hospital was dark and eerie, with faint beeps and random screams from laboring women in the background. They checked my dilation in a tiny, dimly lit room without windows, and left me bleeding on a bed with a gown to change into and a bunch of paper towels to wipe myself. Something softer would have been nice, but maybe they like to rough you up for what's to come.

I was barely four centimeters dilated. Four centimeters is when they admit you into the hospital. I was put into a room next to a screamer, and I wondered for a minute if maybe I should have waited to come in after all. My room felt like a suffocating cubicle, my husband felt useless, and my body was shaking uncontrollably.

Contractions are like road construction in your uterus. It's like the baby is using a jackhammer to get out, and it's not working. The breathing exercises went out the window within the first hour. I was in full survival mode. This went on for another five hours until I was finally at a five and the screamer had finally gotten her child out. My husband was in the corner, terrified.

I was in so much pain. But even more than that, I was exhausted. After twenty-four hours of hard labor, I caved and got an epidural. Actually, I got a brain. There's a lot of judgment and shame around an epidural. Well, maybe not as much now. I'd been told I wouldn't feel anything at all, that I wouldn't bond with the baby, that it poisons the baby, etc. But my body was about to shut down. And let me tell you, I still felt what was happening, with less pain.

My baby girl was as healthy as Whole Foods when she came out, twenty-nine hours later.

I didn't bond with her right away, or either of my kids, actually. They put this thing on your chest after twenty-nine hours of *what the fuck,* and your crotch being on display for anybody that wanted to stick their hands in it. The baby is like a gooey blob that cries, and everything is hot. And you're told you should feel this big magical thing and kiss it. But all I could think was:

A. What the fuck?
B. Can you get it off me?
C. I need a minute.
D. Do I still have a vagina, or did I lose it in the war?

* * *

We kept her in our hospital room that night in the bassinet. I was in the hospital bed with vagina lips the size of neck pillows, sitting on a frozen diaper for the swelling, and my husband was on the pull-out cot by the window. Harper woke up every two hours to be fed. I woke up to feed her each time. My husband woke up zero times.

The next day was my twenty-sixth birthday. My baby stole my thunder, but I have come to realize that kids just do that for the rest of your lives. Your thunder is now a tiny child's squeaker toy that got stepped on as someone passed by. But it's fine. I'm fine. You don't need attention like a child for the rest of your life, and if you do, there's counseling for that. I spend my birthdays having birthday parties for my daughter now, then I don't have to think about planning my own. We get a whole weekend of birthday bliss. And while, yes, sometimes it would be nice to not have a bunch of squealing nine-year-olds spending the night at my house on my birthday eve...well, it would be nice.

Because I'm persuasive and everyone was healthy, we were able to go home on my birthday. All I wanted was a salad and a quiet, clean house, with my own bed. But when I arrived, I was greeted by four greasy pizzas and eight of my husband's friends who he had invited over. I was puffy from the meds and the extra thirty-five pounds I was carrying, I had stitches in my crotch, and I sat on an inflatable donut with a bunch of people I didn't want to be around.

I was eighteen hours post the biggest moment of my life. I needed to process. I needed space. I needed rest. Instead, I sat in a circle with my tiny baby in my arms, with a pad the size of an adult diaper in between my legs, as leftover fluid from the day before soaked it. I pasted a smile on my face and picked at a slice of Papa Murphy's pizza while the boys talked inside jokes and nobody asked how I was feeling. I stared at the wall, wishing I had stayed at the hospital for my birthday.

* * *

The first couple of weeks were a magical blur. Having a newborn is like playing house. You cook and clean and walk by your tiny sleeping bundle and smile as they make little coos and baby noises. You feel warm and fuzzy inside because you are thinking, *Being a mom is the best and not being pregnant anymore is the best and my baby sleeps and this is so easy!* Blah, blah, blah. Then holy shit—they wake up!

* * *

Harp started screaming on day fourteen...bloodcurdling, stiff as a board, red everywhere, pain in her eyes, clenched fists, screaming. ALL. FUCKING. DAY. and ALL. FUCKING. NIGHT.

At first, I thought it was my milk, so we saw lactation consultants. And then I thought it was something I was eating, so I cut out all dairy, soy, and gluten. So now, not only was I starving, but my baby was still screaming. She was projectile vomiting about ten times a day across the room. Projectile vomiting basically to the forty-yard line. It was insane. Sometimes it would hit the wall, and I would watch it slowly drip down as I tried to console her.

The amount of times we went to the pediatrician in the first year is embarrassing. I basically WAS a pediatrician after all was said and done. What they were once calling colic was then replaced with reflux after it had lasted more than three months. So then I was giving my baby crushed up antacids in a syringe and watching her spew it across the floor twenty minutes later, along with any milk or solids she had gotten down in her previous meal.

I didn't sleep the first year. I was up with Harper every twenty to forty-five minutes of each day and night. My husband told me he needed rest so he could work. I wasn't to bother him at night. My friends started to worry about me. The only time she would sleep was when I was running or driving.

So I ran. And I ran and I ran, and I ran. I ran in the rain, I ran in the snow, I ran after I had already run that day. I ran in circles. I thought I was running for sanity, but when I look back, I realize I was running for my life, and from my marriage. I was exhausted, I was malnourished, I was dizzy, and I was alone. Just me, a screaming child, and a stroller.

When I went back to work my sitter would call and text me, completely panicked that she was doing something wrong because of the constant screaming. I felt bad. Not for my baby—I mean a little bit—but mostly for the sitter. I decided to quit my job and stay home and let her scream at me instead. I was certain nobody could put up with that for too long if it wasn't their own child. I'd just cut my losses and do the job myself. I felt helpless.

My husband spent the first year of our baby's life working 8 to 5:30, then going to happy hour with colleagues or friends after work. He went on work trips, and out to dinner and drinks with friends on the weekends. There was golfing and boys' trips and basketball games. He even took up sailing lessons because apparently, he didn't have any family obligations. Why not pick up an all-day hobby when you have a newborn?

* * *

I remember one night I had been driving Harper around for half an hour just to give my ears and her tiny lungs a break.

I was incredibly dizzy, and I couldn't stop crying. I knew it wasn't safe for me to be behind the wheel. I swear driving sleep deprived is just as bad as driving drunk.

My hands had been trembling all day. My mind was too shot to race. All I could think was *WHY? and HOW? How could something so tiny make me so miserable? How was I going to make it out of this? Was I going to get in an accident? Did anyone care?*

When I pulled into my driveway, a friend was waiting for me and just as I said "I think she's asleep," my daughter let out a bloodcurdling scream. I fell to my knees in the driveway and started sobbing, my body shaking uncontrollably. She looked at me and said, "Go to bed. Take a sleeping pill, and don't get up until the morning, I've got this." And so I did.

I woke up seven hours later and went into the other room where my friend had set up what looked like Curves for babies. She had arranged every bouncer, walker, pack and play contraption I had, and had been rotating Harper through it all night. Neither of them had slept more than twenty minutes.

This was one of the best gifts I have ever received in my life, still to this day. She looked at me and said, "I don't know how you do it. You deserve so much more." She was talking about my marriage, my support. Not my baby. I had been doing it alone, and she was the first person to see me.

I didn't have a single girls' trip or night out that first year. I didn't have a single feeding off, except the few times my parents came to visit. I didn't get a single stretch of sleep more than two hours minus that one night. There wasn't a single day that I wasn't expected to have dinner on the table. If I left to run an errand, I got a text within thirty minutes asking when I would be home. And when I did get home, it was twenty questions about the thirty minutes I was gone.

I didn't get a single affirmation from my husband. I was exhausted, and I was mad. Nothing felt right, there was no peace in my life. I felt like I was standing in a flame that I didn't know how to put out, holding my daughter.

* * *

Eventually Harp did grow out of the screaming. It was exactly three hundred sixty-five days and probably four hundred seventy-three runs later. I'll never know why. But on her first birthday, she looked me in the eyes and smiled at me, as if to say: "I'm sorry I was a dick. I was preparing you for something. I'm here now. Let's do this. I love you." I was finally consistently getting two hours of sleep at a time, and I felt like a new woman.

I started to enjoy my baby. We spent the days learning about each other and walking to the park. Every smile was healing, every laugh felt like home. She never did nap more than about twenty minutes, but I learned to be very efficient with my time. I learned to love her busy and curious spirit, and I quickly learned that the fire in her soul was here to stay. I began to love her for it, yet it would take me years to fully understand.

5: Oops, I did it again

Somehow, I got knocked up again. I blame it on lack of sleep or maybe getting one night of full sleep. Either way, while I knew in the back of my mind that I needed to get out of my relationship, I knew that I was stuck. I also think that I was trying to convince myself that my marriage could get better even though I knew it wouldn't. I wanted to believe in us. I wanted to feel loved, I needed to feel seen. I didn't want to be the first in our friend group to get divorced. I didn't want the shame and guilt. I just wanted normal, whatever that meant. I also knew that Harper would be a terrible only child given her track record, so I needed to give her a sibling. Girl had gotten every second of my attention for a full year, and there were no signs of her sharing me.

One-hit wonder number two—or is it a second hit? It sure felt like a hit.

* * *

I got pregnant with June shortly after Harper turned one. I guess I figured I should just continue being sleep deprived, because once I got out of it, I'm pretty sure there would be no going back. I was still changing diapers, might as well tack on a couple more years of wiping tiny butts and having the life sucked out of my tits. I had always wanted two kids. Mostly because that's what I was familiar with. People want what they grew up with for some reason, even though circumstances are vastly different. Not to mention I was getting the hang of it, and I really liked having a purpose other than making dinner and folding laundry.

I'm not completely sure I was cut out to be a mom, but I'm not sure anyone really is. Sure, some people are naturally more nurturing or better with kids, but are we really cut out to be anything? Or do we just do things because we want to, knowing we care enough to learn along the way and put effort into them?

The pregnancy was a blur—I had a baby that kept me busy. All was well and the grapefruit and maple bars were abundant. My vagina had mostly healed, and I was finally getting the hang of how to take a baby to the grocery store without having a meltdown (Her, not me. Okay, sometimes me.) I took a shower almost every day, and Harper and I laughed a lot. I continued to run most days while pushing a stroller with a twenty-pounder in it. She pointed out flowers and cars and anything else she could barely say, singing whatever song she knew at the moment the whole way. I felt healthy, good, single, and numb. But I was also nailing it.

* * *

Six days before my due date, I had my thirty-nine-week routine appointment. I remember this day so clearly. It was a beautiful winter day, not a cloud in the sky, and so cold you could see the breath leaving my body. I had just eaten an Egg McMuffin, which was a big craving that round. I probably should have gotten two in hindsight. I pulled into the parking lot, and as I parked the car, I had a feeling she was ready.

My OB did all the things like sticking her fingers up my vagina, asking personal questions, and the obligatory "how are you?" I was never sure how to answer that one. *I'm fat, Karen, my ass is the size of Uranus, or someone's anus. My husband is a dick who is never around and not helpful when he is, other than knocking me up anyway. I'm seconds away from another stretch mark and my twenty-one-month-old throws more tantrums than anyone warned me about. When I run, it feels like there's a leprechaun with a jackhammer on my cervix, and I want a vacation and probably a wife and four gin and tonics without being hungover.*

But instead, I politely smiled and said, "I'm good. How are you?" I'm sure they know that's bullshit. And I have really grown to hate that question.

When she measured my belly, she went silent. I started to panic a little bit as I realized that she was speaking in slow motion and I heard her say, "Youuuuuu neeeeeeed tooooo gooooo toooooooo thhhhhhe hoooooospiiitaaaal riiiiiiiiiiight awaaaaaaaay."

Ummm, excuse me? Can we go back to the how are you question? Please elaborate and/or define right now. Because right now could be like ambulance status or right now could be like go pack a bag and be there today at some point.

She gave me a tiny smile, and I realized that she had a plan, that we were okay, and that I might be overreacting for the first time in my life.

She went on to explain to me that my amniotic fluid was leaking. I was wondering why I had stayed so small this round. I thought maybe the running was paying off, and I was one of those cute small pregnant girls this time rather than the blueberry I was last time. But turns out, my girl didn't have any water to swim in, and that's why I was so small.

I was given an hour to phone a friend to come stay with Harper for the night and grab an overnight bag to head to the hospital. I called my husband and told him it was go time, and for once, he listened because the doctor said it and not me. I was to start the induction when I got to the hospital. It seems like a lot of women freak when they hear the word induced. I didn't give a fuck. *If that's the fastest and safest way to get this girl out, I'm all in.*

We rolled in at about 1 p.m., and she was born a few hours later. Everything was so much faster this round. Maybe it was the Pitocin, maybe my body was ready, maybe it's Maybelline, or maybe it was this girl's temperament. I remember minutes before she arrived, my husband told me he was going to Starbucks to get a coffee. I'm pretty sure I've never looked at someone with more disgust in my life than I did at my husband in that moment.

To hell with that idea. First, what do you think you are, tired? Second, I'm at a nine here buddy. If this baby doesn't fall out of my hole, then my stomach might, so you should probably stay.

I told him he could get a shitty cafeteria coffee or nothing because there was no way he was going to be at a mediocre coffee chain, paying for an overpriced, burnt Americano, while I was pushing a six-pounder out of my crotch. He went to the cafeteria and within one minute of him getting back, I pushed twice, and we were parents all over again.

* * *

The first two weeks were magical. They trick you. She just laid there like an angel and slept and cooed, and Harper thought she was okay enough. So basically, I was winning. Being a mom of two was cake, and I was thinking I may as well start a blog as soon as I could figure out how to put my clothes and makeup on before getting spit up on.

Anyway, again, it was all good UNTIL SHE WOKE UP

... and she screamed

... and I screamed.

* * *

How the FUCK was this happening again?

My friends and family swore it wouldn't happen again. There was "no way" I could have two screaming babies. I watched people eat their words over the next few months as they faded into the background and watched me struggle. Nobody could believe it. I couldn't believe it. I started resenting everyone around me for telling me this wouldn't happen again. I found myself upset that I had believed them in the first place. *What a fool.* Of course it could happen again.

I started wondering what I did in my previous life to deserve this. Karma is a bitch, and in the moment, that bitch looked like my baby.

I put my twenty-one-month-old and my newborn in the jogging stroller, and I ran. I ran because I was tired. I ran because I was alone. I ran because it freed me from feeling anything but strength. I ran because it created space between me and a screaming child. I ran because it gave me a sense of control. I ran to release. I ran because I felt like maybe if I lost the last ten pounds of baby weight my husband would pay more attention to me. I ran because it made me feel valued. I ran because I knew the steps that I was taking were creating a path for me to get out. Step by step, I ran.

Lucky for me this was just the old hundred–day cry. ONE HUNDRED DAYS. Also known as colic. Now, if you add those two babies together that is four hundred sixty-five days of bloodcurdling, inconsolable, hit-your-head-on-the-wall screaming that I endured. Alone. However, I am eternally grateful that someone higher saw me at the end of my rope and decided to give me a happy baby on day one hundred and one. I'll take it, and I will forever be happy in return. But in order to be forever happy in return, I had to get out.

* * *

I filled my days being the best wife and mother I could be. I put on the face. I played the game. I took Harper to dance (until we got kicked out for screaming), and we did museums and zoos and parks. I cooked, I cleaned, and I had sex when my husband was in a bad mood, so I didn't have to endure the mood swings. I bought my baby girls clothes and toys with money that I earned doing hair from my home. My husband didn't know about that money.

You see, if I told him about the money, he would want it, which would be fine if he understood that women and children have needs. These kids were outgrowing their clothes every other week, my body was also changing constantly due to hormones and baby weight, and the fact that I was rivaling Forrest Gump's running. Fuck, sometimes we just wanted to buy a new nail polish or get an ice cream or go to lunch without being questioned, so I provided for our needs. Just the three of us. If I happened to put any of it on our joint card, he wanted to see a receipt. Heaven forbid I spend more than sixty dollars at the grocery store without explaining myself, without proof that I didn't get cash back.

What I didn't realize at the time was that I was already building a life without my husband. I was trying to construct a solid home inside myself instead of looking for a home in him. I needed space to let go of the foundational trauma that he had laid down for me.

* * *

I needed to make my own money, so I texted a friend who worked at a local fitness studio that had childcare and begged her to get me a job. I was willing to do anything to be able to work out for free and have free childcare. There was no way my husband was going to let me leave the house to work out in the morning before he left for work. He was completely incapable of being a father AND getting ready for work at the same time. God forbid a child wake up before he did.

My friend quickly let me know that she was opening a spin studio of her own in a few months—complete with childcare—and she suggested I come work for her.

SURE! No problem. Sign me up. Front desk? You got it.

She said, "You should teach! You'd be great!"

I must have been extremely tired because I had a huge fear of speaking in front of people. Who did I think I was to work out in front of people and speak at the same time? "Hello, my name is Lianne. I say awkward things and I make jokes when I'm uncomfortable. And yes, I have a filter but it's a little questionable most of the time."

I drove to the co-owner's home a few days later with my baby in tow. Harper was with a friend. I was about five weeks postpartum. She greeted me with a huge smile as I walked into her gorgeous home looking slightly haggard, lost, and confused.

This was my first time meeting this woman. I looked to the left and in her home office were two spin bikes.

Shit. Oh no no no no no no no. NO. I thought we were going to chat.

She started talking a million words per minute and before I knew it, my feet were clipped into a spin bike. There was music on, and my baby was on the floor looking up at me from her car seat also wondering WTF was going on. *Is this the interview?*

I'm pretty sure I was in jeans. She was bopping along like she was going on a short walk, and I was huffing and puffing and trying to keep the beat. Also, my vagina wasn't ready for that kind of abuse. It was still swollen and bruised and felt like it was hanging down two inches lower than it should ever be. Every move felt like I was jamming my lady bits onto a hammer. But I played it cool as my extra six inches of stomach skin flapped to the beat.

This was just a few years before the country was saturated with SoulCycle-esque studios. I have never felt more uncoordinated or out of shape in my life. I felt like a blind baby giraffe on a run with cement blocks on my heels. *Is this how all new clients feel?*

We were chest pressing (hitting my face on the handlebars), tapping it back (being assaulted by the tip of a bike seat), I was dripping sweat on her white carpet (sorry I can't afford to clean it), and she was just bopping around asking "isn't it fun?" Between huffs and puffs and under-my-breath what the fucks, I think I said yes. I might not have responded at all. We will never know because I'm pretty sure I blacked out.

Before I knew it, she was talking to me about training, and I was on my way home with a re-broken vagina and a promise to be back next week. I didn't walk normally for at least four days. I still don't know what they saw in me that day that was inspiring other than desperation, but maybe they were desperate too. Either way, I am forever thankful that two points of desperation make a right. And hey, maybe desperation can be determination if you use it correctly.

* * *

When it came to my new job, things got a little tricky. I eventually started teaching 6 a.m. classes because the girls finally started sleeping better, but then I would catch flack if I got home at 7:15 and a kid had woken up at 6:45. My husband couldn't figure out how to shower if there was a child awake. *(Welcome to being a parent, buddy.)* This slice of independence was literally my first glimpse of hope in being able to make it on my own. It was a glimpse into a different future, one that felt like mine.

I was determined to teach. I so desperately wanted to make a name and a life for myself, but it was never going to work if I couldn't fill the room. And if I couldn't fill the room, I couldn't make more money to create my own life and get out of the hell I was living in. Something had to give.

I taught an 80s-themed ride one day at noon. I was wearing pink glitter leggings with a blue thong leotard over the top. I had a belt over my leotard, leg warmers, and I teased my hair so big that I'm pretty sure it looked like brown cotton candy. My face was caked with makeup so thick you could have written your name in my face with your finger.

I walked into work, ready to dominate, and not one, not two, but three people came that day. There was one man in the back corner, one woman on the side, and one woman who came in late to the front row. Was that my rock bottom? Maybe? Actually, as I'm typing this, I'm thinking that yes, despite all the other shit my life had handed me, that was it.

Can rock bottom happen when you are doing something you love? Yes.

Is rock bottom the moment you decide to make a change? Yes.

There I was, on a stage, with a microphone, for an hour—in front of three people. THREE. And about song four, I said, "Fuck it." FUCK IT is rock bottom. (Mind you there are different levels of fuck it, but this was the real deal.) I was making a change.

Things got weird that class. I owned who I was, I asked for more, and I expected more. I danced in that thong leotard in front of three people. I laughed. I cried. I let my guard down, and I also let my blue eyeshadow drip down my face with each bead of sweat.

I took up space without fear of judgment. I was vulnerable and I loved it. They would either come back or they wouldn't, but that was who I was. I had been suppressed for years, and it felt good to let it all out.

After that day, my classes started filling up. Those three must have told their friends because the attendees multiplied like weeds in a field. I didn't even have to wear the thong again to get them to show up.

People were raving about me and my personality. They loved that I was slightly self-deprecating yet wildly uplifting. They liked my weird dance moves. They liked my jokes, and they liked my motivation.

They saw me.

Have you ever been seen? Like truly seen? I was twenty-seven and had been married for five years and had never been seen—not by my husband or my family.

Let me tell you something about truly being seen. It's powerful and wildly terrifying. It's remarkable to be vulnerable enough to show people every corner of your being and to be one hundred percent okay with it. To have people open their arms and say, "Yes. You. This. We want more." Or on the flip side, it's a "no thank you, not for me." Which is equally cool because you don't need to be for everyone. That's boring and it's not real. I always say, "Just because they aren't for me, doesn't mean they aren't great." And I mean it.

Just because I'm not for everyone doesn't mean I'm not great. (Say it together now.)

Raw honesty. That is how life should feel. I tasted it. Then I craved it. People liked who I was, they celebrated it, they accepted it—no strings attached. Yet at home, I was being questioned and manipulated and picked apart, not being celebrated for my actions and my words and who I was and what I brought to our home. I wanted to be seen at home. But work is what kept me going. My rock bottom also formed my new foundation.

Teaching became my release, my home, my safe space. Work became my family. It felt good to form my own relationships and have conversations outside of my husband. Two kids and a job were what mattered most because that felt like all I had. My husband didn't like my new independence. He didn't want me to go to class unless I was getting paid. The studio was my safe haven. He would ask why I would go work out if I wasn't teaching, what the point was. It wasn't acceptable to take time for myself and things that made me happy. He saw it as a threat, taking away from him.

"Why don't you run? It's free."

When would I run? The middle of the night? I have two, forty-five-pounders and we live in rolling hills. Also, this is free too.

I was slipping, and he was losing. It was over.

6: Abuse? Is that you? I can't see you.

Let me start by saying, I care about the father of my children. We married young, and our relationship wasn't healthy. Neither of us was perfect, and there were still beautiful moments within my wretched reality. I had a roof over my head and two amazing daughters. And although he didn't know how to show it, I do think he cared about me. A lot of healing has happened in the past few years. People change. We are both now in a much better place, separately and together.

The amount of times I asked for couples counseling over the years is almost comical (in a weird and twisted way) because the amount of times my husband was willing to go was zero. He was under the impression that counseling was only for people who were about to get a divorce. I was under the impression that that's where we were headed. We needed some serious help with communication, but he didn't think so.

But I couldn't keep being shut down with condescending talk. Every word ate away at me like acid burning through skin. So I didn't say much. I'd already lost myself along with my voice. He'd basically Little Mermaid-ed my ass and stole my voice right out of my body. The only voice I ever heard was the one he created for me that said, *You're not good enough*. It was a tape that played on repeat, but I couldn't dub my own words over it no matter how hard I tried.

For years, my body had been a storage unit, a vault of kept emotions. I had taken the Christian phrase "submit to your husband" to the next level because I had no power. I couldn't do it anymore. I felt like I was going to spontaneously combust the more I held back. Like I was being shaken up in a bottle.

Every time we got into an argument or I tried to state my feelings or needs, he yelled, "You're crazy! I wish you could hear yourself right now." I'll never forget this. I'd think, *I CAN hear myself right now. I am the one forming the words from my own brain, spitting them out of my own mouth. These are my feelings and you are telling me I'm crazy.* Also, my hearing is fine.

These phrases haunt me to this day. They made me timid for years when I wanted to speak. They made me question my own thoughts and feelings when I'd always handled my emotions with a naked and alert mind.

When I tried to share my feelings, he always said I was too emotional and he was logical. He shut me down. He twisted my own words to make everything about him. I started to wonder if maybe I was crazy. *I must be, right?* Maybe if I fessed up to being crazy, everything would get easier.

Every word was spun to have a different meaning. Every feeling was discounted. Anything that he was or was not doing was my fault. I felt stupid, like I was just a housewife. I replayed every conversation in my mind, wondering what I had missed. But I never could see what he was saying. Isn't it logical to want a solid partner?

I started to question my memory. *Did that really happen?* I would write each situation down so I could look over it again. (I realize now that that's what I was doing when we were dating and I saved our email exchanges, but this was eight years later.) He never could quite manipulate or berate me the same way on paper.

I want to say I should have known better, but he always reeled me in. I never had anyone to talk to about it because it was all behind closed doors—nobody would believe me. I didn't know how to bring up the hard stuff to my parents without being parented or being told to go to church or counseling, which I had already tried. I couldn't put two and two together. I thought I just needed to toughen up and change how I reacted.

I grew passive. I let him walk all over me by silencing me. It didn't feel worth fighting for myself because in his eyes, I was never right and he was never wrong. I was constantly afraid of upsetting him. I didn't know what he would do, so it was worth it to just put my head down and keep to myself.

I never felt wanted. I was positive he wished his wife was a little hotter, made a little more money, and gave a little more head. The only time he ever told me I was beautiful was if he was about to take me to bed. He never gave me an unsolicited compliment about my looks or heaven forbid, my brains. I didn't feel good in my own body when I was around him. But I was willing to do anything to restore any shred of peace to end a cycle of abuse.

Our relationship was a dance. He was good at his side, and I got good at mine. I bought him gifts, wrote him notes, starved myself so I could look better, didn't make friends so he wouldn't get jealous, only spent money on groceries, smiled at his work events, laughed as if it didn't hurt when he made comments about my body or character in front of our peers. I let him do whatever he wanted, whenever he wanted, no matter how it affected me.

I felt like I was being eaten alive, there were no physical marks, but the mental ones almost broke me. Nobody knew how he really treated me. "What a good guy," they would say. You never really know unless you are the one experiencing it, and that's what makes it so hard to explain and define for people.

But this stuff will fuck with your head. It will leave scars on every part of your insides, graffiti on your heart. It'll say "you aren't good enough, you are crazy, you don't deserve this, I can't believe you act like that…who do you think you are?" Those internal marks are proof that only you can feel.

I was suffocating, powerless, and completely hopeless. I lacked all control over my own life. I was angry and I was terrified, yet for nine years I didn't shed a single tear. I became completely numb.

* * *

He was a master at his craft, manipulation was his art. As time went on, he slowly buried me, layer by layer, until I choked at the thought of my own words. My trauma kept leading me back into situations that would repeat themselves.

He would show dominance, then feel guilt, then make up excuses to avoid taking responsibility. Then he'd quickly go back to a more normal behavior, as if it had never happened. He would become extra charming and apologetic, making me believe that he was sorry. And then the cycle would start again, growing more turbulent each time.

His demands kept me isolated. I didn't have any friends to connect with, no one who could vouch for me. I basically had to hire my friend as my nanny when the girls were babies just so I could see someone regularly that I liked. There was no network for me.

A friend sent me an article about emotional abuse. I read about acts of isolation, verbal assault, humiliation, intimidation, or any other treatment that diminishes your sense of identity, dignity, and self-worth—chronic verbal aggression. How it is the most suffocating, claustrophobic, lonely feeling in the world. I felt seen, yet anxious, depressed, and alone while my self-esteem was in the shitter.

When I realized what was happening and that I was not in fact crazy, I felt trapped. It's like one day a light bulb went on and I was like NOPE, not me, not you, not today, not anymore. I was terrified and embarrassed. I felt foolish for staying so long, for not listening to my friends while I had them, for having kids with him, for letting him talk down to me in front of people. But it wasn't my fault. I knew that. I was stuck.

Nobody could hear the conversations and silent conversations we were having. *How was I going to prove I needed to get out? That I was slowly losing every bit of myself that I knew to be true? How was I going to disappoint my family? How was I going to disappoint his? How was I going to deal with how hard he would make it? Is there something else I could have done? How much would he twist my reasoning? How was I going to be able to emotionally cope when I was now a robot on autopilot, my emotions needing to be dusted off again?*

I needed to feel something, and I knew the first thing I was going to feel was immense pain and loss. But I also knew that there was so much joy for me somewhere on the other side, and I needed to be open to feeling that too.

One of his family members pulled me aside around that time and voiced their concerns over how he treated me. They had always checked in over the years, but I was always too afraid to tell the truth. *What if he found out I had told someone?* Toward the end of our marriage, they expressed that they were very concerned for my mental health. They could hear my silent cries for help.

* * *

I had started working one day a week in a salon doing hair again. I saw money coming into my account and although I wasn't able to put any aside because my finances were under a microscope, I was able to do some basic math and calculate what it would take to be able to make rent at my own place and pay my phone bill. I was getting closer to independence and freedom.

I was also busy raising two beautiful girls. I fought to balance it all—the meals, the kids, the lack of sleep, the jobs, the highs and lows of my husband. I felt like a joke and a fraud. None of it was easy, and parts of me felt damaged and weak.

At the same time, I looked at my girls and saw my own strength and resilience, my resolve. I didn't want them to grow up and settle for a mediocre life. I was living it, and quite frankly, it was exhausting, and it sucked. I would have been happier to have been married to a toothpick at that point. I couldn't imagine if they were with someone who talked to them like I was being talked to, someone who didn't encourage them to grow.

I needed to show my girls that life was bigger. I felt like my life was a lie, like I was going to snap if one person looked me in the eye and asked how I was doing, so I stopped making eye contact. I was happy on the front and miserable behind the scenes. I was basically a mullet.

I wasn't me, and it wasn't fair to them. I saw something better for myself, for us. Maybe that was the push I needed, but it's hard to say.

* * *

I remember sitting on the kitchen floor talking to my nanny friend one night while my husband was out with the boys, again. She had seen the whole relationship unfold—how alone and emotionally beat up I was, how unfair the situation was. I had gotten to the point where I was deciding if I was going to run my own life or if someone else was. I bawled. I looked at her and said, "As far as I know, I only get one shot at life and I want to do it right."

I didn't want to spend my life inside of a lonely and one-sided marriage. More importantly, I didn't want to stay in my marriage "for the kids." We have all heard that argument. Hell, I had argued it with myself a hundred times. The guilt and the shame of a broken family. But the more I looked at my two sweet baby girls, the more I realized I would never want them to stay in a marriage like mine. They looked up to everything I did. I wanted them to experience big love. The wild kind that can't be tamed and can't be replicated. The kind that is undeniable and insatiable. I wanted them to feel respected and valued. To feel a friendship and a partnership. I wanted them to know a marriage beyond traditional gender roles of a man works and a woman belongs in the kitchen. A marriage beyond money and control. I wanted my relationship to be an example to them of bettering each other, not breaking each other down. I wanted them to look at my relationship and say, "That's what I want." And that was never going to happen there.

I took count of what I thought I needed to successfully get out of my marriage. I had to gain new skills along the way.

I needed a little more sleep so I could function and think properly. This came with the kids getting older. Check.

I needed some sort of financial stability and schedule. This came with teaching and doing hair and having consistently full classes and books. Check.

I needed support, a community of people who saw me and trusted me, believed in me. This came with switching studios and finding my people. Almost check.

I didn't feel like I could truly rely on my family for support without a fight or having to explain myself repeatedly. There was religion, and there was the fact that they really didn't know me. They only knew the version of me they had created in their head. The life they envisioned for me. Daughter gets married, has babies, goes to church, probably gets a golden retriever…yada yada. They also didn't truly know my husband.

Emotional abuse is almost impossible to prove to people. It's hard to wrap your brain around what you can't see. I felt like I was screaming and clawing inside of a glass box, trying to escape, and thousands of people were just walking by me, not even noticing I was there. Or if they did, they would think "she looks fine."

At one point, I wished he would have just hit me because it would have been easier to prove, which sounds twisted and disgusting. But that's how trapped I was. If only I had a mark on my face or bruises on my arms, I wouldn't have to explain myself to all these people. I've never liked explaining myself anyway. I began to think visual proof on the skin would reveal what was going on behind closed doors, and that could have helped me get out. If people see your wound, they believe you, but if they hear about it, there are questions.

Do you know how many women live this way? Most people will move through life without experiencing the trauma of violence or abuse, but that doesn't mean they don't exist. It's everywhere.

* * *

I told my husband I wanted to separate the night before he left for another trip. I had been sick over it and nervous to say it out loud. I had been shaking nonstop for days leading up to it. My stomach had been churning like a tornado for a week. I needed to tell him before he left because I didn't know which way he would swing emotionally. He would either be quiet and sad or have an emotional rage outburst.

I told him I wasn't in love with him, that I couldn't deal with the way he spoke to me anymore. I told him I had given him enough chances. I said I was done, and it was too late for counseling. He didn't hear me before. He didn't see me before. *I wasn't worth the work, so why would I be now?*

He called me from his hotel room twenty-four hours later bawling. I had never heard him cry. He was terrified. He didn't know life outside of me. I was home. I was comfort. I was also his puppet. I did everything. I was our life and he knew it. He begged for another chance. He said he would change. He suggested counseling. He asked for forgiveness.

But I didn't trust him. I couldn't. I said, "I'm not in love with you." And with those words, I said goodbye and laid in my bed and knew it was the final time we would have this conversation.

It had finally happened to me, all those years later and the shit finally hit the fan. I knew I would be the girl who people pitied as she went through a divorce at thirty years old.

I took a big breath and knew I had to dip into the deepest parts of myself—the strength that had been suppressed and shut down for eleven years. I asked it to resurface because I knew I would need it. I was going to have to take who I knew I was and who I wanted to be and make them the same thing.

I was devastated and terrified. I was nervous but strong. I was calm but scared shitless. This was going to be hard. I had no idea what was coming for me. But I was ready.

7: My light

I continued teaching and doing hair, but the studio I worked for reminded me a little too much of my soon-to-be ex...it was toxic, competitive, and slightly manipulative. I decided to look elsewhere and get out of my first toxic relationship (my job) in preparation to get out of the next (my marriage). When it was time to leave my job, I wrote them a letter graciously bowing out so I could part ways and not have the added emotional stress of the studio.

I met my next boss at a dive bar. I needed more space to expand and grow, and I also wanted to be teaching in the city. I was so excited to hear that I had nailed my audition and could get back to doing what I loved.

I remember my first day of training at the new studio. We were in the hallway, and we were learning the new microphone protocol. Microphones in a fitness studio are a big deal. I know my boss would gladly write a book about sound issues, but I'll let her humor you with that later. They were describing rolling a condom onto a microphone pack to prevent sweat from getting in. Everyone was laughing and could not believe that we were rolling magnums onto anything but a wiener or a banana.

And just as we were doing so, a strikingly beautiful blonde woman walked down the hall toward us. She had short hair, was wearing a backward snapback hat, a muscle tee, baggy joggers, and high tops. Her eyes were inviting, big and brown. As she walked by, she smiled out of the side of her mouth and said, "Don't ask me how to use them. I'm gay."

This moment always replays in slow motion to me. I was taken aback by her. Maybe because I didn't know a lesbian in real time. Maybe it's because she came in like a beam of light. Or maybe because that was my first interaction with my soul mate.

Two days later, at 6 a.m., I found myself sitting in the middle row of her class, trying to go unnoticed. But I was like a moth to a flame.

Her name was Steph. She was mysterious. I was intrigued. Her energy was magnetic. She was wearing a red tank and her shoulders were strong, glistening under the down light. She commanded respect. I couldn't stop staring at her mouth, watching the words form as they left her lips. I had never been to a class where anyone had made me work that hard besides myself—I almost threw up.

I had met my match. Game on.

I introduced myself to her after class. She told me that she already knew who I was, which scared the shit out of me.

What did she know? Could she tell that my jaw had been on the floor for the last forty-five minutes? Did she know that I was insecure and drooled on my pillow at night? Did she know that I was desperate to feel anything at all? Was she watching me too?

I started riding with her every chance I got, right next to her, on stage. She was the best. I wanted to be the best.

We made small talk here and there. I couldn't figure out why I was so drawn to her. I also couldn't figure out her relationship with her girlfriend. She couldn't figure out mine either. Neither of us were happy. We were both silently trying to get out, but we never talked about it.

Riding with Steph was part of my routine and kept me sane. She had been preparing to leave for an internship for a few weeks up near Seattle, and I was going to teach her classes, or fill her shoes, if you will, while she was gone. Terrifying? Yes. Doable? Maybe. I tried. I was determined to be seen in this space too.

My first classes waitlisted. I had busted my ass getting to know people in this new space, and clients from my previous studio showed up to support me too. Day one on the job and they saw me.

Steph sent me a text a day later, congratulating me and asking how it went.

What is happening?

We continued to text each other over the next few weeks. Checking in. We both had walls up and we didn't have much to talk about. But we were drawn to each other, so we tried.

8: D is for divorce

I don't believe in regret; the past is where we learn our lessons and create opportunities. Sure, my first marriage wasn't healthy, but I got my beautiful children out of the deal and learned a lot about who I was and the depths of my strength and resilience (up until that point anyway). So while I'm not surprised that we ended in divorce, it's still sad.

I was ready to have the first of many hard conversations with my parents. And by ready, I mean I had no choice because I needed support and I was desperate. It was the next step. As a thirty-year-old woman, I was terrified to tell them. I felt trapped by a religious upbringing that told me divorce was the ultimate sin. I had so much fear of judgment and of disappointing my family.

Over the phone, I told them my marriage was done. They were shocked and they were mad. They thought we could work on it; they didn't understand, and they didn't try. Their initial response was to react. They didn't know about the abuse, that I had asked for help, or that he refused to go to counseling. I didn't have proof of how he treated me behind closed doors, so they didn't believe me. They saw the happy-go-lucky guy that everyone else saw. They had no idea what had been happening the last eleven years in my relationship.

They never asked what my marriage was like, and I didn't feel comfortable bringing it up because I knew their stance on it all. He wasn't cheating, so counseling and books and church and the Lord should solve the problem. I also knew that their marriage wasn't my marriage, and their struggles were different so they would never understand. I was met with comments like "we have had really hard times," including specifics about how long it took to get out of said hard times.

But their specifics weren't my specifics. I saw the way my dad looked at my mom growing up, I heard the way they spoke to each other. Their story wasn't mine.

They were mad about me wanting a divorce, and they were mad that I didn't reach out sooner. But it would have only made my situation worse. I'd often felt isolated and completely unseen in the past when I brought my struggles to the table, and that was the reason I had waited so long to tell them. To them, there was only one way to do things. And if that's not what I was doing, I was straight up wrong.

There was love in their worry, but there was also shame. I felt two completely opposite things at once. I had to constantly remind myself to stand my ground. I didn't want to settle for an average or subpar life.

As the weeks went on, I was questioned repeatedly by my parents. I felt horrible about myself. There was so much explaining. It's hard to explain every one of your thoughts and actions in the midst of so much pain. I'll never understand why my parents' first instinct was to question and blame instead of love, or trust, or hold space for me for a minute. It was instantaneous, like a knee-jerk reaction.

I had hoped for love and respect as they gained under-standing—not questions, accusations, and quick fixes. I must have been "depressed or having a mid-life crisis." It stung. It also made me put up a wall similar to the walls I'd built around my heart during my marriage. Big, thick, sturdy walls. Walls that I am still trying to break down to this day. I was thirty years old, and as I write this, I am thirty-five. I knew me better than they did, better than anyone did.

My dad cornered me and asked if there was someone else. My husband had told him I was cheating. I was pissed and completely heartbroken. *How could they accuse me of anything when I was trying to break free from control?*

My only goal was to be happy, safe, and raise my kids to know an honest and loving relationship. I didn't need this shit.

I started talking to my husband strictly via text or email so I could document some of the behavior. I found myself telling my parents things as they happened, not to make myself feel better, and not to turn them on him, but more to prove my case so they would stop questioning me.

Every time I did it, I hated myself a little bit more. It was exhausting. And I felt dirty. I needed someone to see me, to look at me and say: "Okay yes, whatever you need, I have your back." The last thing I wanted was for people to hate my ex. I was stuck with this guy in my life forever. Kids and years together bound us.

I was empty, yet I still had the capacity for grace. Hate would do nothing. Resentment would do nothing. I wasn't even mad anymore. I was only scared.

I was trying to move forward with the divorce, but it was hard to do when I had no control or access to our finances. I knew I had about $2,000 in my account and by then, I knew I could bring in about $3,000 a month while still being with my kids whenever I had them. This wouldn't be enough, but it was a good start.

I had to get out of my house. He had started leaving every night, which was fine because it was awkward if he was home. But it was also terrifying. I never knew where he was or when he would be back. We slept in our bed next to each other for two months after I told him it was over. I laid with my eyes wide open every night, facing the wall, nothing but tension and a sheet between us. My chest would rise and fall so quickly that I couldn't catch a full breath for eight hours a night, inhaling and exhaling anxiety.

At the same time, he was trying everything to win me back. Every four days it felt like he was a completely different person. One day he was telling me he felt bad for me because I was making a mistake. The next week I would get flowers, he would cook dinner, or ask for counseling. He got up before me to hang out with the kids so I could sleep. He cried. He begged. He started going to church and taking the kids, trying to look like the good guy. He promised to change, apologized, left notes, and told me I was beautiful. Each gesture made me shake, and when one gesture didn't work, there was a period of rage from him before he turned into the next Romeo. I was disgusted. None of it was genuine, and it wouldn't stick for more than a week even if I had bought into it. We would fall into the same patterns.

We played house during the day, avoiding each other but being civil because the kids were around. I dreaded the nights because that's when we would hash things out. We usually spoke over the kitchen island. I felt safe there with a giant quartz slab between us and a door behind me in case I needed to get out.

Some nights he got angry, others he got sad. He told me he felt bad for me, that I was pathetic, that I was making a huge mistake. I explained to him that we both deserve happiness and we couldn't find it together, not with how he treated me. Some nights he would tell me he was afraid he would never meet anyone as good as me. Our conversations were all over the place. There was so much pain on both sides, yet nothing made sense. I wanted to cry but I couldn't, I was so numb after all that time, my tear ducts as dry as the Sahara Desert.

When we talked about our kids, I told him I wanted to raise our girls to be strong, independent women. He replied that he disagreed.

UM, WHAT?! Who doesn't want their daughter to be strong, independent, and have a voice?

When I asked him why, he couldn't form an answer. I often wonder if it's because he did not know how to articulate that he was controlling and liked it that way without actually sounding controlling. He didn't even argue with me. Just a straight up disagree, full stop. He just didn't want them to be like me.

* * *

A few days after this conversation, he came home in the middle of the night, waking me up as he stormed down the hall, getting closer and closer to our room with each thud of a footstep. I started shaking because I didn't know what he was going to do. He flipped my light on and started thrashing through my room.

I was terrified. I think he was drunk, at least I hope so because that somehow makes it a little better. Except it didn't. I held my breath and didn't move, listening as he got closer and louder, pushing things off the dresser, stomping and thrashing around. He wanted me to wake up. He was there to pick a fight with me. I'm sure he wanted to hit something. At one point he stopped for a full minute, I could hear him breathing. He was standing next to me. I could feel his anger, and there was no way I was stupid enough to sit up.

I was doing the whole play dead thing they tell you to do if you ever see a bear. It was the only thing I could think of.

What would he do if he got to me—what would I do?

I was shaking in my sheets as I held my breath and braced myself. So many thoughts rushed through my head in that moment. *How would I escape? Could the kids hear this?*

Did he have anything in his hands? How did I let it get this far?

He finally left and slammed the door. We never spoke about it, but it was time to move.

* * *

My parents had finally seen and heard enough to understand the real picture because of the emails, stories, and texts that I shared. They wanted me out. They wanted me safe. Somewhere along the line, my mom had reminded my dad that their marriage was not our marriage, and that my struggles with my husband were far different than her struggles with him. She reminded him that because not all marriages are the same, not all solutions would be the same.

I found a condo nearby, and my ex and I agreed I would move into it in three weeks. Three weeks sounded like an eternity, but I had almost ten years under my belt. At this point I was still making him dinner. I could do this. I would plan it out so one of us would leave each night for a few hours after the kids went to sleep, and we would start alternating weekends. There were occasions where he left for days at a time, and I had no idea where he was going because he wouldn't tell me. There were also nights when he was clearly dressed to impress. It was weird. And it felt dirty. So much malice.

And there I was at my second rock bottom. I had flipped two beautiful homes, been comfortable in my finances, and was about to be a single mom living in a tiny outdated condo in Lake Oswego, Oregon. Home of too much Botox, too much filler, and too many housewives that knew too many details about everyone's life but their own. A town full of rumors and money. Somehow, it felt like the best pill to swallow. My pride was out the window anyway.

* * *

I started trying to get things in my name. My credit card had been blocked, and I was given an allowance of $200 a month to buy groceries and basic household supplies. If I needed more for any reason, I would have to ask him. He was protecting himself.

I called the phone company to try to get off the bill, but they told me he had to authorize it. I knew that he was trying to track my texts and my calls, and I was terrified and felt beyond violated. When I asked him to release me, he said no. He said it was HIS phone plan. Up until then, as marriage states, I was under the impression that it was OUR phone plan—that it was shared. I didn't remember signing a prenup for our AT&T bill. He was watching me, and he wasn't going to let up, even if getting off the phone bill saved him thirty bucks a month. Passwords were changed, accounts were locked, and I was refused access.

I had a hard time having reasonable conversations with him, so I took to my old email tactics to try to have productive conversations and get my point across.

You still seem to think this is so sudden. This started in our dating life. The patterns have not changed. I remember emailing you about the same things when I was in beauty school. I was always the one pursuing you. From day one I put the effort in. Through the years you continually chose friendships over me, you were not there. You watched basketball while I was in labor. You went out with friends on New Year's when we didn't have babysitters. Harper almost killed me year one, and you went on boys' trips, to games, to beers. I was exhausted, beaten down, and completely alone. You couldn't figure out a plan for my birthday and instead went to a soccer game.

There are so many moments when you did not choose me, when others mattered more. Important moments. I understand I am breaking a vow, but you also broke your vow when you weren't there for me. When you put me second, your wife, the mother of your kids. You broke my trust. I felt disrespected, neglected. I asked for help, you couldn't give that to me. I put a wall up, I got stronger, and I realized what I deserved.

I have tried for years to communicate with you. To tell you, to ask you to do things differently, etc. This is not sudden. You always talked down to me, twisted the words, made me feel stupid for feeling a certain way, got defensive. You would talk to me one way and apologize later. And then do it again, and again. Never learning that every time it hurt, and every time it pushed me further away. I've given you 12 years now to see me, to hear me, to love me, to put some effort in.

I feel like you have "loved" me in a very controlling, manipulative way. Even this last email when you stated, "You are free to go," as if you own me. It's hard because you do not see how you have treated me, talked down to me on repeat for all this time. How it has wounded me in so many ways. For years I hid my emotions in fear that they would be abused if spoken aloud. I refuse to be talked to or treated this way. The damage has been done. It's beyond repair. I have known for quite some time that this is what had to be done. It is not sudden; it is not a new life or whatever story you are telling yourself. This is years of being unhappy.

Our kids, these girls, they are so incredible. I do not regret our time together. These kids are so special. There is no doubt in my mind that they will continue to feel loved and supported. You are a great father. We will always put them first. We will show respect for one another in front of them. We will lift them up, hold them close, and cherish their dreams. Moving forward, I hope we can keep our pride aside and really focus on what is best for them. No doubt it will be a hard transition. But if we continue to work together, we can make it as smooth as possible.

I would like to go to mediation. I think if we are willing to work with each other instead of against each other, this will be a much easier process and save a lot of time and money that would be better spent elsewhere or saved for the kids. There are some useful forms on the mediation site. It would be great if we could get started on them and try to come to some terms together before we go in. We can talk about it. I hope this gives you a bit more clarity.

We spent the next seven months bouncing between mediators and lawyers and anxiety attacks. I found a piece of paper near his briefcase that noted his strategy was to drag his feet. I have to commend the man, he did a damn good job with that. I was told at one point that I didn't deserve more than $200 a month in child support and alimony combined.

Was I on some sick and twisted version of candid camera? Do men really think that women have no value? That it's not equal?

I didn't work per se because I stayed home with our two kids who were too young to go to school, and he was too cheap for daycare. To him, that type of work wasn't deserving of half of the assets. Being a stay-at-home mom had no monetary value to him because I didn't get a paycheck. He clearly had never stayed home with the kids, or he would have known that raising children at home is literally the most demanding job in the world. He also told me that he didn't respect what I was doing so I didn't deserve the money. Like you could put a price on actions.

* * *

I got smart and called the credit card company to get a log in. I could see the card being paid off from our checking account, but I couldn't see why the bill was so high or what was on it. I was only spending my allotted $200 a month. His paychecks were no longer going into our accounts, so he would transfer just enough money in to pay the credit card off each time.

I got the log in from the company and went to do my own investigation. There was a $169 charge to a PayPal account called Girl Friday. *Was this a stripper? What the fuck was this charge?*

I knew he was watching my cell phone, and I had checked to see if my house and car were bugged. A friend and I spent hours searching every corner of my house along with the inside, outside, and underside of my car for cameras or microphones. There's nothing like thrashing through your own belongings when you feel like you're being spied on.

Was he hacking my computer? I tried every Google search I could find and found no evidence of the PayPal account. I called the credit card company again and asked what the company Girl Friday was. They said it was linked to tech services and gave me the name of the actual company. I Googled it. As I clicked the link, my heart stopped beating and I couldn't breathe. He had hired a private investigator.

I immediately texted him and asked him about it. All while trying to uncurl my fists and swallow the boulder in my throat. My veins felt like they had lava in them. I was overcome with disgust, fear, and rage. He couldn't believe that I was looking at the credit card bill or that I'd gotten access. He kept asking me how I found it. I couldn't possibly be smart enough. After all, he was the only one in the relationship with a brain. He lied and wouldn't tell me what it was until I finally told him that I knew. I asked him to fess up. I didn't want to play games.

It turns out he had hired the investigator to follow me a week prior. I have never felt more violated than I did in that moment.

The private investigator was a woman, which felt like a violation of girl code in and of itself. She had followed me to my friend's house one evening before Christmas, as I had nowhere else to go. She had been waiting in her car with her lights off down the street until he called her and told her I had left the house. It was my agreed night to leave. He'd known that, so he set me up.

She took photos of me and my car along the way, trailing me. Meanwhile, I was just trying to get out of his sight, probably blasting my music, having no idea that someone was on my tail for twelve minutes. She took photos of me getting out of my car and walking into my friend's house. All for $169. I would have felt better if she had charged more. *Did he find her on Craigslist?* She could have been a murderer or a real stalker for that price. She also had an AOL email account. There's nothing sketchier than a live AOL account in 2015. But the guy was cheap, and he got what he wanted.

When I found out, I felt bad for exposing my friends to my situation. He didn't need to know where they lived. I didn't need him harassing them or showing up at their door. I wanted to protect them.

For the next year, I drove with my eyes more on the rearview mirror than the road. I pulled over multiple times on the freeway or street to let someone pass because they had been behind me too long. I was sure I was being followed. I would sit on the side of the road and cry, shaking, traumatized, as cars whooshed past me. To this day, I still wonder if someone is following me. I check my rearview mirror like a nervous twitch.

He didn't see anything wrong with it. He thought I was lying, and it was his money to spend. After all, he had the bigger paycheck. I just wiped the kid's asses and apparently his. Even my dad told me he probably would have done the same thing if he thought someone was cheating. I haven't recovered from it. It's a trauma I will carry for the rest of my life, and something I will never agree with. It was completely unnecessary. I was also horrified that this woman was okay spying on innocent people as a job.

We were getting a divorce. *Let me go.*

* * *

A week before moving out, we decided it was time to tell the kids. He insisted that I was the one to tell them since I was the one leaving. Fine. I wanted to leave. And he wanted me to look like the bad guy. However, again, I didn't want my kids to look at our relationship and think that this is what love and respect looked like. I was happy to be the one to tell them, going with my strong woman theme. If you don't like it and it won't change, leave it.

Fortunately, they were little, and they trusted me as their mother. I emphasized that they still had two parents that loved them, that they would get to see us both equally. I told them that they would have two rooms to make their own and the same friends, etc. Fortunately, the only thing they were upset about was the fact that we couldn't keep the dog. I think my ex was expecting them to disown me and see me as the bad guy and hate me. I'm certain he was super dissatisfied with the outcome.

I took a big breath and held them close. We were going to be okay. We were going to figure it out, and I was certain that every single one of us, including my ex, would be happier on the other side.

9: Someone called the movers

I'd lost my wedding ring the previous summer. It was the final sign that I needed to leave. The universe was telling me: it was okay, it was done.

June was really into Play-Doh at the time and loved to put anything and everything in it. She would leave it out, it would dry, and we would throw it away. We lost a lot of toys this way, especially Shopkins. I was usually totally okay with it. Why in the world would you make such tiny toys anyway? It's like vacuum bait but then it fucks up your vacuum, and you are left with a crying child and a bill for $200 to Dyson for the repair.

Anyway, I was sure my wedding ring had gotten tossed. I liked my ring, but I hadn't been wearing it. So I was bummed but not devastated. Truthfully, I was hoping to trade it in for cash if needed. I guess I'd have to find cash another way.

One Thursday, my soon-to-be ex was at work, and the kids were playing downstairs as I was packing the rest of my clothes and shoes. Once it was time to go, I had to go fast to avoid any rage. I was moving the next day. I was taking a few things from the house and had ordered a bunk bed for the kids. I could come up with the rest later. He had told me to take whatever I wanted and that he didn't care.

I sat on the floor by my closet, reading a red leather journal I had found from beauty school. In it, I had hand copied letters and emails that my ex and I had written to each other before we got married. All the times he manipulated, pushed, and pulled me. All the times he twisted my words or told me I was crazy. All the break ups and get-back-togethers. They were right there. Abuse on every page. Midway through, I had broken up with him, or him with me. And I wrote, I hope *I don't end up with him*. That was the end of the diary. One hundred blank pages left. Suffocated words that I never released over the next ten years.

I hadn't even let myself write on a blank page as I knew the truth would come out. And although the truth would set me free, it wouldn't be that simple. It was like the truth would set me free, but with a clause. The clause being: "Not before it fucks you up and hurts the people around you. Not before you deal with their emotions before your own." I looked down at the pages and tears started spilling out of my eyes. My hands were trembling. I had known all along. I knew. I felt heavy but oddly light at the same time. Like floating with a weight vest on. I had been silently suffocating ever since I wrote the last sentence.

The light from our window was shining on me in the closet. I tucked the diary into my duffel and turned around to grab the last pair of shoes I had, as something shiny and bright dropped right in front of me and hit the floor. If a tiny piece of metal could sound like a siren when it hit the carpet, that's what I heard. It was my wedding ring. It was blinding me as I stared at it and it stared back at me. I slowly cocked my head to the right.

What was this? Was it taunting me? Was I hallucinating? Then to the left. *No, it was closure. Hell, I don't know.*

I slowly reached out to grab it. It was real. The moment lasted ten minutes in my head, when in reality, it was only a few seconds that the ring held my gaze.

How the fuck did it get in my shoe? Was God real? Because if he was, where was he in all of this? Why didn't he help fix my marriage or make my husband nicer?

I held it between my fingers and stared at it while tears stained my cheeks and the carpet underneath me. I felt the last ten years in an instant—the joy and the trauma, all the beauty and the pain. I felt it ALL.

It had come full circle. It was time to go. I never told him I found the ring. I didn't know what to say about it, and I didn't need to deal with one more reaction or set of questions. He would probably want to sell it anyway and pocket the money, but that ring is a part of me whether I like it or not. It's a part of my story.

* * *

My mom, dad, and eight of my friends went to my house and started loading up every box I had packed, loading them one by one into their cars while I was at work. I didn't take much; I didn't care about the stuff. I only needed enough to get by, and the rest I could pick up along the way.

I wasn't stoked about my new place, but it felt safe. When I got off work and showed up, my friends were wearing shirts they had made that said *Team Lianne* on the front. Showing support in more ways than one, painting my walls, putting together a bunk bed for my kids, unpacking my belongings, making a home for us.

There was music and energy. Every time the paint roller went up the wall I smiled. It was a clean slate. This was going to be my first happy home—my people were making sure of it.

The house was going up for sale no matter how bad I fought to keep it. I was very attached to it, but he didn't want me to have it. I had taken a bed, a dresser, some wall decor, an old beat up couch, and some salad bowls. I left every other kitchen utensil, dish, bowl, glass, and piece of furniture. I wasn't going to argue about who got what. It would have been a massive headache that $150 bucks at IKEA could fix. Not worth it.

When he noticed that the salad bowls were gone, he demanded I bring half of them back. He needed four plates back, because "half were his." That's how hellish my life had been. I'm surprised I didn't have to saw the mattress in half. He was out to argue my every action.

I did bring the bowls back, and I saw our leftover belongings laying in the front yard with a sign that said FREE. The color drained from my face, and my heart sank to my stomach. Something about seeing your possessions in front of your home that was for sale, with a sign that basically reads "this shit means nothing to me" will really hit you in the gut.

I walked through the garage only to see that my skis were gone, as were my grandfather's tools. I had already had to give away my childhood piano that I so badly wanted my kids to play one day because downsizing my home meant there was no room to keep it. Everything else in the house was gone. Only a few pieces of trash and a large sofa remained. It was eerie and no longer felt like my home. It felt like a trigger. I had always felt like he didn't need me and could dispose of me at any moment, and that's exactly what he did to my belongings. I felt dirty and sad as I looked around. I was angry. I couldn't even say goodbye, it would feel like hugging a stranger.

I left as fast as I could.

My heart was broken. I didn't know what to feel, but what I did feel was not good. It's amazing that things can seem so valuable one day, yet mean nothing the next. Maybe that's what happens when there is anger and spite involved. Most of all, I felt empty. Our things still meant something to me. But my deceased grandfather's tools were now owned by my ex. My skis from college now belonged to a stranger. Who knows what else I had lost and who ended up with them.

10: New home, who dis?

The weeks that followed my move were weird. I was sick with longing the first two days I didn't have my kids. I tried to stay busy, but when I was home, I walked in circles. I cried. I cried on repeat— like a broken record. I was completely beside myself. I slept in their beds to feel closer to them, to smell any bits of them left on their sheets. They smelled like home. The days felt like the movie *Groundhog Day*. I had had at least one child with me pretty much 24/7 for the last four years whether I liked it or not. I was on the buddy system and suddenly I didn't have a buddy.

I sat in the hallway with my head in my hands and cried for hours, questioning if I did the right thing. *What were they doing? Were they okay without me? Was he going to meet someone and try to tell the kids she was a better mother than me? How would I do this? How would I survive not seeing my children every day? How would I provide for them?*

I had never felt true loneliness until this moment. It shook me to my core. You know the scenes in movies where the person is crying alone in the cold, dark, rain, and the camera zooms out and everything around them is deserted? That was me. I was inside that body, and I was also on the other side of the camera.

Despite the loneliness, I felt an overwhelming sense of peace. During the second week in our tiny little condo, I remember Harper looked at me as we were playing and laughing and asked, "Mama, why are you so much happier in this house?"

I looked at her perfect face and said, "Because this is our happy home."

And the mood forever shifted. I had finally been able to play with my kids, sit on the floor with them, and let them crawl all over me without feeling scared about not making dinner on time or doing something wrong. In our new happy home, I didn't have to fear the backlash or the guilt of my ex. I had a space to heal and transform, to learn to trust people, and to shape my own future.

I had moments where I was humbled too. I had owned a beautiful home and now I was living in a dated, dark condo where I could hear my neighbors below. Neighbors who would immediately ask us to keep it down if my three-and five-year-old ran down the hall. It was an impossible situation to explain to a small child. The carpet was stained from the previous owners and there was no outside space for my kids to play, just a parking lot.

I went between feeling empowered and embarrassed. The girls shared a tiny bedroom and my kitchen was the size of a single closet. I also had a balcony big enough for two chairs and zero standing room. At least the balcony had a view of Mt. Hood on a clear night and enough space for me to sneak a cigarette when the stress was too much to handle. Everything was dated and had a film on it from whoever had previously lived there. Layers of stories that weren't mine that not even paint could cover. But it was my home—our home.

Our surroundings weren't ideal, but I was doing it. And I knew it. I'd created a space where I could breathe. A space where we could create the life we wanted. One that felt good for us. Where we could grow and mess up and rise up unapologetically. I knew in that moment that I did the right thing. The three of us would be fine. We would write new stories here and then we would leave. We had freedom.

I spent my days trying to work two jobs and build a life for myself while also fixing up the condo to feel like a home and being one hundred percent present and available to my kids whenever they were with me.

I drank a lot of gin, usually starting around 3 p.m., and I smoked a cigarette a day. I never drank enough to get drunk, but enough to take the edge off and get rid of the fear that he would come beat down my door. Enough to make me feel like a lighter version of who I was in the moment. Enough to lift the extra ten pounds of stress off my chest and layers of chaos and confusion from my mind, to shush the voice that told me I wasn't good enough and fill the emptiness I felt inside.

* * *

I never slept more than three hours out of sheer anxiety or the fact that he would always wait until the evening to send a disturbing or completely out-of-line text, just in time to rile me up before I was to settle down. It put me in an instant frenzy, my heart would race, and I would be short of breath for hours, wondering how and if I would ever fully get out of this mess. I was certain he was going to try to make me miserable until the divorce was final.

11: Do I even like flowers?

Transitioning out of my marriage had been the hardest thing I had ever dealt with in my life, so I started to think about what we do for people when things get difficult. The most common theme always seemed to be flowers. I've never loved the idea of sending flowers. What was the point if they were just going to die? Like, here you go, here's seventy bucks that you cannot spend, in a vase.

I don't remember loving them as a child. My dad would get my mom roses, and I've always had beef with roses. Maybe it's the cheesy romance that goes along with it. Or maybe it's the fact that in high school, a classmate dropped off two dozen red ones on my porch one Valentine's Day with a balloon that read: "Do you wanna monkey around?" I was mortified and did NOT want to monkey around. And carnations just meant you were cheap or someone had died. I do remember loving daisies and wildflowers and picking them on walks, but maybe because they were so innocent and unassuming. Something about them seemed more pure and simple.

I thought about the three times my ex really did buy me flowers. A random birthday, Mother's Day, or another obligatory occasion. And I just got mad. Every time.

Don't do it because Hallmark told you to. I don't want obligatory flowers. I wanted flowers that said: "I love you, and here's a random gesture to show it." In the moment, I would try to be appreciative, always trying to wrap my brain around the real sentiment behind flowers. But then I'd watch whatever sentiment it was fade and die as the flowers started to droop, and the pollen and petals fell onto my countertop. It was one more mess to clean up and one more vase to wash.

I thought about the flowers that were sent by others after I had kids. How I would sit on the couch, completely exhausted, and see the droopy half-dead flowers, minutes away from being completely bare as the last petal hung on for dear life. I would stare at the brown water and gooey stems, wondering when I would have the energy to throw them out, wipe up the counter, and clean the rotten smell from the vase. It seemed as though somewhere along the way, someone had made it okay to send flowers in lieu of deeper emotional or physical support. And the world just went along with it.

I started to resent the idea of getting flowers. I told my ex I didn't like them anymore. They just die—just like my marriage did. Why not bring people something that can live on if you really want to share a feeling? A houseplant, perhaps. Or money in a vase that you could spend on something that would be there for more than five days. Or maybe a card, words on paper can live forever and be reabsorbed at any time.

The more I thought about flowers, the angrier I got. It wasn't ever about the flowers in the first place, but it became about the flowers. The gesture, or the lack thereof. And then the mess and the cleanup.

I decided that I never wanted flowers again. Leave them in the ground and let them live. Let's only admire them in their natural state.

PART 2
Get a Wife

12: Sure, I'll be gay today

One of the most repeated questions I got when I started dating my wife was "when did you know you were gay?" This completely caught me off guard because I had never thought to ask someone that or thought that of myself. The only reply I could think of was "I'm sorry, when did you know you were straight?"

The when-did-you-know question seemed, and still seems, like the most uneducated and irrelevant question there ever was. Beyond being caught off guard, I quickly became offended. Every time. I was appalled that people would even ask.

It's not like I shot out of the womb and the nurses said, "It's a girl! She's seven pounds two ounces, and nineteen and a half inches long, brown hair...and she's gay!"

You also don't just wake up one day and think to yourself, *You know what? I'm going to be gay today*, out of nowhere. It's not like I chose to upset my family or was seeking out a way to offend baby Jesus. I didn't want to spend years explaining myself or the reason I fell in love with someone who happened to be the same sex as me. I wasn't looking for a way to make my life more complicated.

The second I showed interest in a woman, I was labeled as gay?

HOLD UP. WAIT A MINUTE.

I understand that it's easier to use labels for people so we can file them away in a little box for gay, straight, Christian, swinger, comedian, airhead, etc. But that's not actually how it works. I acknowledge that many people fully identify as just one thing—gay, straight, bisexual, etc. And that is fantastic. I also know plenty of people who have only ever been attracted to the same or the opposite sex. But that leaves no room for the spectrum of people in between.

Why is it so important to slap a label on someone's inclination to love someone? It's not like humans are a barcode on a piece of fruit that goes down the conveyor belt until it's scanned and placed in the appropriate bag. I don't want a label or a conveyor belt. And I don't want to be placed in a box or a bag. It makes me feel small and controlled, and a bit claustrophobic.

Could we take a moment to shatter our conventional thinking for the greater good? Could we ever just wrap our brain around the fact that you can fall in love with someone? SOMEONE.

* * *

The definition of someone is:

some·one

/ˈsəmˌwən/

pronoun

1. an unknown or unspecified person; some person.

* * *

Notice how the authors of the dictionary didn't put "someone" in any box or category. There's no sex assigned. They are only classified as a person—a human being. Why? Because it turns out that's all that matters.

Carry on.

13: My big gay education

They say you should marry your best friend, so I did...the second time anyway.

This next part is the story about how I fell in love with a person. A special "someone," if you will. That person being my best friend, who's a girl. In fact, she was one of the two houses I would seek shelter at during the worst of my divorce. It happened whether I wanted it to or not. Get over it.

* * *

I was raised in a small town and a big church. Some may look at it and call it a cult, and while I still don't see it that way, I can see how others would. I have fond memories of church, for the most part. I liked the fellowship, the morals, and the community. I see how organized religion is comforting for people, offering answers and hope. I have amazing memories from church camps as a kid. It taught me a sense of freedom in a safe space. As a teen, I remember driving to evening worship with my friends and going to hang out afterward. It was my community and a safe space where I felt like I fit in and stayed out of trouble. A place where I could make my family proud. I think it's the church where I fell in love with people. But I also think it's the church that jaded me.

I can see how churches single people out, making them feel different and unwelcomed. I know how Christians interpret the Bible when it comes to gay people. It was pounded into my head. As was love thy neighbor, don't judge, God made you perfect in his eyes, etc.

I remember the sermons about homosexuality. The pastor and congregation referred to it as a lifestyle. They painted a picture of gay relationships being dark and negative, like it was bad or the ultimate sin to love someone of the same sex. And it wasn't always necessarily about doing something bad, but more being someone bad. It was all very confusing and conflicting information. As I got older, these sermon messages started to sink in. I didn't understand how so many people could hate someone for loving someone else, and if it wasn't hate, it was judgment.

The term *fag* or *faggot* was a thing when I was a kid in the early 90s. The slang *homo* was tossed around in jokes about people. I knew it had a negative connotation in my community, but I also wondered where in the Bible it said it was okay to make fun of gay people, or any people for that matter. Remember the passage about "thou shalt not judge"?

I had listened to pastors talk about how gay people chose a life of sin. Why would someone choose a lifestyle just to be met with criticism and persecution from society? Especially from people like a community of Christians who were supposed to love everyone. Didn't God make them in his image as well? Why would someone choose a lifestyle they felt they had to hide and endure abuse for living? That isn't a lifestyle at all. Why would someone choose to fear who they were or to share who they loved? Also, why would Christians judge them for that? There's no way anybody would choose that.

I didn't know any gay people when I was younger, or at least they hadn't come out yet. Except apparently my great Uncle Dick with the pink seahorse socks and the life partner...but when you are six, you don't really put that together. I'm still very confused as to why coming out is even a thing, or why it must be this grand gesture that takes months or years to work up the courage to do. Speaking and living your truth should be like breathing, yet we are suffocated by society's traditional values and conventional thinking, family ideals, religion, and shame.

I kept my eyes peeled for a gay. *What a specimen that would be!* I wanted to meet one because it was such a novelty. I wanted to make the call for myself whether they chose this dark road or if they were born this way. I pictured someone so loud and flamboyant, wearing rainbows and glitter, maybe even a boa or a sparkly speedo with a high-pitched voice, flailing their limbs around and vogueing down the supermarket aisle, talking incessantly about sex. This is what homosexuality looked like from a Christian perspective. This was the picture that had been painted—sinners being loud and in your face with their "lifestyle."

I remember jabs from my dad and brother, jokes about homos and gays. It was confusing. Each one was like a tiny poke to my heart. It wasn't right, I couldn't laugh. It started to coat my brain, jab by jab, layer by layer, like a protective barrier between me, my family, and religion.

Part of my ex's family had a hard stance against homosexuality. Yet they were able to divorce even though their church taught that both were a sin. Did this make them a hypocrite? Weren't all sins equal? Aren't we all sinners? Apparently not. Why were we still condemning gays?

One of their daughters was gay. She was younger when I met her, not yet "out," but it was very apparent to me that she was gay and had been gay straight out of the birth canal. I loved her. She was smart and confident and curious and sarcastic, just exactly as she should be. She eventually came out to her family and they were devastated. Horrified, even. They agonized over who they pictured her to be and how she could possibly choose a lifestyle of sin. They tried to talk with me about it, I tried to listen. But all the while I wondered how they could look their daughter in the eye and tell her she was wrong, that she wasn't whole.

They were essentially saying to her that she wasn't fully loved. It was like, we would love you more IF you weren't gay. I love you with a clause.

Their disapproval caused a huge rift in their relation-ship. They agonized and prayed for her every day. I don't know where she stands with her family now, but I applaud her for staying true to her heart, even if it hurt.

* * *

When I moved to Portland, I met my first real gays. I worked for a man who was so very clearly gay and had been from the get-go. He was wonderful and generous. He and his boyfriend loved to travel and laugh and go out, just like the rest of us. They were blowing up every stereotype I'd ever known about a "gay lifestyle."

Then I realized I had been brainwashed; it was all a lie. My co-worker and his boyfriend were proof. I loved spending time with them. They became my friends, my family. They attended my first wedding. The boyfriend sold me my first home. They held my babies days after they were born.

They were happy and kind, and they loved each other wholeheartedly. I saw no judgment in their eyes. They were disproving everything I had been told growing up, one day at a time. Just two people, with great style, in love and living.

I started to get mad when people used the word lifestyle in reference to gay couples. My parents knew these men, and quite honestly, they may have been the first gay men that they knew in general besides Uncle Dick. They loved these friends of mine, yet they still believed that their love was wrong. How can you judge your friends? The layers coating my brain were getting thicker and thicker.

I had never thought about my sexuality. I dated boys because that's what society told me to do. I married a man. I had never felt sexually or physically attracted to a woman, so I didn't really give my sexuality much thought. I never had to state if I was straight, or gay, or whatever. People just assumed I was straight because I was a girl. A girl who kissed boys.

* * *

Let's talk about lesbians. Up till that point in my life, my knowledge about lesbians was limited to what I saw of Rosie O'Donnell and Ellen, and the comments about them from people around me. I'd learned a lot about gay people and even had quite a few around me that I loved. They were little bundles of joy and sunshine; they were my friends.

Lesbians, however, get a bad rap. I heard stereotypes that they apparently are either bitchy or butchy. *Dyke* was the word that was used a lot to describe them. In my observed portrayals, they always had short hair and were a bit aggressive and a bit overweight. They wore baggy jeans and t-shirts and had terrible attitudes and disagreed with everything. That's the picture that was painted for me growing up by my television, media, and the church. Steph was the first lesbian that I met in real life. I had heard her reference it before in the hall at work. There were always comments around me of "I'd turn gay for Steph." I was so curious about her in general.

But what did that even mean? "I'd turn gay." Can you just decide to be gay by just turning the key over? I tried to imagine how that even worked. Sounded easy enough.

I often think about that first time I saw her, my light. When I took her spin class and I couldn't take my eyes off her. That was weird in and of itself because I am the queen of looking away. I'm hard to impress. Her, standing on that stage in a red tank with shoulders glowing. She was confident and regal, her blonde hair glistening under the stage light, as well as her muscles. She was mysterious and had this aura around her. And her mouth, I couldn't stop watching the way it moved. *Was it the shape of it? The color?*

She was beautiful. Striking. I was probably staring like a total creep. I'm not even sure I blinked. My jaw was probably on the floor and for all I knew, I was drooling. There was just something about her. It was like I was seeing heaven's gates right in front of me.

She didn't fit the lesbian stereotype in my head. She was stunning and kind and confident, and she wasn't singled out because of her sexuality. She had a tomboy style with enough femininity to appeal to basically anyone—tall, slim, athletic, positive, and radiant.

I was starting to understand how, yes, you could actually just turn gay for Steph. However, it wasn't going to be me. Looking back, I wasn't competitive with her, I was just extremely attracted to her. So maybe I WOULD be gay for Steph.

* * *

Steph and I became friends and started hanging out here and there. I couldn't wait to spend time with her. I was enamored with her energy. I wanted to figure her out. And I wanted to understand how her relationship with her girlfriend worked. They seemed to do everything separate, as did my husband and me. *Maybe this is the way happy couples worked. Or maybe she wasn't happy like me.*

I remember one day her girlfriend told me that she was planning on proposing soon and showed me the ring. I had spent a decent amount of time with Steph alone, at work between classes or a coffee chat here and there, and I had never heard her talk about her girlfriend. *But they were talking about marriage? Maybe this chick just really kept her shit close. Something is off.*

When her girlfriend showed me the ring, I felt more confused, because even though I didn't know Steph all that well, I felt like I knew she would never wear that ring. Not because she didn't want to get married one day, but because it wasn't her style. It wouldn't look right; it wasn't the ring for her.

What was happening? And why did I care?

I decided to be excited for them, regardless, and just wait to see what happened. Steph's girlfriend tried to propose a week later, and it was the beginning of the end for them. I didn't ask Steph about it. I just knew they weren't engaged, and I left it at that. I knew there was a reason they never touched, that she never talked to me about her. It was all starting to make sense. They ended up breaking up, and I left it at that. Until I didn't.

14: That one fateful night

I had received a card from Steph at work, talking about how I was an amazing mother, friend, and instructor. She spoke to my character and my drive and my soul. In my thirty something years of existence, nobody had ever spoken to me that way. So clearly, I decided to write her back. I loved writing letters, and I wanted to know more about her. I wrote, and I wrote, and I wrote. I wrote about her, and how I was always wanting to be around her more, more, more. I didn't realize it then, but this would be the first love letter I would ever give her. When I read it again a couple years later, I did an *oh fuck wow, that was ballsy pat myself on the back* sort of thing. I really went for it in my letter and I didn't realize it. *Way to subconsciously know what you want, self!*

* * *

The last time I had been dancing I was twenty-one years old. It was my bachelorette party. My ex didn't let me go out dancing, not with girlfriends, not with him, not with anybody. I wasn't even able to take a dance class. He would argue with me all day if I brought it up, so I stopped trying. I'm not sure if he didn't trust me, or didn't trust other men, but I'm pretty sure he was just insecure.

I'm one of those people that lets the music take over my body. A song comes on, and it becomes a part of me and the rhythm sneaks into my veins. My body starts to move and I'm more than okay with it, and quite honestly, I can't help it. Even if I could, I wouldn't. Dancing makes me happy. It's cathartic. I love music because of this. I grew up playing instruments and dancing my way through high school competitions and late nights. Music and movement are creativity and therapy for me. Just because it's not for everyone doesn't mean it's not great.

* * *

I arrived at Steph's one afternoon at 2:30 p.m. To be honest, I'm not sure what we were planning to do. We had plans with friends later that night, but she kept texting me and asking if I could hang out earlier. I was without kids that day and dying to get out of my house, so I made it work. I stopped and bought her a tiny paddle cactus as a gift to break the ice. I couldn't figure out why she wanted to hang out so bad, or why I was so excited and jittery.

I'd never hung out with just Steph. But somehow the hours leading up to going to her house felt like years. I was nervous. I'd had a sex dream about her a few nights prior. I woke up in a total panic. *How? Where? Did I subconsciously want this? Was my wanting to be around her attraction? WTF? Did I like it? I've never thought of a woman this way.*

I remember walking up to her door, a little nervous but definitely excited. I knocked on the door, and she opened it with a huge smile and a hug as she let me in. I fit perfectly in her arms, and she smelled like home. It was confusing. She seemed overly excited to see me. I wasn't sure what I was missing. I don't know what I was expecting, but it caught me off guard either way. We decided to grab a coffee from a cafe across the street and head out for a walk. It was fall and the weather was perfect. We had nothing else to do. As much as I knew everything about who she was, we didn't really know each other at all, and I was excited to learn more.

I'll never know if we walked for three hours or thirty minutes. I've never been so present in my life. I was lost in conversation and completely captivated by her sound. I craved her thoughts before they were formed. Her voice danced into my ears like silky glitter fairies.

She seemed excited to be with me, and I couldn't figure out why. In my eyes, I wasn't good enough. I was broken, damaged goods. She was asking me a lot of questions, learning about my life, walking reallllly close. I looked down multiple times and noticed her hands were trembling.

The thing about Steph is, when she asks questions, she's not fucking around. They're like straight-to-your-soul, don't-even-think-about-lying-or-not-answering-make-you-uncomfortable, make-you-think kind of questions. She was trying to figure me out and I was letting her, which was very unlike me. I had locked myself away years ago, but she was chipping away at the lock.

I wasn't sure what we would do when the walk was over. We still had hours before our friends met us. *Why do I want to hang out with her so bad? And her with me? Am I just desperate for a new friendship? Anyone?*

I swear she wanted to hold my hand. I felt it. It was extremely confusing for a "straight" girl like me. She fidgeted with her hands the whole walk, and they stayed shaky. Did I want to hold hers? Probably. Hard to say.

Steph is the kind of woman that could make any living thing fall in love with her with one look. Fuck, I bet she could make a stick fall in love with her. Even gay men swoon. I felt possessive when people looked at her. In my mind, nobody was good enough for her. She was the most gorgeous, kind, genuine, and mysterious soul I had ever met. Everyone was drawn to her. She called everyone babe, and therefore everyone thought they had a chance, or dreamt it anyway.

Later that evening, I was lying on her couch, she picked up my foot and started rubbing it. I didn't think much of it as she was a very touchy person, but it did send a shiver through my body.

She was always grabbing a shoulder and making someone fall in love with her. It was like freeze tag when she touched you but instead, you'd just tense up and be like, *Fuck, I'm in love, now what?* Now that I'm with her, I realize that wasn't a normal thing to do.

I would never give my friends a foot rub, unless they asked, I guess. But I didn't ask. I thought it was just something she did. She was pretty good at it, so I wasn't about to take my foot out of her lap. Not to mention, my feet were a bit muggy and probably didn't smell great as I walked miles in boots with her all afternoon. I found out later that she has a horrible sense of smell which maybe kept her interested that day. We'll never know.

We made dinner and played games and decided to go dancing. I was JACKED. Not only was I making new friends, but I got to go dancing. *What if I lost my rhythm or tried to twerk and fell? What do I do if someone grinds on me? What if I'm not hot anymore and I just look like a desperate housewife in the club, twenty years too late?* But I got over my what-ifs the second I heard the bass from the DJ.

Freedom.

I still have flashes of this night, of the day—her face, her questions, her laugh. The way she would randomly touch my shoulder, stumble on her words, or fidget with her hands. I remember the way my heart would race when she called me babe (mind you she called everyone babe, but I think deep down I wanted to be THE babe). I remember having quite a bit to drink and maybe eating one too many edibles that night. I was experiencing 100% freedom for the first time in my whole life. I was going for it, and I didn't give a single fuck. I had always been under the scrutiny and beliefs of my parents until I got married, and then I was under his.

I was finally just me, doing what felt true to me in the moment. I was dabbling in the luxury of the term "living my best life."

I remember feeling so liberated on the dance floor. Lights flashing, people everywhere. I leaned my head back and opened my arms and let it all soak in as sweat dripped off my forehead. There was one man in particular who wouldn't leave me alone. Every time I turned around, I felt him pressing up against me. There was a constant boner in my back. This should have been another red alert that I didn't like the wein. *Get it off me.*

Enough was enough for me, and apparently for Steph as well. She had been watching the whole thing. She sauntered over, smiled at me, looked him straight in the eyes and said, "Back off my girlfriend."

Time stood still as I heard those words. *My girlfriend.*

And this is the first time my mind thought of dating a woman. This woman specifically. For a moment, I had a pretend girlfriend and I loved it. It happened so quickly. The thought was like a flash of inspiration.

I loved that she was being protective. It felt like she meant the words as she said them. Time slowed down for half a second as I looked at her, taken aback by what she had just said, beaming my face off but also trying to hide it and play it cool. She smiled at me and grabbed my hand, pulling me away from boner boy, and closer to her.

It was the first time she had held my hand. We started dancing. It felt rhythmic. It felt natural. It felt perfect. Closer. It was dark, the music was loud, the lights were flashing, and we were perfectly in sync. I don't know if it was the weed or the booze or the freedom but before I knew it, our bodies were pressed together. I held the back of her head in one hand and watched as my other hand traced down the front of her body...slowly. Starting at her cheekbone, down the side of her face, her neck, down her chest, to her hip, and pulled her a little closer. We locked eyes.

Oh shit—did I just do that?

At that moment, everything stopped around me. It was black, and she was light. It was like a slow-motion picture in the background, centered on us in the middle of the dance floor. Hundreds of people were dancing around us, they were blurry, with the flashing of lights and bass pumping up through the rumbling of the floor. Her face was glowing. I remember the way she was moving, breathing. I remember the way her eyes lit up when I ran my hand down the side of her body. A look of shock, hope, clarity, and excitement.

I felt a buzz pulsing through my veins—certainty. The first certainty I had felt in my entire life. It felt like electricity, cold and refreshing with a warm sting.

It was over. It was the beginning. She was it for me. I finally realized why I couldn't get enough of her. I literally wanted to absorb her into my body. I had officially touched her boob and I was officially done for. I touched a boob and I liked it, and I think she liked it too.

Fuck.

How was I going to do this? My divorce wasn't final yet. My family saw being gay as the ultimate sin, a lifestyle choice. *I have kids, she doesn't. Is it the weed? Am I too drunk? Am I rebounding? Is it too soon? I have to go.*

I felt like Cinderella when the clock was about to hit midnight, like I needed to get out of there ASAP. Except it was 2 a.m., and there was a babe lesbian with my heart.

I knew I needed to sober up, so we took a car back to her place. I didn't want to make a mistake because I wasn't fully coherent. She laid next to me for what felt like days but was probably thirty minutes, my body was aching next to her. She kept saying, "It's going to be okay." I knew in that moment that she was feeling the same certainty. We were going to be together, and we were going to have to figure out how. There was certainty in our uncertainty.

We didn't talk about the moment, the shock, the knowing. She just traced my neck, my torso, my leg, with her long, smooth fingertips, all while trying to reassure me. I had butterflies, I was shaking, I couldn't breathe. I just listened to her whispers over and over again as she got closer. I didn't know how, but I believed her.

I'd told her to meet me at 8 a.m., which at that point was in four hours. I didn't sleep, I replayed the day and the night like a movie reel. I was looking for a glitch or a hiccup that wasn't there. I couldn't believe it was happening. Plot twist! *Was I losing it? What if she wasn't into me in the morning?*

* * *

It was early Sunday morning and the city was calm, asleep. We met behind a building in a part of town where nobody would see us. I knew this would be a huge deal if anyone knew. When she showed up, I felt my insides start to shake. Her face looked like home. I looked down and noticed her hands were shaking again. We started walking down the street in silence, but I knew it was only a matter of time before we had to sort this out. Time wasn't exactly on our side.

I turned to her and asked point blank what happened in her last relationship and why she never talked to me about it. I think she was a little shocked, but we didn't have a whole lot of time here and I wanted to start this, whatever it was, with nothing but complete honesty. I knew we were going to end up together, and I knew there wouldn't be any waiting. We couldn't wait. I needed to ask the questions.

She explained to me that while she cared for her ex, she was never in love with her. She was content but she knew there could be more. In my mind I was thinking, *Ummm, hell yeah there could be. I felt it last night, right now actually.* I couldn't waste another moment. My next question was not aggressive at all...

I said, "What the fuck happened last night?" (Okay so slightly aggressive, but as I said, time wasn't on our side and I was freaking out. I needed to know if she felt the same.)

She replayed the whole thing to me exactly how it had happened, word for word, thought for thought. The world froze for her also, the room went blurry. She felt the electric shock in her veins, she knew she had to be with me. This was happening.

I said, "Look, I have two kids, my divorce isn't final, I'm not 'gay,' my family is religious, and right now the whole city is watching me. This is going to be hard. If you are in it, I need you to be in it forever. I'm not going to play around here, I can't. I have too much at stake." We were running at each other with such intensity, and I didn't want it to be destructive.

She assured me that she wanted it all—the mess, the kids, the fight to be together, and me. She wanted me in whatever form I came in. She said she had asked for me her whole life. She had been waiting for me, for kids. She wanted a brunette with brains and a whole lot of sass (and a side of large ass). Someone who said yes to life and inspired people. Someone who stood out in a crowd. She'd always wanted a family, she just didn't know what it would look like.

She kept saying, "I asked for this, for a big love."

She also told me that she had dreamt about me a few months prior, not just the illusion of me, but ME. For a moment, my sex dream didn't seem so crazy anymore.

I looked into her eyes as she explained that she wanted a big love, and I believed her. While there was a tiny bit of doubt and questioning if she had lost her mind, I trusted her.

My next question went like this, "So, are you going to kiss me or what?"

Her hands started shaking and her lips started trembling as they parted, and she smiled the biggest smile I had ever seen on her. I think my forwardness caught her off guard, but I knew what I wanted, and I knew she wanted it too. We couldn't wait another minute. There was no point. It was a done deal.

Shielding ourselves from the world around us, I grabbed her hand and we snuck into a building inlet. We were set on protecting this feeling that was so pure, a feeling we finally both realized actually did exist. I asked her if she wanted to sit down as her whole body was trembling. We sat facing each other on a tiny step, carefully placed our hands on each other's faces, looked into each other's eyes, and as our lips met, I felt it again—certainty.

Her lips were soft and cool. Her jawline felt like it was made for my hands. We were electric. Her touch made my whole body feel warm. Her lips were shaking, and I had butterflies in my stomach that felt more like tiny little drones taking pictures of every cell and every bit of happiness inside of me and around me in that moment. I also felt like I had baby confetti cannons in my body, celebrating every breath that I was sharing with her. These moments have never faded. I am so thankful for the tiny drones in my body that continue to help me relive this moment.

I felt alive. There she was. My forever. She was mine, but we were each other's. This was it. I couldn't breathe, and I didn't for at least another year.

15: Timing isn't everything, or is it?

I was terrified of the timing with Steph. It would have been so much easier if our love bomb would have exploded a year later. In fact, we even talked about trying not to be together until everything was final.

But it was impossible. When you've waited your whole life for a certain feeling, why would you wait out of fear of what other people thought? (Easy for me to say now. Looking back, I should have just said, "Look, I fell in love. I can't help it. It doesn't affect anyone but me, get over it.")

I was navigating it all. I'd never known anyone to go through something like this. I didn't know where to turn. Divorce, kids, and a same-sex relationship in the midst of it. Then telling the family.

My love with Steph taught me that you can't help the timing of your life, or who you fall in love with, for that matter. It's really opened my mind to the world around me. Society puts so much pressure on people to do things in a certain order and a certain way, checking all the boxes before you get to the next step. I'm here to remind you that there is no right or wrong way. It's individual. And that's what makes everyone unique. It's what makes our stories ours. People are just doing their best, and you can't judge them for that. And if you do, you better check yourself.

* * *

Steph and I met for lunch and a walk five days after that day and night of magic. We waited until the kids were with their dad again. She was shaking, per usual, which I thought was cute and really wished she had never stopped doing. (Honey, what does a girl have to do to make you nervous and giddy all the time?)

She started walking unusually fast and talking even faster. She turned around, looked at me, and threw her hands to the side and said, "I THINK I'm falling in love with you." She was beaming her face off.

Um? You THINK? Or you know? I wasn't sure how to respond. In my mind I was thinking, *I'm obsessed with you. You can't just throw an "I THINK" at me, that's not fair…What do I do with that?*

So I made a little joke of it and was flattered but wildly confused. I knew I was in love with her, but I also couldn't believe that this woman, who had been with someone for three years and never was "in love" with her, was now, after five days, falling in love with me.

We got to the end of the road that overlooked the river and the city and sat down under a giant oak tree. I looked at her, right into her eyes, and gave her a kiss. I took her shaky, cold little hands and said, "Steph, I love you. I'm in love with you."

She smiled and her eyes got all watery as she said it back. She then explained that it was insane to say that to someone on day five of dating, so that's why she had said "I think."

I laughed and realized that we, in fact, were insane. But there was no use waiting if we knew. We decided in that moment that we needed to apologize to everyone in our lives we had ever made fun of for saying "when you know, you know."

We both confessed that we knew the night we went dancing. We call it "that fateful night." She had waited five days (a year in her mind) to try to tell me how she felt. And while she didn't quite nail it, it was adorable and perfect and something I'll never forget.

I started building our life together in my head. It was perfect in my mind. In reality, it was a war zone. I was scared shitless, my stomach like a constant tornado. Every time I went to see her, I felt like I was driving through landmines, and everything was grey until I got to my little rainbow named Steph. I was scared, but I wasn't. I was certain about us, though uncertain of how and when we would get to build this life.

Most of all, though, I was present. I was feeling for the first time since I was nineteen years old, and I was feeling it all. I was warm, no longer numb. I was smiling and excited. My heart was full and broken all at the same time. Tears would squirt out of my eyes for no reason. They were happy tears for a change, tears of love and belonging and certitude. A sign of life as I had been dried up for ten years. I was coming alive.

We saw each other when we could, but it was complicated. I hadn't told my family or even my friends. I wanted my divorce to be final—I had kids to protect. I was deep enough with rumors, shame, and judgment as it was. We spent a year hiding. We would skip town when we could afford it, and when I didn't have the kids, just so we could walk down a street together and hold hands. She would come over after my kids were asleep and leave at 5 a.m., so they didn't know.

We didn't sleep. We talked and laughed. And we dreamt. We made love and ate way too much charcuterie and burgers and drank way too much whiskey. Then we did it all over again until she had to leave. Our moments were precious. She always said she would never take sleeping next to me for granted. We weren't able to for a year, and we couldn't stand to be apart. We were already sure a lifetime wouldn't be enough.

Every moment we weren't together, we were texting each other. We covered a lot of ground and compromised the integrity of our thumbs with all the texting. She poured her heart out to me. She explained her first true love and that she never felt she would feel that again, until there was me. Only this love, our love, was even bigger. I saved these texts so I could remember the words, revisiting them in moments of weakness.

I had never known true love, but I knew this was it. One look took my breath away, one sentence left me beaming. My cheeks were sore from smiling 24/7. We would laugh and laugh and just say "owww" because our cheeks hurt so bad, pressing them in with our palms as we smiled even bigger. I hadn't smiled in years, let alone continuously. I was obsessed and addicted. We would always say, "I'm obsessed with you, but not in a creepy way." Because honestly, it was kind of creepy how attached we were. But we didn't care. We were going to do it; we were doing it. One fucking step at a time.

We would go out randomly in Portland, but every time we did, someone who knew us would see us, and we'd hear a rumor about it two days later. Some were true, some were not, but all were damaging. This was the problem with being a nano-celebrity in a small city. People knew us, and we didn't necessarily know them.

For the first time in my life, I felt bad for celebrities. Privacy should always be respected; you never know what people are dealing with or going through in their personal lives. I'll never understand why people decide it's their business to share other people's lives anyway. Someone sharing that we were together with the wrong person could have completely shattered everything that I had been working for, and the security of my kids. I had no idea how long the divorce would drag out, but we were trying to keep our love hidden for the sake of my family.

Steph would meet me for five minutes before work, to sneak a kiss. We would send twenty pictures a day to each other, and each one gave me enough butterflies in my stomach to lift me off earth. When we hung out in groups, we avoided each other, but you could feel the vibration between us. Everyone could. We were magnetic and the energy was undeniable. Not to mention we had hearts shooting out of our eyes, and we were the idiots who thought nobody around us felt it too.

Steph made me better. I made her better. We broke down each other's walls. She taught me that I could feel again, that it was okay to cry, and that my thoughts and words were valid. She stayed present with me while I listened to the whispers of old stories in my head, while I was hurting and healing. I taught her to have more fun, to show herself to the world more. We learned vulnerability in new ways. We cried after sex; I didn't have to fake my orgasms anymore. We pushed each other, all the while pulling each other closer. Our bond was made of cement. We knew we were unstoppable. We knew we would end up together, we just didn't know how.

* * *

My ex was dating as well, I knew it by his tone. It would change when he was happy. There was so much back-and-forth. We spent a very expensive day with our lawyers and a retired judge doing mediation, going room to room to negotiate child and spousal support.

I asked for less support than I was entitled to. I also asked for the amount to lower each year. I didn't want his money, but unfortunately, I needed it while I got on my feet.

Meanwhile, all that he asked was that his lawyer honor his strategy, which made my life an expensive living hell.

Mediation was depressing. My heart broke not being able to sit at the same table to negotiate with someone I had lived with for years. A stranger carried our most private information, and our feelings, between rooms like a carrier pigeon. How can two people who had spent half of their lives together not be able to sit in the same room and talk about their own belongings? We were both so hurt.

My lawyer and I sat across from each other on the twenty-third floor of her law firm's office building at a table built for ten. It was a gorgeous day outside, but there I was breathing recycled air in a cold glass box. I honestly think mediation should be held on your living room couch where you can wear your ugliest sweatpants and drink vodka.

Yet there I was in business casual and heels as I realized that marriage is all about government, and not at all personal once things go south. My soon-to-be ex-husband sat in a replica of the same room just next door with his two lawyers, only a wall separating us. It was sterile, to say the least. And he was paying double just to stick it to me.

As the day went on, it became all business, and the feelings mattered less and less. Can this happen to love? It just went cold.

I eventually had to leave and use the restroom. I was having a hard time holding it together, knowing my soon-to-be ex was one wall away, fighting for every last nickel and dime because he didn't care enough to help me land on my feet and provide the same life for our kids that he could. I was sick over it.

As I was walking back from the bathroom, I passed him in the hall. It was the hollowest hello I have ever felt. Our eyes met for a split second, and it was enough to make mine drown in tears. I was heartbroken. I wanted to fall onto the beige carpet and scream. I still cared so deeply for this man, and all he wanted to do was hurt me out of his pride and pain.

We finally agreed on terms and went our separate ways, each being walked out by the team representing us at different times, so we didn't have to see each other. It was two weeks until our court date, and we had settled. We just needed a judge's stamp to finalize. I felt relief knowing that I could move forward.

* * *

A week and a half later, the phone rang. It was my lawyer. I thought she was going to tell me it was final. Instead, she told me that he wanted my most recent pay stubs. I couldn't believe it. If I didn't care so much about my new home, I would have punched a hole in the wall or thrown a chair off the deck. He was still questioning me and making my life a living hell. He didn't believe my income numbers. I had been showing him my pay stubs every other week. Still being controlled and monitored because legally I had to. I felt trapped as his puppet once more. But he knew I was capable, and he was watching the numbers grow. Our court date was three days away and would cost tens of thousands more. But for what? The same fucking settlement.

I was exhausted and completely depleted. Literally running myself into the ground working nonstop and fighting my way out. I had lost twenty pounds. I didn't sleep. The stress was wrecking me. I was constantly sick and looked like I had lived seventeen years in one. He didn't care.

Eight thousand collectively for a day of mediation was out the window. If he pushed this, we would end up in court with another 15k bill and the same outcome. I couldn't believe it. *Groundhog Day.* I sent him the statements and he pushed the court date—again. It was six months out. I was devastated and ready to surrender. I'd get a third job if I needed to just to be done with his games.

I heard nothing more for a whole month until I got a notice in the mail from the City of Portland stating that my marriage had been dissolved. He had finally signed the papers. We wouldn't be going to court. I assume he realized it was the best he could do. It took over fourteen months until my divorce was legally final, although it felt like years.

* * *

I know a lot of people are stoked when their divorce is final, and to be honest, I thought I would be too. I remember when I was twenty-two, I had a hair client who was getting a divorce, and she said that she and her ex went out for a drink after they got their final papers and cried. I was confused. I'd heard about other women having divorce parties in Vegas, something that you celebrate with a giant "fuck yeah" and a party. But when my client told me that, I thought, *What a painfully raw and beautiful way to end things*. It opened my mind to the fact that you can care about someone so deeply and still not want to spend your life with them, no matter the circumstances. It was beautiful and tragic. I knew that would be me.

While I felt a giant release of pressure, I also felt an extreme emptiness and a pain I have never experienced again. I didn't know if this is how I was supposed to feel, or if I should tell someone it was final. But with shaky hands and trembling lips, I read the letter, set it down, went onto my tiny balcony, lit a cigarette, and sobbed uncontrollably for two hours.

The finality of it all was terrifying even though it was the right thing. I was flooded with memories, the good ones. I think it was part of the healing and the letting go. I wanted to leave it there instead of drowning in bitterness and hate. I also wanted to forgive him to neutralize the power he held over me. I wanted to forgive him so I wasn't holding onto anger and resentment. My girls didn't need that in their lives.

It wasn't time for a rejoicing, so I kept it to myself. I've never rejoiced it. It stole away years of my life. And it was excruciatingly painful. Every day got a little easier to breathe, like I had been pinned down by a giant stone that was slowly rolling off my chest. I kept it close for another week until the pain subsided just enough for me to breathe and look toward my new beginning.

16: Building our life

I thought Steph was crazy for sticking by me through my divorce, especially because there was a whole other battle to "come out" to my religious family. Judgment is a real thing. People were already wondering, whispering, fuck...it felt like they were shouting. I also felt extremely scared to lose her. She was my constant and the only sense of home I had ever known.

We started telling a few friends, one by one. None were surprised and all were supportive. People told us we had hearts shooting out of our eyes when we were together and looking back at photos, I see it too. *Joke's on us, honey.* They saw that we made each other better and they said, no matter what, they would have our backs.

We had, and still have, an energy when we are together that lifts a room, whether we walk in the same door or opposite sides. We have the capacity to turn a mundane meeting into an event to remember just by being next to each other. It's unreal and terrifying, but it's also the most powerful energy I've ever been a part of.

We continued to travel so we could keep it hush-hush for a couple months more until I could tell my ex. Our first trip together was to LA. We got an Airbnb in West Hollywood. She went a couple days before me, and I remember the flight down like it was yesterday. I was nervous and counted the seconds until I got there. I got in a taxi the second I landed and it could not have been a longer ride. We were texting each other the whole way. As the taxi pulled up, she was sitting on the curb waiting with her infectious smile. I smiled as I noticed her hands shaking as she ran to open my door. She wrapped her arms around me and kissed me so hard. I teared up.

Safety. I couldn't believe we were here, in a space where nobody knew us.

We spent the weekend learning about each other, working out, and daydreaming about our life, which usually just meant professing our love to each other. She kept telling me she was going to marry me. She insisted between cocktails and bites of charcuterie. To be honest, I wasn't sure I wanted to get married again after how horrible it was to try to get out of my previous marriage.

My ex and I had been together for ten years, and it was an expensive and, ultimately, impersonal mess to get out of. If we had been in a committed relationship for years and decided to split, we could have kept our tens of thousands instead of spending it on lawyers' fees. People would have been sad, sure, but I don't think we would have faced the judgment and criticism from the world around us had we not signed that one piece of paper years ago. But I knew I was going to be with this woman and if marrying her is what she wanted, marrying her is what I would do. We were never going to break up, so it didn't really matter to me if we got a county court involved or not.

She had insisted on buying me a ring from that fifth day when she exclaimed that she thought she was falling in love with me. It seemed to be more of a promise ring, but I think it was an "if you like it, then you shoulda put a ring on it" type situation. The modern-day promise ring. Girl wanted to claim her stake, and I wasn't going to stop her.

On the last day of our trip, we were walking around Venice when I heard her yell from a doorway, "BABE! BABE! Come here!" I was like, *Ooooh, shit.* I knew she had found what she was looking for, and I knew there was no stopping her. There it was...a beautiful hammered gold band; beat up, scratched up, and imperfect. So imperfect that it was absolutely perfect, just like our love. It was expensive. I told her she was crazy, but there was no stopping her. I didn't know it at the time, but she ordered it the second we got home.

When we were together, nothing else mattered. Yet, we had this seemingly insurmountable checklist of things we needed to do before we could truly be together. Daunting tasks that could only happen with time, not to mention holding space for each unique reaction.

Finalize divorce
Tell her family
Tell my family
Tell my ex
Tell our boss
Tell friends (one group at a time)
Tell kids
Survive telling these people

I knew my ex was dating someone, but I still felt so much fear when it came to having any type of conversation with him. I was still completely paralyzed by the thought of his reactions.

The stress was wearing on me more than I'd like to admit, more than I even knew. The stress of not wanting to disappoint people, of worrying about what other people thought. I told my family and my ex around the same time. I needed to start to live my life without hiding, especially my happiness.

It's funny how people's reactions to our lives can make us feel like we are doing it wrong. When in fact, it's just that— THEIR reaction. It has absolutely nothing to do with you.

My family was devastated that I got divorced because in their mind, I was their little girl who was to grow up, get married to a man, maybe buy a house and get a dog, pop out a few kids, and live happily ever after while my husband provided for us. And here I was...throwing ANOTHER wrench in their plan. I know it would be devastating to them, completely shattering what remained of their vision for me.

* * *

I wrote an email to tell my parents. It was my way to say everything I needed to say without anyone's emotions interrupting or their questions throwing me off.

Mom and Dad—

I have wanted to tell you something for a long time...but I realize I have felt a lot of shame. I felt a lot of shame telling you about my need to divorce X. I felt a lot of shame talking about the past 12 years of my life and how I had been controlled and belittled every single day. Constantly fighting. I am starting to realize that there is no shame in telling the truth, and I don't want there to be any shame in telling the truth. My life has not played out the way "it should have"... but I think, in reality, it has. I have never felt happier and more free even amidst the exhaustion of this ongoing battle that I'm in.

With that being said, I have fallen in love over the past 6 months. I have experienced something so true and so real, something I never believed existed until now. I have never felt more respected, valued, loved, pushed, certain, supported... I have truly never been so happy. I have never wanted to share something with you guys more, yet been so afraid at the same time...All I have ever wanted was to find my person. And now, after being with someone so toxic, a person to love me and my kids no matter what the circumstances. It's amazing that during such a dark time, when I least expected it, I found it.

I am dating Steph. What started as a really amazing and nurturing friendship has turned into something so powerful and so real. I realize this is going to be an issue for you, but when I see her, I see a person. Not a man, or a woman...I see the person that loves me for me. That cannot wait to see me, to talk to me, to push me to love more and give more. The person that wants to be a part of my girls' lives and raise them to be strong, courageous, and smart women. The person that is dying to hang out with my family. Someone who makes me laugh so hard I can't breathe, that I can tell absolutely anything to without fear of judgment. She is my best friend, my confidant, she fights for me, she pushes me, and she catches me when I start to fall. She is the only person who has the words and the courage to tell me the hard truths when I need to hear them. She feels like home.

And so, I feel shame...I feel shame because I grew up being told divorce was bad. So, when I was being abused on a regular basis, I didn't want to let you down, I didn't want to let myself down. I feel shame because I grew up being told it is wrong to be gay. I do not see myself this way. I fell in love with a person. I had no idea this person would show up like she did. I don't have another way to explain it and I really wish I did. It was a complete shock to me but also something so undeniable that I didn't want to let it go. I have learned to trust myself a lot over the past few years, to stick up for myself and show my kids what it is to live a life full of truth, honesty, respect. I write this to let go of some of that shame. I want to share this with you. I want you to know us and to really see us. We are better together and it's a really powerful thing.

Let me know when you want to talk. I love you.

I hit send and suddenly I could breathe. This was the last big thing. I didn't give a shit about what anyone in the city thought. I needed my ex to know and my family to know. Her family was all in from the day we told them. My friends were too—it made sense to them, no questions asked. That was helpful.

I got a text shortly after from each of them. Thanking me for my honesty and telling me they weren't ready to talk. And another weight was lifted off my shoulders even without knowing how they were feeling. My truth was out there, and their reactions had nothing to do with my reality.

17: Reaction! Reaction! Read all about it!

When I got the call from my parents, I think I blacked out. Or maybe I stopped caring. I vividly remember sitting on the living room floor of my condo. There was a mirror in front of me. It's such a clear memory because I looked up multiple times during that call and looked at the woman staring back at me. Every time I looked into that mirror, it was a reminder of who I was, that this was MY life...and I was doing it right. I was too skinny, but somehow, I looked stronger. I saw a woman who finally felt free to be who I was, the happiest version of myself. I looked at every piece of myself and my heart. None of it was different than it was years ago. I was just happy.

My parents loved Steph as a person, as my friend, but they just couldn't wrap their brain around the fact that Steph was a woman and that I loved her as more than a friend. There was question of it being a rebound. Of when. Of how. Of why. So many questions and so much explaining. Suddenly, I had that feeling that I had learned in church—I was bad, and there was nothing I could do about it.

Over time Steph and I both had ongoing conversations with my parents about our relationship and challenged each other's views on the topic. Steph was much more patient than I was; she had been explaining being gay her whole life. It broke my heart that she had to do it again with my family. But she was determined to build a relationship with them. I had a harder time, always wondering why I couldn't just be happy and not have to explain myself. It's always easy to believe in something wholeheartedly, but it's truly hard to tell someone their love is wrong when they are sitting right in front of you. I didn't have the luxury of the in-person conversations with my parents as we lived states apart. To be honest, I'm not sure I could have handled that anyway.

Everyone seemed to be taking my divorce and my new relationship personally. I had just explained my way out of a toxic relationship, and here I was explaining myself into a loving one. As a grown woman, explaining yourself to anyone, let alone your parents, must be one of the worst feelings. Especially when you have to do it on repeat. It made me feel so small, like I needed approval, or like I was doing something wrong and would be scolded. I was glad there were thousands of miles between us because I could feel the tension and concern through the phone. I couldn't imagine how suffocated I would feel if they were closer.

For the first time I was following my heart instead of societal norms. I was finally living my truth, my life, my happiness—not what someone else had envisioned for me. True happiness did this to me. I didn't want anyone remotely close to me unless they were one hundred percent on board. There was no going back, and nobody was going to ruin this for me. I didn't need to answer everyone's questions about why. I needed to trust myself.

Building that trust in myself meant that I'd embraced what was important. I was so certain about Steph. A kind of certainty I had never known. A kind of certain that would never leave me, even if I tried to walk away from it. It was a different certain from when I thought my first boyfriend was for sure the one for me, or that I was definitely pregnant from dry humping, or that I was going to be Mariah Carey when I grew up. I was more certain than I had ever been about anything in my life.

When Steph looked at me, nothing else mattered. I wasn't afraid of much, but when I was, one touch from her gave me any strength I needed to get through. She made me feel beautiful and safe. She challenged me. She pushed me so hard, to the point where it could be annoying because sometimes you just want to be lazy and status quo. But she always pushed me to be better. She saw me and knew I could be better. She still does. She made me laugh, uncontrollably...the kind of laugh that makes your stomach hurt, and maybe you snort, maybe you don't. She made me speak, which was and still will be one of the hardest things for me to do in my life.

I have always been an internal processor, especially after spending years with someone who stifled my voice. I learned to swallow it all, constantly feeling a lump in my throat. I am good at being quiet. But my babe insisted that I was even better at being loud and heard. She believed that my words had value and continues to push me to speak when all I want to do is internalize.

She danced with me, she asked me questions, she challenged me when I was being a brat. She believed in me. Quite frankly, I think she thought/thinks that I might possibly be the best thing to walk this earth, which is funny because I constantly think the same about her. I always wonder how I possibly scored someone so perfect in every way. Even more so, someone so perfect for me.

All of that to say, if anyone else was going to question what I was doing with a WOMAN directly after a divorce from a MAN, I didn't give a single fuck...not even a nano-fuck. She was it for me. I was done-zo and if you had an issue with it, you weren't for me. As far as I was concerned, everyone could stop worrying about the fact that the love of my life also had a vagina.

* * *

The next person I had to tell was my ex. At this point all our interactions were via text or email. I needed everything to be documented. We had an agreement that if we introduced anyone to the kids that we were dating, we needed to tell each other first, and it needed to be serious. The kids knew Steph before we started dating, but they didn't know we were together now. I wrote him the morning after I told my parents.

> X, out of respect for you and our agreement, I just wanted to let you know that Steph and I are dating and I wanted to tell you before I told the kids or made it public.

His response went exactly like this— Ok, thanks.

I wasn't even mad, in fact, I was elated that it didn't say fuck you. I was beyond relieved. I knew he was dating someone at that point, who he had already introduced to the kids as his girlfriend, so he really had nothing he could be mad about. I knew she didn't live here and that she would come stay for a few days at a time. I called him out on it a few days later, asking if I could meet her since the kids had. You can imagine how that conversation went. He twisted the agreement around. But I also didn't care. I just wanted to know who this new chick was, eight years younger than me and feeding my kids candy and Twinkies. I only knew the age difference because I knew her name and that she was a nurse, and well, it was 2017, and the internet is a wild place full of information. (And your girlfriends are like free detectives when they care about you.)

I sent my brother an email around this time also, explaining the situation, but also assuming my parents had already talked to him about it. I never received a response from him. Four years later, I'm still waiting for it. And that sucks.

At some point, we told the kids and I wish I had a really awesome story about how it went, but the truth is, kids are kids. If you raise them to know that all love is equal, they don't really give a shit if you are dating a woman or a man. They loved Steph so they were excited, and nothing really changed other than they now would see us kiss or hug here and there, which they actually liked. Have you ever noticed how affectionate and full of joy your kids become when they see you happy? To this day the kids' faces light up when we flirt or kiss. They just run over and hug us. I love it.

* * *

During this time of coming out, I just kept thinking about how dramatic it is. But more importantly, I was thinking how painful it is for some. How unnecessary it is for you, burdened under a pile of guilt and shame, to sit your loved ones or friends down and tell them who you are and that you are happy, all while being afraid that they might disown you.

I kept thinking about how I wasn't going to give shame that much power. I wanted to change the whole coming out thing. I wanted to throw it away. It felt so dumb. The best way I could do that was to just blast social media all at once. People were already whispering. Let's give the people what they want. Rip the Band-Aid off, if you will, and let my love and happiness bleed all over them.

It was Valentine's Day. People were posting about their significant others, and I was just waiting until the right moment to break the internet. I had a few Polaroids from Steph's thirty-fifth birthday a couple days prior. In two of them we are smiling and goofing off, and another one I held her face in my hands, planting a big juicy kiss on her while she wrapped her arms around my waist. I took a photo of the pictures in a pile on the counter and wrote, "Love is patient. Love is kind…and sometimes, love looks a whole lot different than you expected." I hit post, walked over to my beautiful girlfriend, and said, "It's done." And I planted another one on her, just to seal the deal.

Her jaw hit the floor. She couldn't believe it. She had been so patiently waiting for me to say it, so we could move forward. Every day that we had to hide felt like a lifetime, and now it was over. I could almost feel the city talking about us, people screenshotting the latest drama and sending it to their friends. Their suspicions were finally confirmed. Judgment be damned. I could feel the city rumble under my feet.

I. DID. NOT. CARE. I felt so fucking good. Freedom at its finest. You want to feel freedom? Take who you are and who you want to be, make them the same, drop the mic, and walk away.

When I finally came back to my phone a few hours later, the support was incredible. Hundreds of messages saying that they were so happy for me and proud of us. They shared how they could feel the energy when we were together and how they wished they could find what they could already see we had. Any stress I had about the situation was peeled away as I read message after message. Good people just want people to be happy. I was happy, everyone could see it.

I can only imagine what my ex-husband's friends and family had to say about the situation. To his religious family, I was making a lifestyle choice, a choice that would get you a one-way ticket to hell. And I guess if we are being technical, I did make a choice. I mean, you can't choose who you fall in love with. That shit smacked me in the face when I wasn't looking. But I did choose love over fear, and over everyone else's vision of what was right for my life.

That was my lifestyle choice. Love over hate. If I go to hell for that, at least I got to live with the biggest love of all while I was here. But I'm pretty sure I'm not. I mean, isn't God love? Didn't God intend for us all to love one another and not judge? Didn't God create me and this beautiful woman of mine "perfect in his eyes"?

* * *

In the end, everyone moves on when they realize you are happy and there's no drama to be made. When they realize that it doesn't, in fact, affect them. When the person you are constantly talking about doesn't turn around and run with their tail between their legs, the chattering loses its luster. At that point, I was happier than I'd ever been, and so was my ex, whether he wanted to admit it or not. There was nothing to be mad about.

18: My parents bought a shithole

Somewhere in the middle of all this, I bought a house. Well, let me rephrase that—my parents bought a house. Nope, still not right. My parents bought a shithole, and my name was on the deed.

I had to get out of that tiny condo in Pleasantville, and there was a house for sale nearby. It was a mid-century modern in a great school district. And I could afford it. But my parents had to be on the loan for the first year until I could prove income. Apparently when you are a stay-at-home parent and can't prove two years of steady income the bank doesn't think you are capable enough to pay a mortgage. They were happy to help, but man, writing your parents a check for your own mortgage every month at thirty-two-years-old really is a blow. It felt like they were teaching me how to eat from a spoon again.

The house was a foreclosure. Small, dated, smelly, damp, vines growing through the walls, and mold. You could barely see how to get to the front door behind overgrown bushes. One look at it online and I was in love. Anyone else in their right mind would have run the other way, which is precisely why I didn't tell my girlfriend. It had been on the market for almost a year and was about to go to auction so clearly everyone had been running the other direction. But I knew if I didn't buy this one, I'd never be able to afford another house in the neighborhood. I also saw all the potential under years of neglect. I saw our home—our future.

So I bought it. And I told my girlfriend later because I thought she would leave me. Okay, not really, but I didn't have time to convince her that I was a genius.

I'm going to have to ask her, because this part of my life was such a clusterfuck, but I do recall she was pissed and very skeptical. Although, I'm not sure why. Just kidding—I know why. I made a huge life decision that was going to include her because we knew we were going to get married, but I didn't ask her about it. Clearly, she would have to move into this house with me. Looking back, that was kind of a dick move, but she's happy about it now. (Right, honey?) I couldn't have anyone questioning me. I was confident in what we could do to the place with a little money and a ton of sweat that I just couldn't try to convince one more person that I was doing the right thing.

When I finally brought her to look at it, it took her breath away...but not in a "wow this is incredible, I love it, I'm in awe, and you definitely made a great choice" kind of way. It was more like a "someone just kicked me in the stomach, what the fuck did you do, how can we get out of it?" kind of way. She looked like she was fighting back tears and scared out of her mind while I bopped around from room to room on damp carpet and pee stains and spiderwebs and told her all the things I planned on doing to the place while yelling, "Isn't it great?!" She didn't say a word. She just looked around with the biggest eyes I've ever seen and a very dull expression. (Honey, I'm sorry I did this to you.)

Needless to say, it was unlivable. I bought a home for our family that we couldn't live in. We spent hours and hours every day after work and all weekend scraping ceilings, ripping up carpet, wrestling layers of linoleum, replacing subfloors, tearing down walls, raising ceilings, replacing pipes and old toilets, and scouring the internet for the cheapest fixtures we could find to make our run-down house a home. The number of dumpsters we filled was astonishing. Also, the number of times we had old flooring or a random bag of drywall overflowing from our trash bin was embarrassing.

Once we had it down to basically the studs, Steph started to get excited. Well, she got a little excited when we tore out the ceiling, but she could finally see my vision. She had been blindly trusting me until then.

We got to a point where there was a working bathroom and a sink, so the kids and I moved in so we could sell the condo. We continued to do everything we could to make it our own and only hired out what we absolutely couldn't figure out. Thank you, YouTube.

When it came to the landscaping, we decided to have a landscape party. Which is only fun if you own a chainsaw. And I do. It's also only fun if you have willing and able, buff friends, which I do. The same friends who showed up in the *Team Lianne* shirts and helped me move out of my old home were, yet again, showing up to help me create a new one. We rented a fifty-ton dumpster that was placed in the front yard, turned on some music, and went to work. It was seven buff ladies and Steph's brother. Every bush we pulled up had another fifty-year-old variety underneath it. The amount of trash in said bushes was worth another dumpster. We had dozens of bamboo shoots sticking up higher than our house. There were stumps on stumps on stumps. I wasn't sure there was earth under all that shit. It was like someone went to the nursery in 1969 and said, "I'll take one of everything!" before planting it all and walking away.

People were strolling by our house, staring and wondering what the fuck was going on with a bunch of ladies tearing up a yard with rap and EDM blasting in the background. I looked around and realized how gay we all looked in our flannels and cut offs, with chainsaws and clippers and biceps. That was about the time we started calling our house the Lesbian Rehab Center. Welcome to the LRC. We looked like a wild pack of lesbians, and it was awesome. We were having a blast and cracking up all day. I love my friends.

We made progress on the house day by day, my amazing girlfriend moved in with me, and we continued to build our life together. Step by fucking step.

19: Let's get married then

When I was going through my divorce, I vowed never to get married again. It was insane to me how signing one piece of paper could make your life a living hell to undo if needed. A state and people you never knew held the power to your future and got to decide when your relationship was over, or if it was over at all. Did you know in some states, you have to be legally separated for six months before you can even file for divorce? That's one more trip to the ole courthouse. That really blew my mind. Thank you, Oregon, for not going that far.

To get a divorce, it was so complicated to connect with the right people and sign the right things and wait for them to okay it all. It really should have just been between my husband and me. I could have just taken some Wite-Out to the marriage certificate and BAM! There you go—divorced.

Yeah, my ex had a strategy of dragging his feet, but the system basically added ankle weights and made it that much harder and slower. It was like slogging through sand with the wind against your face for a full year, occasionally getting completely wiped out by a sneaker wave. Breaking up is so much less messy, and I feel like people judge a lot less. Breaking up seemed so easy and soft, like clouds gently blowing apart. Married with kids and divorce? End of the universe. Dating with kids and a breakup? Super sad, but people get over it.

All that to say...I got engaged.

We went to Mexico for a friend's fortieth birthday. The trip was short, but we had booked an extra day to spend together before we had to come home. We spent the days lounging by the pool with friends, enjoying big group dinners, and well...that's about it.

The resort was gorgeous. It was small and had a private beach, hammocks, fire pits, farm-to-table food, beautiful colors, and friendly staff. There were no other resorts within a couple of miles. It was relaxing and perfect.

Steph and I spent hours having conversations about our future and then spent more hours having the same conversations again. We were aligning our goals and our hopes and our dreams. Getting excited about where our life could take us with our big love holding us afloat. She was asking me question after question, starting with "So, if we were to get married..." And once that conversation was over, and I answered all the "am I ready for this and do I really want to do it?" stuff, she would ask again. She was like a parrot repeating a question.

On our last day, we decided to take a couple of the cruiser bikes from the resort down a dirt road to a neighboring town. We'd heard the surf wasn't so big, and we could swim a little more easily in the water. Everyone else was leaving that day anyway. We thought we may as well have our own adventure and see something else before we left.

Steph was incredibly off that day, which I had never ever seen in her before. She was extremely fidgety and bouncing around like a balloon on a freeway, full of air and nerves. We walked to the bikes, and Steph said she forgot something and ran back to the room. I was slightly annoyed because she was acting so weird, but I was usually the one having an off day, so I tried to give her some grace. Key word: *tried*. I ran out of grace after about minute seven. I tried to give her the benefit of the doubt, *Hey, maybe she had to use the restroom.* I didn't have my phone, or I would have called her. But I also didn't want to leave in case she came back a different way and we lost each other.

About twenty-five minutes later she came bopping up to me smiling saying, "Ready to go, babe?" She had some excuse that I clearly didn't care to remember. I was too annoyed to care. I just wanted to get on with our adventure. We hopped on the bikes and headed up the windy gravel road. On the way into town, we passed beautiful homes with amazing ocean views, and some old farms along the way. We breathed in the clean air and breathed even harder as we raced away from off-leash barking pit bulls on the road who chased us and nipped at our heels.

The sun was hot, and the beach was full of locals and tourists, but we didn't care. We grabbed a spot at a restaurant on the beach and ordered a beer and a taco and watched a band play while the waves crashed behind them and the kids ran from the water.

Within twenty minutes of lunch, my stomach felt like it had a clamp on it. It felt like someone was twisting and jabbing it with a steak knife at the same time. We continued to explore as I was thinking it was probably a gas pain and would pass. We had another beer and made out in a cave and decided to head back up the long winding road, past the beautiful houses, through the field and the fence, down the hill with the dogs chasing us, and back to our beautiful spot. All the while, the waves of pain were taking my breath away one by one. My stomach grew tighter and tighter.

We had planned a room upgrade for our last night there. We felt like after all the shit we'd been dealing with, we deserved one night in the beachfront suite. And by deserved, I mean, we work hard for our money and that's how we wanted to blow it. Steph opened the door and walked me in. As my jaw hit the floor, she gently picked it back up and sealed it back on my face with a kiss and asked, "Do you like it?"

I'm not sure I had ever seen anything more beautiful in my life (the room, not the girl). Kidding. But really. It was open air and tall ceilings and a huge bed that I couldn't wait to spend time in, and a balcony, and a bathroom the size of our house.

It was late afternoon, and we walked out to the patio for some fresh air. You could see the waves crashing a couple hundred yards away. It smelled sweet like summer and flowers, and all was quiet except for the ocean.

We were sitting at a square table; I was facing the ocean and she was facing me. Before I knew it, we were having the same conversation we had had twenty times already that weekend. "If we were to get married…" By then I was wondering if she was forgetting my answers or maybe quizzing me to make sure that I said the same thing every time, so she was certain I was certain. Or maybe so she was certain. It went a little something like this:

"Okay…so you really want to get married again?" Steph asked.

"Yes, honey. Only to you," I replied.

"And you would want to do it soon?"

"Yes, honey. It really doesn't matter when. I'm going to be with you either way, so if we are getting married, there's no need to wait other than to please other people's emotions about the situation."

"And you think the kids would be excited?"

"Yes, honey…babe, we have had this talk a million times this weekend."

"I know. It's because I want to ask you to marry me," Steph blurted out.

"I know honey—"

"Like right now. I want to ask you right now," Steph interrupted.

"Holy shit...um...okay..." *awkwardly picks up chair and turns to face her*

I immediately started shaking and crying as I turned my chair. She was beaming her face off, smiling so big, as she stared straight into my eyes. She was really doing it, she was proposing. I couldn't believe it. *Why here? Why now?*

She looked at me and held my hands with her trembling hands and said all the things that we had been talking about. She said, "I want to do this now, I need to. I want to be with you. I want you to be my wife. I want to build a life with you and those two curly-headed girls. You are my home."

Before we knew it, I was blurting out, "Yes! Yes! Yes!" And there were tears squirting out of our eyes, and I was probably choking on my own tears. My cheeks were soaked, and I felt like I had just been hit with a love bus. It all happened so quick.

She pulled out a ring made of palm leaf and put it on my finger. She wasn't planning on proposing but I guess when she knew, she couldn't stop herself. She had fashioned a ring for me until we could pick one out together. She said she didn't want to pick one without me anyway because I am so particular. Go figure. Lucky for me, I had kept a seashell with a hole in it that I had found on the beach earlier that day that fit her ring finger perfectly.

I have honestly never been more surprised in my life. It was so simple. Intimate and perfect.

After a glass of champagne at the bar and a call to her brother and my best friend, we spent the rest of the night fighting over the toilet in our suite. What I had felt earlier in my stomach was food poisoning and not nerves. It was the most unromantic engagement night of all time, but it really solidified the "in sickness and in health" part of our relationship. We still laugh about it and how we need a do-over in that beachside suite.

20: I don't need a permission slip

I was now in a world that I had only seen from the outside. The gay world. It was exciting and freeing, yet everyone always told me there was something to fear. I quickly started to realize that I was basically at a disadvantage before I even fully got to experience true love. That people would soon see me a certain way before even developing a sense of who I truly was because I was now gay.

I wondered if my friends now thought I had been previously attracted to them. I had women telling me they wished they would have made out or slept with a girl before they had gotten married...like it was a fun game or some sort of novelty. I could hear whispers of old peers saying "did you hear about Lianne?" I suddenly had women coming to me confessing that they were married to a man but in love with a woman, as if I could guide them into a new and better life.

My mind wanted to explode because that's not how it happened for me, but I didn't want to explain myself. I didn't want to be everyone's go-to straight-turned-lesbian. I was proud of who I was, but I was quickly realizing what it meant to be a gay woman. Even if I didn't view it that way, society did.

Before falling in love with a woman, I thought Pride was something gay people celebrated because they knew how to have more fun than straight people. In fact, I envied it. I had previously discounted the blood, sweat, and tears it took for them to be able to be who they were in public, and to be accepted for it. It didn't even cross my mind that people didn't think they deserved the same rights as everyone else or how LGBTQ+ people are abused and even killed for who they are. And as I looked around, I realized that *them* was now me.

It's isolating to understand that people can go on living their lives knowing that they don't have to worry about their rights being taken away. That at any moment, someone I don't know can tell me my marriage is no longer valid. That I'm different and I'm wrong. That people are actively voting and protesting and wasting their lives to have my rights taken away. It takes incredible strength to be able to live as an openly queer person in a world that tells you that you are wrong and less deserving.

* * *

I felt completely liberated at my first Pride. I felt full of light and love. I looked around at thousands of people and realized what it meant to truly be an ally, and that I (despite what I had previously thought) had not truly ever been one to my gay friends. I needed to show up for more than the parade and the glitter and the parties in June. I needed to show up every single day and use my voice and my platform. I needed to ask them questions and have conversations with people like I was having with my parents. I needed to celebrate their accomplishments as individuals and couples, throw them their own damn pride party. They still needed me to have their back even though it was legal for them to get married. Nobody ever questioned my relationship with my husband from a moral standpoint, yet people always do when you get two of the same sex organs involved.

I had to brace myself for the first time I would hear a man say "what a waste" under his breath when Steph and I walked by holding hands. Or a mother saying "I don't need my kids to see that" if we kissed. I didn't know how much it would sting to hear "it's fine if you're gay, I just don't need you to rub it in my face" when all I was doing was giving my wife a hug. I had to brace myself for the first time I heard a rumor that I had a bad experience with a man so now I was gay. Or that people wonder if my wife is gay because she didn't grow up with a dad. Do we really need an explanation to love who we love? Are we really going to give men credit for pushing us a different direction? Didn't think so.

I had to shore up for the comments and the stares and the questions. I had to learn to be on high alert in public group settings. These are things I didn't realize actually happened as a straight woman. That was my privilege. And now it is my privilege to help change it.

* * *

My parents' reaction to Steph and I getting married was less than ideal. Remember that sunny day in Mexico where I was ever so impatiently waiting for my lovely girlfriend to meet me for a bike ride? As it turns out, she was FaceTiming my dad to ask him for permission to marry me.

In her words, she said she had just straight up told him that she was going to marry me. There wasn't a whole lot of asking. But she respected him and wanted to let him know. They were still getting used to the idea of us even being together and trying to wrap their brains around the fact that I was insistent that this was not a rebound. He didn't really say, "Yes, please marry my daughter, I give my blessing." He just said, "I'm concerned."

We called them the night after we got home to tell them the news. Steph was so excited. Meanwhile, I had a pit in my stomach, the kind that makes you think you might shit yourself. She was sure they would be fine and couldn't wait to call them. I was sure they would be like "what the fuck is wrong with you?" I honestly didn't really want to call them until after the wedding. I had already put them through two heart-wrenching situations in the last two years. I didn't think they could handle a third. We sat down on the couch and dialed their number, so I could let them down yet again.

I couldn't speak. I just sat on the couch shaking, so Steph told them that she had asked me to marry her and that I had said yes. My dad just said, "Huh...okay?" I could hear the disappointment in his voice. My mom started bawling. She raised her voice and it started shaking as she told Steph to stop talking and that she wanted to talk to her daughter. Steph sunk into the couch and her shoulders slumped in defeat. In that moment, she felt inconsequential...like she was just an other of sorts.

My mom proceeded to scold me and tell me that she wanted me to have time to find myself. Her statement and her tone instantly made me cry. Not because of her words, but more because if my parents didn't see that I knew exactly who I was after fighting alone for years to get out of a marriage and finally being happy for the first time in my life, they really didn't know me at all. And that was devastating.

After we got off the call, Steph asked if I thought they would have reacted differently if she were a man. I was speechless, disappointed, and completely embarrassed.

I could feel their disappointment from thousands of miles away. I could almost hear their hearts racing and see the looks on their faces, utterly broken. I felt like I'd have to spend years explaining myself and my happiness, why and how we were so great together. I didn't need permission to divorce him, or to love her. I wasn't asking for validation; I was asking for support. I also felt completely let down, like their love was conditional. Like they wanted her to be a man. Like I wasn't equipped to marry again. Like they knew my life better than me.

The guilt and the shame were almost unbearable. I couldn't care less about their blessing. This was my life, and I was finally living it the way that was for me and nobody else. And I was finally happy.

Needless to say, we didn't speak for a while. I got an email two days later from my mom, apologizing. She said she had been sick and had been on steroids for a few days and her emotions got the best of her. It was a nice gesture, but their words, spoken and unspoken, have stayed with me.

* * *

We planned the wedding for later that fall so we could figure out what we wanted it to look like and let the dust settle. Steph moved in and we continued to build our life, our home, and our family. My parents came out to visit a couple of times before the wedding, but we didn't speak about it until two months before. They never asked, so in my mind they weren't coming. But when we finally did bring it up, it's because their wedding invitation was burning a hole in my pocket.

I hadn't wanted to send it because I couldn't deal with the rejection of it, or the lecture that I wasn't ready, or that it wasn't right. How horrible to have your parents decline your wedding invitation? I couldn't wrap my brain around it; however, I knew that it was a possibility.

Steph and I had gone back and forth on what kind of wedding we wanted and all I wanted was to go to the courthouse, just her, me, and the kids, but she didn't want to do that without her family. We decided to get married in a hotel lobby with a dozen of our closest friends and family, and then have a party two nights later with about sixty guests. Our friend was willing to let us use her event space for the party. It was raw and slightly unfinished, with a view of the city...absolutely perfect for us. Not totally put together, not totally known, slightly hidden, and cozy.

We sat my parents down to tell them the plan, and I finally had the courage to speak for myself. I was trying to be bolder and more honest about who I was so I could collapse the space between expectation and disappointment. I was so hurt by how they had handled everything in the past months, I felt betrayed. I was also tired of being worried about and treated like a child. I was a thirty-two-year-old woman with two kids and a one-way ticket out of an abusive marriage that I'd silently fought to leave. Then I'd grabbed a one-way ticket into my wildest dreams. There was no backing down.

I told them the plan and told them we had an invitation for them. I didn't want them to respond right away, I wanted them to think about what I was about to ask. I didn't want them there because they loved me, or they cared about her. I told them I only wanted them there if they truly supported our relationship and what we were doing...and then I handed them the invitation.

My mom couldn't look at me—she was staring at my dad as his eyes filled with tears. I could feel the concern filling their bodies and their attempts at keeping it away. He waited a minute and then he said, "If it's okay with you, we would love to be there." And that was that. They've been one hundred percent on board ever since.

It was all very confusing. I wondered what had changed. *Were they really okay with it? Did they really support us?* But I wasn't going to question them. Simply put, I was sick of being questioned and I was just ready for everyone to trust each other.

Did it all hurt? Yes. But that was their process. Had I hoped it would have gone differently initially? Absolutely. But I learned so much about them and myself. I learned how to stand up for my beliefs and how I wanted to raise my own children in the meantime. While I still have some trauma around it all, I am thankful it happened.

We got married on November 2. And even though it was far from perfect, it was perfect to us.

21: Tell me more

Being in a relationship with a woman is like winning the lottery with an everyday payout. Being MARRIED to a woman, however, is basically like having an early access pass to heaven and still getting an everyday lotto payout. Win-win.

It's annoying how annoying we are. Remember when I said I wanted to absorb her into my body? I still do. I still look at her and think, *DAMMMNNNNN, she's mine? How did I get so lucky?* I still want to rip her clothes off every time I see her and kiss her so hard that she gets the chills. But at the same time, I don't want to kiss her because then her mouth would be busy, and I really want to hear every single thing she has to say and stare at her lips. And I don't know about your wife, but my wife has A LOT to say. But our communication is so good.

The most frustrating part of it all is that we almost overcommunicate. And it's only frustrating because I wish everyone could overcommunicate. It makes things so much easier. It's vastly different from my previous marriage, or any relationship with a man for that matter. It's almost as if we are the same gender or something.

But we talk so much and then we make sure that it's clear, and that we understand the feelings and the timeline. We want to learn every cell and every corner of each other, and we are sure that a lifetime won't be enough time, so we keep talking. She takes care of my thoughts, my emotions. She is my safe haven.

We talk from the second we wake up to the second we go to sleep. We talk when we are at work, mostly about how we can't wait to see each other and how we can't wait to work with each other one day. Because being apart feels like the worst possible thing on earth when you have finally found your home.

When we're apart, we count the hours until we can be together, and we stay up later than we should just so we can get more time together. We're often mad that we have to sleep at all. I wake up early every day just to have an extra thirty minutes to breathe her in while I drink my coffee and she lays on my chest. I stare at her skin and watch the air enter her body, convincing myself that somehow, it's even more pure as it leaves her lips than it was when it entered her body. I have to believe that there are miracles inside of her, things I will never know that I only wish I could see.

My wife is magic. She is perfect. I am in awe of her every day, every hour. She is also the most gorgeous thing I've ever laid eyes on and gets prettier by the second. I don't know how she does it. She's the kind of woman that makes any gender appreciate her.

We basically orbit each other in our home. I cook, she cleans. If I'm doing laundry and walk away for half a second to stir something in the kitchen, she swoops in and takes up the laundry where I left off. If she's cleaning the floor and has to take a call in the other room, I'm right behind her finishing the project. We don't even have to mention it. It's almost as if we finish each other's—well, you get the point. If I'm exhausted and don't feel like cooking, she excitedly says "let's get takeout!" instead of insisting I burn myself out to save twenty bucks.

We work as a team, it's fluid. We are like water swooshing around one another. There is no comparing or keeping score. No "I do this, so you do that." There is no I did more, or I earn more, so I get this. It's all equal. It's easy. It's fun. And nobody has to worry about getting knocked up.

We have impromptu dance parties and when I cry, she cries. And when she's scared, I comfort her. We tear things down and we build them back up. We lift each other up with words and actions. When I want to shut down because of old habits, she waits. She is patient and kind and waits until I am ready to speak even though it makes her uncomfortable because she has a different communication style. She is my biggest fan and I am hers.

Pursuing your partner doesn't die when you get married. Steph and I continue to date each other. Not like a "where do you want to eat tonight?" type of date. It's more like the type of date that you go on when you are learning about someone but can't get enough. So we pursue each other.

My favorite thing to do is set out an outfit for my wife, new or old, and a card telling her why and just how much I love her in that moment. I then drive to the store while she gets ready. But I don't just drive to any store, I drive to the liquor store because we are lesbians and don't like flowers. If I'm going to buy her something, it's going to be practical. And whiskey is practical.

I then drive home and ring the doorbell like I don't live there and somehow, even though I know what she is going to be wearing, when she opens the door my jaw hits the floor because she looks absolutely stunning, and I almost drop the whiskey bouquet I brought her. After obsessing over how drop dead gorgeous she is and patting myself on the back for landing her, I ask her if she is ready. I then proceed to open the car door for her, wherever we go, and take her for a drink and a snack at two or three places we have never been before.

I want her to feel loved, like she is worth the planning. I also want to show her off, because she is gorgeous, and she is mine. I then get sick of showing her off and bring her home and invite myself to stay the night. Then I show her how much I love her in the sheets.

* * *

Making love to a woman is the best. There, I said it. Women are intuitive. We know what works and what doesn't, and we know how to get there. We don't have to train the other sex on what feels good and what doesn't. It's natural, and its mind-blowing. It's fun!

There's also never any pressure to have it or not have it. We laugh during sex and sometimes we cry, and it's always beautiful. Then we pass out in each other's arms, skin to skin. We understand each other and we make eye contact, and there's absolutely zero pressure to fake anything because we don't need to. It's the first time in my life that sex has felt safe.

There are no gender roles in our relationship. There is no *man* or *woman*. I got asked this question a lot when we first started dating, even still sometimes to this day. "Who's the guy?" What does that even mean? Like who's on top? Who calls the shots? Who earns more money? Who wears less makeup?

We are a team and it's fluid. Not having that pressure is so liberating. I don't want those society-created roles in my house. Ever.

We love to leave little notes around the house for each other, little surprises on random days. Things like "I can't believe I get to be married to you," "I am so proud of you," "you are the sexiest woman I have ever seen," or "I can't wait to do *xyz* with you someday." It's amazing what a sentence can do for your marriage.

We make each other laugh. Like the kind of laugh where you can barely breathe, and liquid joy starts squirting out of your eyeballs. She encourages my quirks which allows her space to get a little more silly, a little more weird.

We encourage each other's ideas. Sometimes I hope that she doesn't encourage my idea because I'm trying to talk myself out of something because I'm afraid. But she pushes me. We all need someone to push us. When I say maybe she asks "why not yes?" When I say no, she respects it. When I say, I'm going to do this crazy thing or write this book she says "hell yeah you are, girl. I support you." And then she asks what I need to be able to do it. We don't question each other. Get a wife like that.

* * *

We take interest in each other's interests. Look, if my wife wanted to learn to drive a race car, I would learn with her even though that sounds terrible. If she wanted to dress up as clowns on Saturdays, I'd probably do that too. I've always wanted to take dance lessons, and she will take them with me even though her hips don't move. We support staying true to ourselves while growing together.

Our marriage is easy. I'm not saying that because we have never had an argument. We have. There are plenty of times that we have hurt each other or misunderstood one another. We both have habits and triggers from old relationships that unexpectedly resurface. And we have to navigate those moments.

But compared to what I was in before, our marriage is absolutely perfect, and I wouldn't have it any other way. This feels like how I always imagined marriage should feel. To be honest, it took me a while to trust that this was how it would stay. But it has, because we are supposed to be together, and we work hard to nurture our relationship. We have an insane amount of respect for each other. She is my forever, so we work for it. We fight for it. We are so thankful for each other every single second of every day.

I am proud of the marriage we have built, and I am proud to model it for our girls. And while I'm not sure it's healthy to love someone as much as I love her, I'm convinced that my heart might stop beating if I ever were to lose her.

We always say #getawife. It's the best decision I ever made.

PART 3
My Fuzzy Little Head

22: I'd like a mammogram, ma'am

I'm not really a boob girl. I never really felt myself up much. I've always been known for a perky backside, so I never gave my chest a second thought. I did get a boob job after my second daughter sucked the living tits out of me, and after my divorce. The truth is, after kids, my boobs were like saggy empty sacks. Those old, limp flapjacks couldn't even fill out a training bra.

I am petite anyway, so finding tops that didn't fall so low as to reveal the girls had been hard my whole life. But after kids, I didn't have any tissue left to hold shirts up at all. So, when I say I got a boob job, it was literally the smallest implant they make. Just a few ounces to fill those suckers back up to youth. I didn't want to look augmented like the boob jobs I knew from 2003, or the women I'd seen trying too hard to be something they were not. I just wanted to be able to fill out a B cup. Perfect tits. And perfect tits are what I had, or that's what I thought.

* * *

Steph and I went on our honeymoon to Thailand about six months after our wedding. It was really my first time abroad (sorry, Mexico), and while I've always felt like I was living the YOLO life, I was mad at myself for waiting so long to get to another part of the world.

The Thailand trip was one I had always imagined taking. When I arrived, I was hit in the face with perspective. What a beautiful country—the people, the food, the water, the culture, my wife. I was the asshole that got to vacation here. I was so humbled and so thankful.

About four days into our trip, in our second location, I was getting ready to head to the beach. As I was putting on my bikini top, I felt an itch near my nipple that I can only describe as coming from the inside out. No matter how hard I itched, I couldn't scratch it. As my fingers were going back and forth, vigorously digging to satisfy the itch, there it was. The lump.

Now don't get me wrong, my first reaction was to freak out. But my second was to keep this little secret mystery lump to myself and not to tell my wife. I was thirty-two at the time, healthy, fit, no family history of breast cancer, and finally living an honest, big, and bold life without restrictions. That little pea-sized fucker wasn't going to stop me.

Instead, I just pointed the itch out to Steph, along with the red rash I had created just outside the line of my swimsuit top and went about my day, pretending like the itch and the lump weren't there. I just wanted to honeymoon and not be stressed for once. We just chalked it up to a fluke thing, maybe a weird bug bite. I hadn't told her about the lump part. I skipped right over it for the time being.

That itch only happened one more time. But I knew something wasn't right. My health had been feeling off for a few months. I was exhausted all the time, couldn't keep weight on, was constantly dizzy, and had a sinus infection every two seconds. I had had multiple blood tests and doctor's appointments prior to our wedding and the honeymoon but everything looked normal in my labs. Doctors chalked it up to stress, told me I was fine, and to essentially get on with my life. "You are probably overdoing it," they said. Or, "You could be stressed out."

I know my body better than you know your iPhone screen, so I kept feeling the lump. It was still only about the size of a pea.

* * *

Fast forward about five weeks. I was sitting in my living room and felt a cool rush down the front of my right breast. And then another, slightly electric rush, almost like an engorged feeling. It's hard to put into words, but it was not a normal sensation. It was almost as if the cold-water stream that comes from the fridge was inside of my boob. I felt the area where the lump was again. This time it was quite a bit bigger and longer, an irregular shape. My internal dialogue said, *Lianne, don't be stupid. You know something is wrong.*

But here is the thing, I once fell off a punching bag onto my head on the concrete during a photoshoot for Lululemon Athletica apparel and didn't seek medical help. I certainly had a concussion. I once broke a rib and sprained two others and still worked out like a maniac with back tape on and zero downtime. I was doing push-ups nine days post breast augmentation.

I refuse to take medications even when I'm miserable. I'm stubborn. But the way I see it, I just refuse to let things get in my way. And I knew that whatever this devil lump was, it would stop my life, a life I felt like was finally just starting.

I got over myself and called my OB. I saw her assistant. God bless her, she was the one that took my IUD out the moment I started dating Steph. She's sarcastic as well, and we celebrated the fact that I no longer needed contraceptives of any sort. We even took a picture of me tossing it in the trash to document a good time. But there was no celebrating this visit.

After changing into the gorgeous bile-colored hospital gown, I laid on the table just so she could open said gown. (I'll never understand why they have you dress down to put a gown on just to open it up. Just let me just remove my top, we can skip the modesty, and then you won't have to leave the room for twenty minutes. You're going to see the girls either way.)

I laid back, gown open, lifted my right arm above my head, and immediately when she started to ask where the lump was, her hand slid over it and she said, "Ohhhh, there it is." She followed that with a couple of adorable, but very sorry attempts at finding "normal" lumps elsewhere in my breasts. She was trying to make it more routine, less scary. But we both knew it wasn't. I was referred for immediate imaging at another clinic for a full mammogram and an ultrasound. She also left me with a promise that it was "probably nothing, but we need to be safe."

That's when shit got real. I was nervous and I was terrified. What I was suspicious of in my head was confirmed by the tone of her voice. I already had an issue with false hope. I realize people need to say something, and maybe she truly believed that it was probably "just nothing."

But I was already annoyed because it took me back to when people told me it was impossible for my second child to come out crying nonstop, yet she did. I believed them and then I was let down, and then I was mad. I would have preferred if she just said "I'm so sorry you have to get your boob smashed, please keep me posted on the results," instead of giving me a sliver of hope when I knew I was fucked. My gut said it was cancer, and remember, my gut is god. My OB's assistant is not.

Being self-employed, I don't have the best healthcare coverage. So when they say it's *rushed* or *immediate*, what they really mean is take a number, take a seat, and don't hold your breath. I went to the imaging center three days later. I walked in wearing a silk cheetah button-up top, matching shorts, and black Air Force Ones. If I was going to do this, I was going to do it in style. I said hello to another beige waiting room with the same bulk patterned couches and HGTV playing in the background. It didn't mute the feelings in my head of "is this really happening?" or "am I going to die?" But it was a nice suggestion I suppose. I looked around, sat down, and thought to myself, *I don't fit in here.* Everyone was old...and sick.

I was called back for my mammogram first. I had heard horror stories about getting your boobs smashed between two pieces of glass. I must admit, I was kind of excited to see what all the hype was about and if I could handle it. My friends would love to have an insider scoop on a mammogram before they hit forty. Besides the tech having the most anxious energy I've ever encountered, it wasn't so bad. I wondered if I should offer her a Xanax from my bag, but I figured she wouldn't understand my sarcasm.

* * *

Squish squish bish. It's fascinating how many ways they can squish a boob. They carefully take your boob in the palm of their hands and place it on a piece of glass. They tilt your head to the side so it is smooshed up against another pane of glass, like a small child pressing into a window that you just cleaned, while they lower the last pane of glass on top of your boob that's been placed on a flat surface like a slab of meat, then they press it down. They adjust the boob and the glass multiple times to get the right pictures. You can't move, let alone blink an eye.

Did it hurt? Not for me. Was it uncomfortable? Yes. Do we need to be so dramatic about mammograms? No. I wonder if fear is what makes mammograms hurt more for women, that and denser breast tissue. That being said, my mammogram was taking a long time, and the longer it took, the more I knew the outcome.

Steph was in the room with me but had to stand behind a weird divider to avoid the radiation exposure. She couldn't even hold my hand. She was listening and watching the whole thing, trying to make it all okay, telling me it was going to be fine—but I knew it wasn't. None of it was okay, I shouldn't even be here. False hope. I just kept telling myself, *It's okay to not be okay.* But I felt like I needed to hold it together for her.

They sent me to another beige waiting room where I sat for a good twenty-four minutes before Ms. Anxiety brought me back in for more imaging. More imaging is not what you want. You want a "looks good, go home." We walked back into another tiny cubicle of a room with a giant boob smasher in the middle, and again, my wife stood behind the partition. This honestly became the theme of my life. My wife, watching me be brave, with absolutely nothing she could do, trying to make me feel better, trying to make it all okay. The technician kept pointing out calcifications. I didn't quite know what that meant but at this point I knew it wasn't good.

FUCK.

I was then taken to get an ultrasound for further imaging and to measure the exact size of my lump. The room was dark and sterile and had a heavy energy to it. It felt different than the ultrasound rooms that I had been in when I was pregnant. This one felt full of lost hope and confusion, doom and shattered dreams. Something told me they didn't lie to you in this room. They didn't tell you it was going to be okay or that it was "probably nothing." There was truth in this room.

I plopped down on the bed and waited for the next technician. The goo that the tech put on me to slide the wand around was slimy and cold. They don't bother to warm it up to make you comfortable like they do when you are pregnant— that would be too happy. I kept looking at her for any sign of concern, but she was a well-trained robot. For the life of me, I wouldn't have been able to tell if she had just won the lottery or if her cat had just died.

After about ten minutes of ultrasound and awkward silence, she left the room. She told me she had to check with the radiologist and would be right back. However, her right back felt like an eternity. The waiting was more painful than the mammogram for sure.

She entered the room with a small older woman by her side. She was wearing a lab coat and had tender eyes. Her head was tilted about twenty degrees to the right, the tilt of concern. The tilt a dog makes when it's trying to understand a human. The tilt I gave my baby when she was born because I thought she would understand me better. There was a crease in her brow. She was the radiologist.

* * *

She told me the lump was "concerning." I think that's a way of saying "you have cancer," but I'm also blunt and have realized that people have a hard time giving it to you straight. I pretty much blacked out after that...she said something about the shape of it being irregular and the calcifications.

I said, "I need you to tell me right now, is it cancer or not?"

I knew full well she wasn't allowed to say, but I also knew full well that she knew, even without a biopsy. She said in her experience, which was clearly a lot of years, she was positive that cancer was the only thing it could be. And then, for the first time, I was asked if I had any family history of breast cancer.

They left us in that dark room alone, Steph started shaking. I had woken up a somewhat normal thirty-three-year-old, ready to go sling some hair and make some money to pay some bills, and I would leave this god-awful room with cancer. As far as I knew, it was a death sentence. So now I was no longer normal. I was a thirty-three-year-old, still about to go to work, but with what I knew was a death sentence—cancer.

This radiologist had pulled the rug right out from underneath me, turned my world upside down with one concerned look and a cock of the head. I was so confused. One moment she looked so sweet, and the next moment my dreams had been shattered. She didn't even apologize for ruining my life. She just left.

This was the moment I started to plan my own funeral. My mind was swirling.

Who would take the kids? Could Steph pay the bills alone? Would she marry again? Would my kids remember me? Would people be sad, or would they move on in a month or so? I didn't want a funeral. Was there a way to make a funeral fun? Could there be a DJ? Or would they slowly lower me into the ground on a grey and rainy day while everyone wore their darkest shade of black? Would I be able to watch said funeral or "celebration of life" as a white ghost? Or could I also wear black? I'd want to wear something designer for sure. Or would I just be a speck of dust that didn't feel anything at all—something that people stepped on every day, not knowing it was me, pressing me into the ground as they walked by and the memories faded?

It is an odd thing to think about burying yourself while you are still alive. It's completely unfair and something you cannot help but do when you are catapulted into these situations. When you are "normal" and young, how you die and how your legacy does or does not live on never crosses your mind. But the moment that someone steals your normal, it's all you can think about. I couldn't even stop myself. Every time I tried it was like an avalanche of thoughts wiped me out of the present and into the grave. Little did I know, I would bury myself again and again over the next couple of years.

I couldn't even cry because they had left me with a phone and number to call to schedule a biopsy. I had to stay in control. I couldn't break down now. It was only going to get harder.

I resorted back to robot status. The loneliness of my disease started at that very moment. Nobody was going to call and make the appointment for me, no matter how tired or scared I was. They were going to walk away, and I was going to rely on myself for the next step.

I left the center with an order for a biopsy of the breast tumor and lymph nodes on the same side. It would have been way too convenient to just get it done that day. So, we waited. Because waiting is fun when you are told you have cancer and given NO OTHER DETAILS, like what stage it was, or if it has spread to your brain, and/or if you will die next week. I just kept thinking, *Wait, I'm not equipped for this.* I was taught how to be nurturing and attentive and respectful and responsible. But nobody had ever taught me how to fight for my life.

I cancelled my clients for the day and called my dad, boss, and ex-husband to fill them in. You would have thought I had merely stubbed my toe by the lack of reaction from my ex. I felt exposed and guilty telling them the news, like I was letting them down somehow. I didn't want to stress anyone out or be a burden. Nobody I told knew what to say, or what to do. I didn't either. I didn't know what I wanted to hear or what I needed for that matter.

I got home, crawled into bed, laid down, and said nothing. I knew nothing about breast cancer other than women get it when they are older and a lot of times you die from it. I knew nothing about MY cancer, just that it was in my body. I Googled and then tried not to Google. A couple of lone tears would randomly escape my eyes and roll down my cheeks as I looked at my wife and had nothing to say. She was speechless for the first time since I had met her. I knew she was spiraling, but I didn't know how to save either of us.

We went to lunch at what turned out to be another dimly lit environment with no people in it. You would have thought we hated each other by our lack of interaction. It reminded me of when you see a couple who are clearly miserable on a date, so they just scroll through their phones while sitting across from each other. Only we had left our phones at home and we were sitting next to each other, facing a wall. We had put ourselves in time out, completely shocked, terrified, and frozen. I don't even know if I ate anything, but we were trying to carry on.

There was no carrying on.

I was supposed to teach a fitness event that evening downtown and I decided to go. I wasn't going to let cancer slow me down yet. I wasn't ready to let anyone down yet. I'm not sure my logical brain was working at the moment, but my emotional brain was on high alert. In my mind, this could have been the last event I ever taught. I was still lacking crucial information about my timeline. I also wanted to go because movement had always been my medicine and my clarity. I wasn't going to let cancer change that.

So I taught. I was present. I was in a body that was fighting for me but also against me. I will never forget that night. I cried my eyes out as a hundred of us moved our bodies together, trying to remind myself what a gift it was to move without giving away my new informal diagnosis. I was trying to hold myself together in the most normal way I knew how.

* * *

Eight days later, I found myself in another beige waiting room. Different day, different imaging center. My wife and I were called back to the room where I would have an ultrasound-guided biopsy of my breast and lymph nodes. The assistant was young. She looked about three years older than my seven-year-old, so ten. Okay, so she was likely around twenty-six and probably had never thought about the fact that she, too, could get cancer at her age.

I was injected with three vials of lidocaine to numb my breast. I was getting a core needle biopsy. Basically, a hollow needle is used to go in and take tissue samples of the areas in question. Just a casual needle to the tumor. I'm not good with pain meds, as in, I think I might be immune to them. I don't feel much pain relief when I do take them, so I don't usually bother taking them. I wonder, *Why put chemicals in my body if it doesn't even work?* I feel EVERYTHING.

I laid flat as the doctor leaned over my chest, coming in at an angle with a giant needle that would take flesh from my body. It was extremely painful, like she was jamming a dagger into my boob with her whole body weight—a dagger that had a stapler at the tip. I told her I could feel everything and she replied "hold on," and she kept going, holding me down with the weight of her upper body and one arm, and guiding her needle through my breast with the other. She was guiding the needle from one side of my boob, through my nipple, to the other side to get a sample of the tumor. She had to do this while avoiding popping my implant. I was being held down on a table, fighting tears, feet locked so tightly together so I wouldn't budge, jaw clenched, breath held, wondering, *What the fuck was happening to my life?* I could feel every turn and jab of the needle as she went in and out trying to find the right part of the tumor.

I was certain I was breaking my wife's tiny, bony, fingers as I squeezed her hand in an attempt to find relief and a way out of my situation. I heard a click-click, like the cocking of a gun. And just like that, the doctor stole tissue from my body and pulled the needle out.

We weren't done though. She still needed to biopsy a lymph node. At this point, my arms were falling asleep behind my head, I was extremely dizzy, and I was starting to feel like I might burst into tears at any moment. She pierced the needle through my side, threading deep into my armpit. I held my breath as she placed a tiny metal marker shaped like a staple in the tumor and the tested nodes to mark where they had been so it would be easier to see on imaging moving forward.

This was the beginning of my life as a pin cushion.

When the needling was over, they decided it would be a comfortable time to send me back for another mammogram. There's nothing like a good squeeze of the tit after the trauma of having a wide gauge needle in it for an hour.

When the images of my second mammogram were done, the tech realized that none of the images had been saved. I would have to do it all over again. I had been in the clinic for three hours. I was really practicing patience, but this was one of the many moments that I almost snapped. I was in so much pain, had spent hours being poked and prodded, and now—you fucked up my third mammogram in two weeks? *Ummm, excuse me, but who fucks up a mammogram, ma'am? You had one job.*

After the biopsy experience had come and gone, I had the pleasure of waiting. Again. I kept wondering when someone was going to tell me that it wasn't real. I was waiting for the phone to ring and for the person on the other line to tell me it was a false positive. Please, someone tell me this was the world's most cruel joke. Fuck, I'd have been on candid camera with this joke if it meant it weren't real.

* * *

Six days later I got a call. Confirmed. Invasive Ductal Carcinoma (IDC). The radiologist said, "Your full pathology will take a couple of days, but this is really aggressive." I swallowed the lump in my throat and replied, "Great, so am I." She laughed as she hung up. No good luck, no anything.

I suddenly went from feeling like I was going to fuck this shit up to this shit was going to fuck me up. *What was happening to me? I never get scared.*

The good news was it wasn't positive in my lymph nodes. The bad news was that they needed more imaging, but an MRI this time. They still weren't convinced it wasn't in my nodes, and my tumor was bordering between stages.

23: Cat's out of the bag

I work in fitness and see about three hundred different faces a week. (Un)fortunately, Portland is small, so people know me in this city. I had randomly been subbing out my classes for last minute appointments, and I knew it would only get worse. The news coming out was inevitable as people would start to wonder. I knew if anyone asked what was up, I would have my first fall-apart since God knows when. I needed to keep it tight until it could come from me.

I didn't intend for social media to become an outlet for me, but I'm so glad it did because what happened over the next few months was truly amazing. A few days after my diagnosis, I decided to just get it out there and blasted social media with the news.

It honestly felt good to let it out. I have an amazing community that is so supportive, and although at times I can feel overwhelmed by attention, I wouldn't have it any other way. The initial outpouring of love and support was big. Really big. I will always be thankful for that. I had more people reach out than I could count. Really more than I could respond to. I didn't have a problem sharing my story, but what I DID have a problem with is hundreds of people giving me ALL their advice, stories, or questions.

It all started the day I publicly exposed the most earth-shattering thing that was going to happen to me in my lifetime, for all I knew. I had only known of my diagnosis for a few days, and I honestly didn't know much about it. Yet I'd already been smothered with "if anyone can do this it's you!" and "So-and-so had it and they are fine now!" And that was just from the few friends and family I had told. I hadn't thought about the fact that of course people would try to console and relate.

As much as I appreciated the good things, I didn't have any idea how jarring some of the comments would be. And to my entire being no less. I used to say that type of positive thing to people all the time when trying to make them feel better or when I was trying to relate. It seemed like the right thing to do, and I clearly didn't even think twice about it. But from the viewpoint of the sick person, these sentiments were so far from comforting, even highly offensive, that I decided to document as many of my raw moments as possible. I wanted to talk about life as a cancer patient—what was helpful, what was annoying, how it felt to be me, how it felt to be anyone fighting cancer. I wanted to educate people, so they knew what to say, or what to do and not to do if this happened to them or someone around them.

* * *

Until that point, what I knew of breast cancer was a pink and fluffy world of Breastie Retreats and sisterhoods. I was thrown into a world I didn't belong in, and I couldn't relate to the brand that was breast cancer, or the people in it. People were sending me cards that said: "Put lipstick on and handle it." And it had a red lipstick and a compact mirror in the package. I wanted to throw the lipstick off a cliff or shove it somewhere it didn't belong. Putting lipstick on would not handle anything, and it definitely wouldn't save my life. I realized that this picture of breast cancer didn't even come close to what it was all about, what the fight looked like, or what the majority of women who fought it represented. It was complete bullshit. I started to wonder where the truth was and why society was telling women that even when we are fighting for our lives, we need to be soft and pretty. It's not a feminine disease, and it's not ladies only.

Why did I need heels and lipstick to sit through a chemotherapy infusion? Why should those items make me feel any stronger than my leggings, tennis shoes, and a bare face? Why was there such a soft, girly filter over all things breast cancer? Why would I need to cover up my chemo chapped lips with lipstick? Why are we trying to look like we aren't sick? Why did we need to smile and act tough on the days that we felt the weakest? Was it just to prove that we had a pink ribbon as a badge of honor and a lifetime membership to the Breasties Club?

The message was wrong. The message IS wrong. I didn't want to hide anything. I wanted people to know that it wasn't all pink ribbons and lipstick—that it wasn't just fluff and sisterhood. It was gritty and fucked up and a battle for any gender, and it even affected girls who loved to wear black and hated red lipstick. Nobody was talking about it, but it needed to be talked about.

I sat down, spelled it out for the world, and pressed post.

5.9.18

33 days after my 33rd birthday I was told I was sick. That there is a 0.44% chance of getting breast cancer at my age and that I, in fact, was in that percentage.

I have breast cancer.

8 days later and it's still so hard to spit out. I am healthy, no family history, I'm short, had my kids young...I did everything right, but it happened to me.

I have a long road ahead of me that could take a sharp turn at any second. I ask for your support and I ask for your patience if I don't respond to you right away or at all. It's a lot to take on and I want to do it while being as present as possible with my wife and kids.

Things that are helpful right now...laughing, showing up, not complaining about stupid things, not taking your body or your time for granted, being present, talking about normal life.

Things that are not helpful right now...hearing about everyone you know or have known that has had breast cancer, long sympathetic gazes, offering me booze...'cause I can't drink it, telling me I'm going to beat this, asking ALL the questions, bombarding my wife with questions on my diagnosis and how she/we are doing.

When the doctor called to confirm my biopsy results, she said, "Your cancer is aggressive"...and I said "Great, so am I."

Cancer chose the wrong fucking girl.

* * *

I wanted to let people know that I wasn't going anywhere. That I was going to stay online and in studios and show them what it looked like to truly fight for your life every day. I was going to show them whether they wanted to see it or not.

It's uncomfortable to witness pain, to truly watch someone suffer. There were a variety of responses to my frankness about my process. Some people didn't see me, or they chose to look away because they couldn't handle it.

On the other hand, there were plenty of people who rushed to share their own remedies for the situation, or ways to improve my general happiness. Suddenly there were hundreds of responses on my post and hundreds more in my inbox. People offering advice, asking questions, telling me I was a fighter, saying if anyone could beat it, it's me—that So-and-so had it once, or twice, or they died.

I was sent every cancer coloring book that was ever made. I was given invitations to try do Terra oils (because we all know that that's the real cure for cancer). And bonus for the person who sent that because if I liked it, I too could make an income at home selling oils! I was sent links to articles and links to other humans that were miserable and would probably be offended if I reached out. I was sent head wraps in the ugliest shades of pink, and journals on journals (unfortunately none with a lock like the real journals we all know from third grade). I also received enough robes, pajamas, and blankets to furnish a boutique hotel slumber party.

So I guess if there was ever a time to let myself go, it would have been then. There were flower deliveries like someone had already died, and I was really looking forward to cleaning up the dead petals while I cleaned up my life. I love cleaning anyway, why not send all the things that will die? There was a new box of some sort of "fix" on my doorstep every day.

* * *

Being diagnosed with cancer when you are supposed to be at the age where you are building a life, family, and career is terrifying enough. I'm sure it's terrifying at any age, but this is just what I know. It's like cancer says: "Welcome to the latest horror movie. You are the star and I'm trying to kill you." And in that movie, there are people watching you, but they can't help you and some just disappear altogether and never return. There's no script, so don't fuck it up. And welcome to the Breasties Club where everything is pink and fluffy, and we talk about cancer for the rest of our lives. You can't get out of it. Good luck."

Some people I had known all my life started to fall into the distance, and people I had never met were coming forward. People in our most intimate support systems seemed to disappear overnight. The ones who stayed started to treat me a little differently. You could feel their fear like dry sand on your skin. You couldn't always see it, but sometimes you could hear it in their tone, their words, or if you were lucky, you could catch it on their face and it stuck with you when you left them. The thing that made it most apparent was the distance they kept or their need to fill any silence when they visited.

I was now in the category of *sick*. It's a different sick category than when you have the cold or flu, or hand, foot, and mouth. Or God forbid, herpes. I was the sick that people prayed they would never get. The sick they pitied, that people avoided because it made them uncomfortable. The sick that killed people. Some people treated it like they could potentially catch it if they were too close to me, like it was a cold that lingered in the air.

I was insanely lonely from the day I was diagnosed to this very moment that I am writing this portion of the book. I'm not sure why all the outpouring of love and support left me feeling so empty. I still have friends, not as many, and they are available to hang out when I need them. But nobody asks how you are when it's over. It's like it's over and done and life goes on as usual, but it doesn't.

This loneliness never goes away. It's completely different from the loneliness of wanting a partner or being alone on a Friday night, or even feeling like nobody understands you. It's a loneliness of facing your own fate yet outliving yourself...like seeing another universe. There's no way to get rid of it. It follows you like a shadow in every conversation and every interaction and every step you take. Although I was not alone during treatment, there are people in the cancer community that understood. But at the same time, others didn't understand at all.

This loneliness is more emotional than physical. It's there even when trying to share the intimate parts of the fight for my life, all while people discounted my experience by saying "be positive," "you've got this," or "this girl that lived down the street from me had breast cancer too and she's fine now." These comments were so invalidating. It's basically like if someone told you they won a spelling bee and you said, "Awesome! I got a gold medal in the spelling Olympics!" Just don't go there.

Nobody really wanted to hear about your stare down with death. I was straight up suffering, and that made others straight up uncomfortable. It was brushed off with "what else is going on?" as people assumed, I didn't want to talk about it, and I assumed they didn't know how. Everyone wants to hear a positive story. It's much more appealing. But they weren't ready or willing to hear what was real.

There were so many moments that it felt impossible or pointless to share my experience. I knew so many would just look away, as if it brought too much pain. But that's what I wanted—not to cause pain, but to show that pain was part of life and that you can find beauty in the experience of it if you are willing to sit with it.

Our society teaches us to make things better. And when we can't fix something, we get uncomfortable. It's hard to be present with what you cannot fix, to sit with it. (And from my point of view, apparently, it's almost impossible.) This was even hard for my own wife. When I would post a photo that was raw and real to try to educate people, I was met with so much sympathy and "you've got this" cheering because that's what everyone wanted to see. A hero, someone who gave people hope, a cancer warrior with a smile. And while I did smile, it was so much uglier than that. The warrior with a smile was a fraction of my experience. It didn't feel like cheering. Instead their words were a way for them to minimize their own fears. Society doesn't educate us on how to talk about hard things.

24: Please don't say that: A cancer friend's guide of what NOT to do

The things that people say to you when you are diagnosed are unreal. Even if they are well intentioned, think these phrases through before letting them escape your mouth. Let me break it down for you from a sick kid's perspective.

"My girlfriend had it a few years ago if you want to talk to her, she's totally fine now! You should talk to her!"

Is she? Is she "totally fine now"? Have you asked her? Does she love the fact that her boobs (and probably nipples) were removed and she can't feel her chest anymore? Is it fine that she can't reach her hands all the way over her head anymore? Did she just wake up like it was all a dream and not think about it again? Is she not a little upset that it put her life on hold for a couple of years and she lost herself a bit during treatment? That she never felt the same afterward, in body or mind?

Did she have the same cancer as me? Most likely not, so our treatment will be different. Not to mention her treatment was different anyway because a lot can change in five years, or however many years. Because who knows how old she is and when she had it. Do you think she likes being everyone's go-to when someone gets diagnosed? Reopening a wound that she probably spent years healing? Is she as sarcastic as me? Did you mention this to avoid your own discomfort over a life-threatening disease? Because if not, we won't get along. I think I'll find my own cancer buddy, but thank you. I think someone who is in it right now might be more helpful.

"So-and-so had it twice, and now she's good!"

You're an idiot. And how you think me hearing that someone's cancer CAME BACK, but now they are healthy can make me feel better is beyond me. I want to believe that this is a one-time horror story for me.

"Thank you for sharing your journey."

Now, I may be alone on this one here, but the word *journey* makes my blood boil. A journey sounds fun. A journey sounds like something that you might actually want to participate in, like there is a magical unicorn involved that takes you across land and sea to eat lollipops and see beautiful spaces. Riddle me this: how are we supposed to use the word journey to pump our veins with toxic poison and get our boobs chopped off? It's not a journey.

"My sister had cancer, and she was just like you. She was fit, healthy, young, and we had no family history. She was going to beat it, we knew it, until she didn't. Our biggest regret is that she didn't leave notes for the kids or have a lot of photos with them. Write your kids letters, take pictures...you never know what will happen."

I'm sorry, but did you just tell me to prepare to die? Holy shit. This one shook me up for a good three weeks. Actually, let's get real—I'm still shook. This message was beyond out of line, especially to someone who JUST learned of their disease and didn't ask if anyone knew anyone who had had breast cancer, let alone died from it. I am so sorry about your sister, but I have no idea who you are, and this is completely irrelevant to my situation. You didn't even state where and when things went south. We could have had a completely different treatment plan and stage of cancer. Not to mention, this is just, again, totally out of line. Comments like this made me feel like people were projecting their grief on me, the newest cancer patient on the block.

"Have you tried (insert weird diet or rain dance that cures every form of cancer imaginable)?"

Oh, wow! Why didn't this come up as a cancer cure when I Googled it? I've spent hours researching and this never popped up! You could make serious money, and not to mention history, if you told someone of this amazing cure. Also, I had NO idea you read my pathology report and that you were a part-time oncologist and could treat my specific cancer! What are you doing working at Nordstrom, you little genius? Take off the Tory Burch, put on the hazmat suit, and let's fix me!

"You are so strong." "You've got this." OR "You are so brave."

I don't have a fucking choice, Carol. Would you just sit here and let something kill you? Not fight back? But, thank you. Of course I am. Also, don't say the same thing to someone fighting for their life that you would say to someone running their first 10k.

"If anyone can pull off a bald head and no eyelashes, it's you."

Yeah, I'm such a trendsetter and I CANNOT WAIT to rock this look. When you see me, you will absolutely wish you looked this way too. Girls across the country are going to be pulling out their lashes, trying to look like me. Razor sales will go up and lash extensions will go extinct. You know you are lying, and this sentiment doesn't make a single person feel better, so just put a cork in it. Nobody wants to look like a real-life mannequin or dildo. This compliment is just not a compliment. Save it.

"If anyone can beat this, it's you."

This comment made me feel so much pressure. Thanks, but what if I don't? I know you just didn't know what to say, but that was the wrong thing. Plain and simple. I appreciate you believing in me, and I hope you are right, but cancer kills. It just does. And what a fool I am if I let myself believe that it couldn't take my life. This is a disease. It kills over 40,000 women per year. I wasn't even supposed to get this shit in the first place, so I don't consider myself out of the woods on it taking my life. Also, if I don't beat this, and hundreds of strangers and friends told me I could, how bad would I feel? Or how bad would they feel, for that matter? Shit happens. Let's not be naive. Also, save this for someone that has the stomach flu. They will feel like a goddamn champion when they beat that shit. Get out of here with that toxic positivity.

"I don't know how you do it."

Again, this is meant to be a compliment. But it is a selfish compliment. It's like they are trying to tell you how strong you are, and then they get to feel like they said the right thing. Here's the thing. I AM strong. But I am strong as fuck physically. Mentally, I'm just like anyone else. Sure, I had a few things that were inconvenient and hard over the last few years that bulked up my mental muscle, but we are all born with these mental muscles. It's not that special to keep going. I'm no different than any of you. You would all do the same thing.

We keep going every time we wake up and decide to go to work, have a hard conversation, or change a poopy diaper. You can either sit back and cry and let it kill you, or you can exercise your mental muscle and keep going. That's the only choice. If you do choose not to, you die. I hate to break this to you, but your life is going to hand you so much shit over the course of it, so you might as well start oiling your mental machine sooner than later. "Every fucking step" is what we say at our house. Step by step by step. That's how I do it. And I will do it again the next time life hands me lemons. Except lemons are delicious...so it's more like, next time life hands me moldy grey meat.

* * *

Here's the deal. I've been an asshole too. Nobody knows what to say when shit hits the fan. We all stumble over awkward words and stories and wish we could just pull them back into our mouths right after letting them escape. We are human. The way we place ourselves in the world and tiptoe around subjects change, depending on the circumstances and the objective.

But now I know what NOT to say. Honestly, I think when you don't know what to say, instead of trying to fix it, or trying to comfort someone by saying something that makes YOU feel better, there are really only two things that work. It's called pause and acknowledge. Don't fix.

Here are a couple perfect options for you to use.
1. "This sucks, I'm so sorry this is happening to you."

2. "I don't even know what to say…What is helpful to hear if anything? How can I support you?"

The number one rule of cancer support is: DO NOT try to relate. You are not them, and your friend's cancer isn't theirs, so there is no need to bring it up. The second rule: DO NOT try to fix it. You most likely can't. Just let it be the shitty situation that it is, and be available, ready, and willing, for whatever they need. Third rule: DO NOT project your emotions on them. They don't need to swim through your tears while they drown in their own.

I was able to group people into what I'm calling *catastrophe categories* throughout my treatment, and it really helped my mental state. And yes, I know I said I don't like putting people in boxes. These boxes are real though, and once you identify your behavior, you can then work to escape said box.

You have the comparers.

"So-and-so had it, and it's been three years. Now she's fine!"

"Oh, yeah, I was nauseous once when I was pregnant. It was horrible, so I totally get it."

"When my mom went through chemo…."

You wonder what the point of talking is because these people will always one up you. They want to file you away with comparable stories and just put you in their pocket like you're a tiny, sad minion.

There are the probers, the ones asking all the inappropriate questions.

"What's your prognosis? What's your treatment plan?"

"How are you feeling?"

"When do you get your new squishy boobs?"

They use this information as new gossip to fling around over cocktails or get "worried" about via a group text with friends. It's so fun to have the latest gossip on the cancer chick.

You have the fixers. These people say...well, you'll get the idea.

"Eat this! Do this!"

"Have you called this person? Have you tried this?"

"Celery juice! Rub kale on it!"

"Put a bird on it!"

"Just take whatever herb capsule twice a day! Wheatgrass shots!"

"Essential oils! CBD!"

"Pray and it'll disappear!"

These are all well intended, but mostly without substance. And I didn't ask for quick fixing.

You have the ones projecting their discomfort with comforts.

"God never gives you more than you can handle."

"If anyone can beat this, it's you."

"Lean on Jesus for comfort."

BLAH BLAH BLAH. These people want to fast forward with blinders on to a happy ending because they are so uncomfortable and out of touch with discomfort. Also, if God is in control and created everything, then God gave me cancer, so why would I pray to him to take it away? That feels manipulative and unfair. And if that's the case, God forgot to love me as much as he loves you because you don't have cancer.

Projecting people also love the phrase "whatever is meant to be will be." People say "it wasn't meant to be" when something doesn't go their way, or they are uncomfortable facing the facts or the truth. I started to wonder if they would say that if I died. "She wasn't meant to be." Like my life wasn't meant to be lived or I wasn't supposed to be on this earth?

Finally, there are the groundhogs.

These people pop up out of the blue. They're the ones that you haven't talked to in years, or you had a falling out with, or they burned you. Now you are taking care of THEIR emotions. If something happens to you, they feel good knowing they did the "right thing" by reaching out. Maybe they are Band-Aids, trying to cover an old wound they weren't willing to repair by showing up and pretending they care now that you are sick. I had a lot of these. I just smiled and graciously thanked them while seeing straight through to the heart of their intention and guilt. Guilt must be a bitch. Don't be a groundhog, or a Band-Aid for that matter.

* * *

I bet you are wondering which one you are now. It's okay. We have all done it. Like I said, I'm guilty of it too. I for sure have told people in the past "you got this." And now I know not to. What I should have said is "this sucks, and I'm so sorry this is happening." And then I should have shown up in a way that was helpful.

What cancer patients really need is true empathy. But what cancer patients usually get is sympathy. People seem to get them confused. There's a difference. Empathy is trying to understand someone's feelings as if they were your own. Sympathy is acknowledging another's feelings and being sad about their misery.

Empathy requires you to truly try to connect and understand someone's pain. THEIR pain, not your own. THEIR discomfort, not yours in relation to the situation. Empathy keeps the pains separate. True empathy doesn't even have to use words. The most honest script for empathy that I can come up with is what was mentioned above: apologizing for what's happening and asking what you can do to help. That opens the door for further discussion and understanding instead of shutting feelings down with a quick fix to avoid being uncomfortable. It's not at all fancy, and it's definitely not flowers on a doorstep.

We are all learning here. And empathy is a muscle that needs to be worked on regularly. So no, I'm not mad at you if you said or did any of this to me. And no, you don't need to send me an email or a text apologizing.

25: You better check yourself before you wreck yourself

Being able to afford decent healthcare in the US when you are self-employed is a joke. Because I am "healthy," I never planned on getting injured. And I've had my children, so I purchased a fairly basic health insurance plan. Why would I need anything else?

Lesson learned: never assume you are healthy. My mind was blown that I worked out for a living, ate relatively clean, didn't smoke (except for a pack during my divorce), and yet I had cancer. The whole "but you don't look sick" thing is a joke. To be honest, I looked great up until this point. Sick looked good on me.

Now, don't get me wrong, I still pay a pretty penny for my health insurance plan and should be able to find a doctor that I feel comfortable with, but apparently that just isn't how it works. I was told I only had a few within the network to choose from. Basically I couldn't decide which surgeon was going to cut me open. They were just going to assign me one.

Before I could make an appointment of any kind, I had to establish primary care so they could refer me to all the specialists I would need to see. Why go back to basics when I was already needing a specialist? I was livid. It didn't make any sense and seemed like the biggest waste of time and resources. Apparently, a positive malignant biopsy isn't enough to get you an appointment with an oncologist, you have to go talk to a family doctor first so they can check your blood pressure and your pulse. By then, I was living on the phone on hold for physicians, appointments, information, anything! (God bless unlimited minutes; not sure what people did twenty years ago.)

Communication is lacking in the healthcare system. It was hold music and commercials on repeat. I can't tell you how many times I heard the same advertisement with an older man saying "healthy foods can be delicious..." or "did you know that getting eight hours of sleep a night..."

Just answer the damn phone.

I finally made an appointment to establish care, which was my nineteenth tipping point of that particular week. I sat down at a family medical center I'd never been to, and the physician's assistant walked in shortly after. I didn't even meet my primary physician.

"When did you feel the lump? Did you notice it yourself? Do you have a family history of breast cancer? Do you drink alcohol?"

Not only were all of these questions irrelevant at this point, but every fucking person I called asked them. Why they aren't saved in the system, I'll never know. Also, I'd like to know what the magic number of alcoholic drinks per week is. *Is there a number that won't give you cancer? Is this information even relevant or are you just using it for a general study?* Either way, it's enough to make you crazy when you have bigger issues at hand. By the time I left, I wasn't sure people at that doctor's office even knew what breast cancer was. But I felt confident they could diagnose the shit out of a common cold.

After the most pointless appointment of my life, I walked out fifty dollars poorer, with referrals for an MRI, an oncologist, and a breast surgeon. *Let's go.*

* * *

One of my goals in life was to never have an MRI. This was alongside my many other goals that include traveling the world, being all-around happy, winning an award of sorts (for something or other), being obsessed with my spouse, and meeting Ellen. Actually, getting an MRI had never crossed my mind, so not getting one wasn't a real life goal. But looking back now, it would be. I never thought I'd be in a position to need one because I lived in a safe bubble and well, apparently, I'm naive.

Ever since my children were born, I've had a really hard time being in places where I don't have control, where I can't get fresh air if I want it, and where I can't get out fast if I need to. So places that aren't great for me are airplanes, apartments, or hotel rooms without a balcony, and I don't know...MRI machines!

The amount of times I've nearly passed out on an airplane BEFORE we even took off is embarrassing. I'm the one that basically strips naked before takeoff because I get panicked and hot, and there's no air coming out of the tiny vents. I'm also flailing my limbs with no rhyme or reason while simultaneously pressing the call button on repeat, just to ask the flight attendant for a cup of ice to dip my fingers in so I can literally chill the fuck out. This all happens while trying not to let my world close in on me. Flying with me is fun, I promise.

Thirty minutes before my MRI, I popped half of a Xanax. Because claustrophobia. And not half because I didn't need a whole, half because I needed to be coherent enough to remember anything important that they told me afterward.

I was taken to a changing room to put a hospital gown on. Does anyone know why they make hospital gowns one-size-fits-all? They are basically like a king-sized bed sheet with a hole at the top for your head. I also wonder why they are all the color of bile, or why I had to wear two if I was just going to take them off and one was big enough for seven of me. I threw the nasty hospital grippy socks on and went to wait for my nurse to help set my IV and send me into the black abyss.

I kissed my wife goodbye while trying not to look into her eyes before I walked away. I was afraid that if we locked eyes, one of us would break. It couldn't be her because I needed her to be strong for me. And it couldn't be me because she needed me to be strong for her.

There was enough fabric on my body to make parachutes for a family of four and a baby blanket with the leftovers. Any pride I had left was trapped under the yards of cotton I was tripping over as I tried to act cool and walk down the hall to get my IV. I swear the staff just watches that stuff and laughs. But I walked down that hall like it was the goddamn catwalk at New York Fashion Week.

The IV was placed so they could pump blue dye through my veins that illuminated any cancerous cells in my chest and underarm area. The nurse that was helping me asked if I had a music choice for the MRI. Of course, I did!

"Old school hip-hop, please."

He laughed like he thought I was joking. He told me most people wanted something calming. *I was serious, Chad.*

I was escorted past rows of computers and staff reading the images of people's tumors and injuries. These people were about to know more about my fate than I did. They all looked up as I walked by and gave me a nod. It was sympathetic and cold, with a slight look of confusion, because I was so young. But they knew why I was there. I smiled and waved as I walked by.

I can only describe the MRI room as the inside of a bomb shelter or industrial refrigerator. It was bright white, with no windows, and caution signs were plastered everywhere. There were also more locks on the door than I was comfortable with. I laid down, face in hole. There were two cut out slots under my chest, one for each boob. The machine would take the photos under my chest area that were needed to help determine more about the stage of my cancer and the proximity of the tumor to my nipple. This determined whether I would get to keep my nipples during my mastectomy surgery and if I would need radiation.

MRIs are loud. It basically sounds like you are in a tiny hole, and they are doing massive construction or demolition all around you, with jackhammers. My first round of imaging was cake—only three minutes.

It's funny that they ask you what music you want to listen to because you literally cannot hear it. However, in the thirty-second break between rounds of images, you can.

First song? Ice Cube: "You better check yourself before you wreck yourself." *How ironic. What do you think I'm doing here, people?* I cracked my first smile that day. Round two was five minutes. Done.

Second song: "Y'all gonna make me lose my mind, up in here, up in here." Again, I started to laugh. *How appropriate.*

Round three is when I started to panic. I realized I didn't check the door to see if I could escape if I needed to, and now I was face down in a tube. *Breathe. Breathe. Breathe.* Click.

"Back that ass up." *Ridiculous. Can the techs hear my music? Tell me they are laughing.* Each round got a little bit longer and a whole lot louder.

As time went on, I felt my anxiety building up. I was telling myself to breathe and counting to twenty over and over again, in an effort not to pass out. The last ten minutes is when the blue contrast was put through my veins. They warned me through my headphones, over the music, telling me they were about to administer it.

It was cold as it entered my blood. I could feel it running through my body from my arms, then torso, then down my legs to my toes. I felt very alone at that moment. I wasn't scared, just alone—in a tube in a hospital basement, naked, strapped down, and now looking like a Smurf.

When it was over, I lifted my head as they rolled me out of the tube so I could check the door. I needed to know if it was open. The room felt like a vault. There was no getting out without someone coming to save you.

Check MRI off the list of things I never wanted to do and add it to the list of things I never want to do again. I put a smile on and said thank you on my way out the door, shuffling out of the hospital as fast as I could. Why I have to say thank you when it comes to these things is beyond me, but I'm a lady with manners. So thank you, I guess.

More waiting. And when you are waiting on news about a disease that could take your life, each hour feels like a week and each week like a year. It's a brutal mind game of time.

Am I dying? Technically, yes.

Am I going to get a second chance? Time will tell.

* * *

Meanwhile, the flowers were rolling in. A new delivery every day to my doorstep. Sympathy—something else I didn't want. A way for people to say something without saying anything at all. Each time I looked at the flowers, I wanted to feel hope. Instead, I just felt hopeless. Just like these people felt when they didn't know what to say to me, so they sent flowers instead of words, thinking the blooms would say enough. But they just made me realize that something was desperately wrong with me. It got to the point where I just left them outside, I couldn't handle it, whatever the symbolism was.

26: Break it down for me

I am in the public eye more than I'd like to admit. Portland is a village, not a city. Our buildings look like Duplo blocks instead of towers. It's cute. I have taught up to a dozen classes a week for the last seven years, so I know people. A lot of them. And they know me. Maybe it's because I'm so friendly. (Just kidding.)

I have a love-hate relationship with being recognized because at home, I'm an introvert, in contrast to my extrovert work persona. I feel bad for celebrities who don't get a lot of privacy because I have felt a smidgen of that over the years, being overly exposed when I am vulnerable. This was going to be no exception. Hell, maybe it would make me famous. *Waiting on Ellen's response to 492nd email.*

There was one woman who reached out after my diagnosis. I think she might have been an actual angel, and I think she saved my life. She happened to work for the top breast surgeon in Portland. The one that my insurance (that I pay for) denied me being able to see. Yet, if I'd had state-funded insurance or was homeless, I could see this woman. (Like I said, the system isn't working.)

She reached out to me after seeing my post and offered to let me come into their office, free of charge, to go over my pathology report. By then, I had no information other than I had Invasive Ductal Carcinoma, and that it was aggressive. That's enough information to be sure that you are dying and that you need to arrange your first and last trip to Barbados, and your hearse, within a week of each other.

I was on day thirteen or one hundred of ugly crying. I'm not sure because I wasn't sleeping and everything was grey, and well, is crying ever not ugly? Trying to hold your shit together is extremely hard when you are waiting on a prognosis and being treated like a number at the DMV. It should be illegal for them to hold information from you and not tell you the second they get it back. It's enough to make you crazy. Well, crazier since you're dealing with too much already.

This woman was a breath of fresh air. I immediately hugged her and started crying. She handed me a tiny tube to spit in, a saliva genetic test to complete while we were chatting, so they could whisk it off to the lab. This was to test for genetic risks of other cancers, as well as my current breast cancer.

I had just had coffee, which meant I now had dry mouth, so in between sentences I squeezed my cheeks together and swirled my tongue in an awkward attempt to create enough coffee-colored saliva to fill the tube in front of a person I had just met. She was casually talking as I was nodding and ever so politely spitting one tiny drop at a time into a tube while most of it dripped down my chin.

It's a good thing I don't get embarrassed often. I had a feeling this was the first of many times I would just have to humble down. I had already gotten used to every doctor seeing my tits.

This angel of a woman talked me through each word on my pathology report.

Cancer, Invasive Ductal Carcinoma
Grade 3 (cancers are graded 1-3, grade 3
being most aggressive and fastest spreading)

> 78% growth rate (*Let's get this show on the road, people!*)
> 96% Estrogen Receptor Positive
> HER 2 Positive
> Stage 2
> Prognosis: Good.

One in five breast cancers are HER2 positive (HER2+). This type of breast cancer tests positive for a protein called human epidermal growth factor receptor 2 (HER2). In normal tissue, this protein helps breast cells grow, divide, and repair themselves. But if something goes wrong in the gene that controls the protein, your body can create too many of these receptors. The cells throw a rager, and then grow and divide uncontrollably, which is what makes it so aggressive. Basically, my cells threw a house party that got a little out of control and my body called the cops.

She explained that being HER2+ was actually a good thing because there are so many more targeted treatment options for this specific cancer. Therefore, the treatment success rate was higher. She also referred me to the plastic surgeon they called The Boob Whisperer. Sounds sexy, right? And talked me through my recommended treatment plan, including why I should get chemo before surgery, etc.

God bless this woman. And why couldn't I just come to this clinic?

We hugged. And as we left, I took my first full breath in two weeks. Maybe I wasn't going to die at thirty-three.

* * *

It took what seemed to be a lifetime, but what penciled out to only be two weeks from D Day (Diagnosis Day), to get an appointment with an oncologist that I trusted.

We walked in and waited. The waiting is super fun and something that I excel at. I noticed the choice of all beige everything and the lovely gown I was going to have to put on while she left the room for the twelve minutes that they always do. *It literally takes me thirty seconds to undress. Please, just stay here.*

I was reading the posters on the wall. One for cancer-induced insomnia, a picture of a kitten, and puppy just fuckin' snoozing. False advertisement. First, I'm almost positive those animals didn't have cancer. Second, they clearly didn't have insomnia because they were having the best rest of their lives in the photo.

Am I going crazy? This all feels like a joke. I started looking through the cancer pamphlet in the magazine rack, there was a picture of a senior citizen on every page. *Yo! Kids and young adults get cancer too!* This is why we all walk around with no fucking clue about how hard this is. Because nobody tells you that you, too, can get cancer before you are sixty-five.

Two knocks later and in walks my oncologist. Her hair was dark and looked unkempt. She wore hospital clogs and a floral blouse one size too big. She seemed rushed and abrupt but also had a tenderness about her. She shook my hand with the usual tilted head of concern and introduced herself as she sat down. It took all but twelve seconds for the questions to start firing.

"Did you find the lump yourself? How long have you noticed it? Do you have a family history of breast cancer? How many alcoholic drinks do you have in a week?"

I squeezed Steph's leg, hoping that she knew that this was now the universal sign for: *Stop me from pushing this woman off her chair and giving her a piece of my mind because I know she is here to help me.*

I immediately felt bad for squeezing her leg so hard. *Breathe.* Mind you, they ask you all these questions but don't tell you whether what you were doing was harming you or not. I'd still really like to know what the appropriate number of drinks a week is to not get breast cancer. And just how many cigarettes can you smoke before you should be worried?

As expected, I switched into the gown/bedsheet/parachute and waited what felt like four days for her to come back in. Breast exam. It felt like my cat was walking on my chest, just pawing, kneading, and padding around my tits. She looked at me and said, "There it is." My mind was thinking, *No shit. We have had three mammograms, a biopsy, and an MRI.* But I decided to keep my mouth shut. *Would anyone else like to feel it while I'm here?*

I changed back into my shirt, sat back down, and proceeded to go over the same information all over again. It was still stage 2, grade 3, HER2+, IDC, and it was still aggressive. Unfortunately, that hadn't changed. She didn't give me any options for my regimen. She just started spouting out what the next year of my life would look like.

In that moment, I had to let go of everything I had dreamed of for myself in the future. Nothing was up to me anymore except a giant will to live, and nothing would go back to normal after this either, mentally or physically.

First, I would have a portacath placed in my chest, which is where the nurses would access my veins to draw blood and give infusions. Ports are indicated for patients requiring frequent and long-term intravenous therapy, such as the oncology population. *I was now in the oncology population.* It is surgically-inserted completely beneath the skin and consists of two parts—the portal and the catheter. Hence portacath.

The portal is usually made from a silicone bubble and appears as a small bump under the skin, in my case it would be very noticeable and large as I am petite with low body fat. It can be punctured by a needle repeatedly before the strength of the material is compromised. So basically, instead of fucking up your vein, they fuck up the port. The plastic catheter, attached to the portal, is then threaded into a central vein, which in my case was straight to the jugular.

Immediately after my port placement, I would begin twelve months of treatment. I repeat, ONE YEAR, of treatment. GULP.

Okay. Break it down for me.

Treatment would be every three weeks. The first six rounds consisted of four drugs and would be the harshest. After each session, I would be sent home with a Neulasta shot pack on my arm that would give an injection twenty-four hours after it was placed to help build up my white blood cells after they had been murdered by treatment, side effects included.

After those six rounds, I would have my first surgery. The remaining ten rounds of chemo would drop down to just two drugs that target the HER2+. They call this regimen TCHP.

Taxotere = poison
Carboplatin = poison
Herceptin = poison
Perjeta = poison

She went on to explain the side effects: hair loss, nausea, constipation, diarrhea, bone aches, changes in body temperature, mouth sores. I kept listening waiting for her to say something positive like, I don't know...guaranteed results, a free trip to Hawaii, ability to miss work without having to worry about income, a chance that it would resolve in three rounds instead of six, a chance to be Lady Gaga for a day—

NOPE. Girlfriend was all business. I guess that's why she gets to charge $600 for an office visit.

Countless people asked why they were doing chemotherapy before surgery. In more or less words, they wanted to watch the cancer die. Because if there were rogue cancer cells in my body that we didn't know about, and the chemo was killing my tumor, it would be killing those as well. If they were to remove the tumor before treatment, it was less direct evidence that the chemo was working. It made enough sense to me.

We got up and said our goodbyes. It's very weird to say thank you to someone who is about to pump you full of poison for a full year, but I did. I was fighting back tears as I walked out of her office. For the first time in the process, I felt overwhelmed. I could feel weakness creeping in.

With my head high, I walked down the beige hall, to the silver elevators, to the beige first floor full of wheelchairs and an oddly buzzing silence. Out the doors we went. I looked up and took a big breath of my new reality as tears poured out of my eyes. I immediately turned to Steph and said, "I don't want to do this."

We both stopped. She wrapped her arms around me and just held me in the middle of the walkway. She said, "I know." There wasn't a day since that moment until about two years later that I didn't say that sentence. But I did it.

27: GI Jane

I decided to shave my head before my port placement. I needed to have control over one last thing in my life. Chemotherapy works by killing the cancer cells in your body, but it kills the fastest dividing cells too, including your hair. That's why some chemotherapy medications cause hair loss. Hair all of the sudden didn't matter anymore. Life did. That part was black and white to me.

Now, I did realize that I am a hairstylist, and not only would I be bald, but I would no longer give a shit about anybody's hair anymore. I was already having a hard time with the vanity of it all. I could only imagine how hard it would be to have clients sit in my chair and complain about grey hair, or something not laying right when all I wanted was to live long enough to see grey hair on my own head. Or any hair at all.

My kids were terrified of me losing my hair, so I tried to search for bald Disney princesses on Google. It was beyond ridiculous. I am not a princess, and we know Disney would never portray them without their long, flowing locks, let alone bald. If they did, they sure as hell wouldn't be in a gown unless it was a hospital gown. Who was I kidding?

* * *

It's terrifying to get diagnosed with cancer. But I do believe it's a different kind of terrifying if you also have young kids. I wrestled with how much to share with them. They were barely five and seven when I was diagnosed. I knew that if this thing took me, there was a solid chance that they wouldn't remember me when they were older. All of my hard work as a mother—countless hours in labor and feeding and packing lunches and holding them while they were sick, consoling them when they cried, and tickling them until they laughed so hard happy tears were streaming down their precious faces—would be forgotten. There might even be a stepmom somewhere down the line.

It was all nightmarish to think about. But I also knew I was their mom for a reason, and I needed to stick around for them. They changed my whole world. There wasn't going to be a day anytime soon that we didn't have each other if I had anything to do with it. I refused to let my kids grow up without a mom. I just wasn't quite sure how I was going to pull it off.

We spent hours explaining my cancer to the kids. If you tell a kid you have cancer, they automatically assume you will die. It's heartbreaking. I soon realized that a lot of adults feel this way too. We gave the girls a play-by-play of what would happen. First noticeable thing, Mommy would lose her hair. This produced the most fear and tears from them. We explained that the medicine you need to kill the cancer makes you lose your hair. They also asked if their friend's dad had cancer because he didn't have hair. *No, girls, he's just an older man experiencing male pattern baldness.*

We explained that I would be spending time in the hospital getting chemo, I wouldn't be able to play as much, I wouldn't feel well, I would need them to be patient, and I would need their help. We also told them that I would need multiple surgeries and that parts of me would look different, maybe temporarily, or maybe forever. The biggest thing was that I honestly didn't know what was going to happen, and I refused to lie to my kids. I asked them to love me and fight with me and give me some grace on losing my hair. I'm sure that was horrifying for them in a world that defines femininity by the length of your hair and romanticizes looks from a young age. I'm looking at you, Disney.

* * *

When all was said and done, I thought it would be better if they helped me shave my head, or were at least there, so it wasn't so scary. The girls stood behind me with Steph, as I walked up to the mirror with my shears, grabbed a giant section of hair, and cut it off. I stared at it in my hand for a moment before I looked up at the woman in the mirror.

I was holding my last bit of control. My bangs. Before I could even catch my second breath I snipped again, I was going for a mullet. Because let's get real, when else would you have a real mullet?

To be honest, I kind of enjoyed it. My wife and kids stood behind me and watched as hair fell to the floor, piece by piece, watching a woman on a mission. I wasn't scared, I wasn't sad, but I do think that the three behind me felt that way. I tried not to look at them as I kept going. If I saw a single tear shed, I would have to stop, and I couldn't stop.

Once the majority of it was off, I picked up the clippers. What most women cry over and freak out about, I welcomed. I watched the remainder of my hair fall to the ground in clumps. It was wildly liberating. It felt like freedom and like war. While I watched, I realized the severity of the situation, but I felt extremely calm, present, and ready.

There was no going back. I was going to battle, and I swore to myself that day that I was going to win. But I still didn't want anyone else to say it. I could let myself down, but I didn't want to let anyone else down. This was the last time in a year that I would feel like I had control over anything in my life.

5.17.18

This one is for the guy that told me I didn't have the right face for short hair. Eat your words, dude.

* * *

Someone once told me when I had short hair that I didn't have the face for it—to my face, while I was sporting short hair. So yeah, I bet that guy feels like a dick now that losing my hair wasn't a choice. Hope you're reading, dude.

28: A port named port

I got my port two weeks after my diagnosis. I was super excited to have a device in my chest because it reminded me every time I looked in the mirror that I was sick. And it reminded the people around me. I'm small, so anything sticking out of my chest would be huge and noticeable. (And it felt like it was. It looked like a giant sperm in my neck.) I would have it for a full year.

I was asked repeatedly what I was going to name my port, and I was wildly offended every time. I wasn't going to give it a name as I didn't want it to be something I was attached to. This was short lived. And to me, it felt like the mark of the beast. It didn't deserve a name, even though it was there for the purpose of making my infusions easier. I only name things I like—my plants, car, animals, and my children.

We arrived at 9 a.m. for an 11 a.m. appointment. Because in the world of cancer and surgeries, there's the appointment time, and there's the check-in time. They are hours apart. Through the double doors, down the beige hall, up the blue elevator, down another beige hall to pick up a phone to tell them I'm there.

The doors were buzzed open wide, and I was so thankful in that moment for the dramatic entrance I was able to make. *Red carpet, please.*

I strutted myself through the double doors a solid four steps before I landed in front of a scale and my nurse. Her name was something along the lines of Kathy, and she looked like she stepped straight out of 1982. She greeted me with a smile and more enthusiasm than I'd ever seen in a shitty situation, or maybe even my lifetime. She had feathered hair and was wearing New Balance sneakers, blue pleated pants, a dated floral scrub top, thick spectacles, and a sweet blue fanny pack that I was slightly jealous of. I wondered what kind of goodness she kept in that thing.

She took my weight and guided me to one of the seventeen cubicles that lined the hallway, each one with only a thin curtain for privacy. Another hospital gown awaited. I laid down on a bed while she hooked me up to the IV to draw blood and get my pre-meds flowing. Mind you, I hadn't eaten or had anything to drink since nine the night before. I was getting a tad hungry, but I was more upset by the fact that we had passed twenty-seven Starbucks on the way in and didn't get to stop at any of them. Your girl gets cranky without food or coffee.

The nurse made jokes about the amazing turkey sandwich the hospital would "gift" me, a.k.a. charge me for, after the procedure. And while it was funny because we all knew it would be terrible, I couldn't help but fantasize about it in my head. *What I wouldn't give for some shitty faux turkey on some shitty white chemical bread with a wilted piece of lettuce and a packet of mayo and mustard on the side.*

After a few failed attempts at an IV, I was feeling jacked to get my port placed. No more rolling veins. (What a great hospital band name—The Rolling Veins. You're welcome.)

Kathy hit me straight in the IV with pre-meds. I quickly realized that the drug entering my body ended with-ycin. I'm allergic to erythromycin and clindamycin. *Are they all cousins?* As my body began to itch uncontrollably, I looked down to see my arms and legs covered in red welts and realized that yes, they are cousins. I seemed to be having a very impressive allergic reaction to the third one in the family. *Typical.*

So I did what I do best and kept my mouth shut because I'm stubborn, and I do things the hard way. I didn't make a peep. I itched. I was red. I could feel hives swelling on my back. But as I looked up at the antibiotic bag hanging from the pole, I could tell I only had about seven minutes left. *I will prevail,* I thought. Like an idiot.

I held my breath so I wouldn't make any faces that would give away my discomfort. I sat on my hands so I wouldn't itch, I didn't want the nurse to know. I felt like I had been there a week, and I didn't want her to stop the meds and order something else. Smack your head, I know. I'm annoying, but I like to think I was being time-efficient and low maintenance. Call it what you want.

With about two minutes left, I let her know, because I was covered in hives and I couldn't sit still due to the miserable itching. She was going to notice anyway when she walked back in the room to a tomato of a human on the bed. She was a bit pissed, but the bag was gone at this point so all she could do was hit me in the throat with some Benadryl.

After two pills, all was calm again. I should have just told her. I figured I'd be in a lot of discomfort in the months to come anyway, so why not start now, build up the tolerance.

I kissed my wife goodbye, and she watched as they wheeled me down the hall into the operating room and into what, still to this day, feels like one of the most traumatic experiences of my life, and I imagine hers as well. This was the first of many times they would wheel me away from her over the coming years. I had no idea what she was feeling, but I was ready to do the damn thing, even though I was terrified.

After twenty minutes of waiting in a hall, strapped to a hospital bed, surrounded by empty hospital beds, alone, I was taken into the operating room. I was awake. They put a sheet over my face, but I could hear everything, and I could feel everything. They shot me up with lidocaine, but the lidocaine didn't work, again. My arms were strapped down by my side so I couldn't move. I felt the first incision, a knife slicing through my skin. I asked for more lidocaine. I felt the second incision, I asked again. It was clear to me that this was how it was going to go.

I held my breath and fought back tears as the surgeon placed a small device into my chest that I didn't want. He proceeded to press with his whole body to get it into place. He was a small man and it felt like he was on top of me, pushing and trying to get it to lay right.

I was stuck, not only strapped down, but all I could see was the sheet and a doctor's silhouette above my face. I could feel his small Asian hands jamming metal and plastic into the incisions in my chest. He kept telling me to hold on, that it was almost over. Like I had a choice! I couldn't even move my legs as those were strapped down also. He pressed, twisted, and pressed again, each turn stinging a bit more than the last. He may have even stomped on it at one point. He then ran it up to the vein in my neck and I felt him clip the end so it could fit.

I felt the stitch tug. I felt the tape pull. I saw the fluorescent lights through the sheet. I heard the shuffling of nurses' feet around me, the hums of computers in the background. There was mumbling between the surgeon and the nurses. The port was hard. It was in my neck, it felt tight, it was stinging. It felt foreign, invasive. And I felt alone.

I wondered if the government had a tracking device in it. It felt inhumane. I wondered if this guy liked his job, if he cared that I could feel him cut me open and press a metal ball into my chest with all one hundred fifty pounds of him. I wondered if he got paid by the port, if I was just a bed with a dollar sign or a number. I fought back tears as they wheeled me back. I felt sad. I honestly felt traumatized.

Is this how it was going to go? Would I have no say? Would I just be thrown around like an object of no value? Hold it together. This is just the beginning. It's going to get a hell of a lot worse.

For the first time of many, I said to myself, "You are going to have to do better than that."

* * *

They rolled me back into my cubicle room where my wife was waiting. I tried to act tough, but she could see right through it. I needed to get out of there, fast. I also needed that turkey sandwich.

Soon after, I had to prove I was ready to leave, so Kath and I got to go on a circular walk around the unit. I'm pretty sure I was drunk, but I can hold it down when needed. As it turns out, I walked the circle straight enough, and even gave some thumbs up and dance moves to other patients on my way out to lighten the mood. Someone was lying in a sheet cubicle every twelve feet. You know me, always making friends. Anything to get me the fuck out of there.

And so I left, still completely in shock. I remember the walk to the car. I had a new device in my neck. It felt heavy and tight. My chest would never feel the same.

For the first time, I felt scared. I was indescribably lonely. This was an experience that I had alone, feelings I couldn't articulate to my wife or the people around me. This is how I would feel time and time again over the next year. I was sad for the rest of the day.

What was happening to me? Did everyone going through treatment feel this way? Why didn't anyone warn me?

Little did I know that I would spend the next few weeks nursing a pinched nerve in my shoulder from that small man jumping on me to get the port properly placed in my chest. Thanks, bro.

When it rains, it fucking dumps.

* * *

Next was the heart scan. This is something that I would need done every three months for the next year, so four times total. Basically, they wanted to make sure that my heart didn't get too damaged from the chemotherapy and targeted therapies. TOO DAMAGED? Thanks, guys. Like a small to medium amount of damage was acceptable. I swallowed that pill and drove back to the hospital only to be greeted by the most beautiful male nurse I had seen in a hot minute.

He had a shiny bald shaved head, so of course I decided to attempt flirting and made some comment about how I was going to have his exact haircut in a few weeks. The thing about making cancer jokes to people that work in hospitals is that they actually feel really bad for you, so they give you a nervous laugh and then it's just awkward. Sympathy. Apparently not every client is as dark and sarcastic as me. Fine.

Continue, Brandon, but do tell me, do I take my top off for you as well? He somehow did an hour scan working so carefully on and around my breast while never actually looking at it or touching it. Impressive.

But at that point, I would have just flashed him. Everyone else had seen them, and they were about to be a thing of the past. But no, Brandon was a gentleman. *Maybe next time. See you in three months.* The heart checked out just fine. No holes, no blackness, not too cold, and beating like a champ. PUMPIN' BLOOD! Great. Thump on, little guy.

* * *

5.21.18

Let me tell you something about cancer...it sucks. It's a full-time job on top of the jobs you have and the family you have and any fun you want to have. It's a pause button on your life when your peers are continuing on. It's stressful. It's terrifying. It's a mindfuck. It's a wallet suck. It tries to tell you you are weak. It doesn't let you eat Pringles and brownies and drink gin. It's perspective. It's physically and mentally draining. It takes away your control. It's dark. It's isolating. It's a joy suck. It tests you and taunts you. It makes you question most things...it's the devil.

As I head into my first week (of one year) of treatment...I feel so loved, supported, lifted up. I am so thankful for the people around me who push me to live this big full life and have my back during this time, who inspire me to share it. When I feel alone, I remember that while my body fights alone, I have hundreds of people holding me up. I don't have enough words, but I will start with thank you. Thanks to my friends, to my team, my family, clients, strangers on the internet...thank you to my WIFE. Thank you for the words, the flowers, the rides, the GoFundMe page, the fist bumps, the laughs...all of it. I am so humbled and so thankful. And as always, if I don't respond, know that I see you and I hear you and the words of encouragement and gestures do not go unnoticed. I'm just busy fighting. I appreciate you. I will try to remember this every time cancer tries to wipe the smile off my face. Thank you is not enough but thank you is what I have right now.

* * *

I taught another community workout that week, with a freshly shaved head and bandages fresh on my chest. My boss opened the evening asking that nobody give me sympathy and just treat me like a normal human because that's what I wanted. She said, "Whatever you do, don't pity her. She doesn't want your pity."

It was incredibly true. Pity is not for me. My grand-mother, though, she wants pity. Her name is Lorraine, and she was always Lorainne-ing on my parade. I just don't play the pity game well. It never gets you anywhere, and who wants people to feel bad for them? I was just a girl publicly going through some shit.

It was an incredibly emotional night. I've never seen people push harder. I imagine everyone was wondering why and how this trifecta of shit had happened to me so quickly—divorce, coming out, then cancer? Or maybe they didn't, and maybe that was just me. But I do know that most of them did feel bad for me, despite the previous talk about pity, and that it was probably a slap in the face to have the person fighting for their life be physically stronger than you. That has to be a mindfuck. And if it isn't a reason to step your game up and do one more burpee, we've got a problem.

Fighting for your life is lonely. It's like watching a car full of your favorite people drive off without you, and you have to walk thousands of miles home. Alone. Without water and without a map.

Moving with people who were stuck in a room with me was my go-to. Experiencing my body for what it was, when the world told me it was failing, kept me going. It wasn't failing me at all, it was trying to survive. We were just having a major misunderstanding.

I started chemo two days later. Drip drip, bish.

29: Round 1

It's odd to feel somewhat normal and then go get a medication pumped through every cell of your body that makes you feel like you are walking straight and ever so slowly into death. It's also odd to know that what you're putting into your body is so toxic that the nurses wear hazmat suits to hook up your IV and your bag of drugs. Yet they so easily pierce your body with a needle and let it slowly drip through your veins until it ravages every cell, only leaving the healthiest behind, and even then, taking healthy cells with it. It's also hard to explain to your kids that the medicine makes you feel worse, and look sick, but will make you better in the end. But hey, parenting is hard and confusing, so yes, pile that on there.

It was my first day of a full year of living life on a three-week hamster wheel. I would be getting infusions every twenty-one days. I popped a steroid as directed and left the kids with my parents as Steph and I set out to the hospital. I was told my first infusion would take eight to nine hours. I was wearing leggings and some layers up top so they could access my port. I had a book and a pillow and a small cooler with fresh snacks that my friends had made for me for day one. I stood in front of the hospital with one finger in the air, symbolizing my first treatment, as I posed for a picture like it was the first day of school. I had no idea what I was getting myself into, or rather, what would be getting into me. But whatever happened, I was going to be honest about it.

I had read a few books about cancer and chemo treatments, but none of them felt like they had prepared me for anything thus far. So I thought, *if I can articulate this any better for people, I will. Because unfortunately, I won't be the last person this happens to.* I would have loved to have had a better picture of expectations painted for me.

* * *

They don't tell you much about the side effects of the drugs. Just the main ones like mouth sores, hair loss, fatigue, nausea, and diarrhea. I really had no idea what to expect otherwise. We walked back into the beige hospital with the beige halls and up the beige elevator to the second beige floor to the first beige room to the right, or was it the left? It was all starting to look the same. The receptionist checking me in was far too chipper to be dealing with cancer patients all day. I chalked it up to lack of windows and exposure to chemicals and took my seat.

The waiting room was full of pamphlets on insomnia and chemo-induced infertility, how to deal with fatigue and medical bills, support groups, and free pastel knitted hats for bald chemo heads. Nobody on the brochures was under the age of sixty-five. Hell, I'm not even sure anyone on the brochure was even sick. The room was almost empty, minus a few people twice my age in wheelchairs with a loved one by their side.

Minutes later they called me back into a large room that was lined with chair after chair, all facing the center of the room. Each chair had a number, a pillow, and a pole to where your bags of drugs would be hooked up. They split it into the left and right sides of the room. Today, I would go left.

I was to pick any beige chair that wasn't taken, most were available as it was eight in the morning. I walked slowly, knowing that I would be there for at least eight hours and I really didn't want to pick the wrong chair. *Was there a wrong chair?* At that point, it was only me and one elderly woman in the room. I chose a chair near the window and pulled up a seat for Steph right next to me. There was nothing comfortable about the room, or the seating arrangements. I was staring straight into a hazardous waste bin where they dispose of thousands of needles a day. But I did have a view of the whole room so I could dissect the place while I was sitting there.

There was a snack bar on the other end of the room. They offered me yogurt, hot chocolate, soda, canned soup, or processed crackers. It blew my mind that this was the best they were going to do for people. I wanted nothing to do with more chemicals and fake foods when I was about to be pumped full of liquid poison like a conventional chicken at Safeway. I was hoping for more of a salad bar situation or really anything that wasn't processed. Wasn't the goal to get healthier here?

A nurse came over to access my port. My port and I still weren't friends. It stuck out of my chest, poked me in the neck, and reminded me that I was sick. It made me shutter if I accidentally touched it while getting dressed and it made me different than my peers. It was a foreign object in my body, and it was still black and blue. We were never friends, yet I understood why it was there.

At the beginning of each infusion, I needed to get my blood drawn. This was to gauge where my white and red blood counts were, as well as track anemia, liver enzymes, etc. If any of these numbers went too far south, my treatment would be delayed. Just stack a little pressure on for good measure. She told me to inhale and as I exhaled, she pushed a long, thick, curved needle into my port. I heard a pop, and I felt a click. It didn't feel great, but I've felt worse.

Game on, we were really doing this.

She took five vials of blood, flushed my port with saline, and left the needle inserted into my chest with a tube dangling from it. She then flipped my seat number to say "reserved" and sent me down the hall, to the next beige office where I would meet with my oncologist to go over said blood work. Each infusion would start this way.

And then I sat and waited, again, in a room without windows. I was starting to wonder if I might have a panic attack. Seemed legit considering the amount of time I would be spending there and my need for fresh air. I scanned the room and there it was, the poster of the sleeping kitten and puppy on the wall that was promoting help for breast cancer–induced insomnia. The marketing at the hospital made my head spin. The animals did NOT have insomnia, nor did they have cancer, goddamn it. They were just taking a nap without a care in the world.

My blood pressure and everything else checked out. My heart rate was forty-eight, which is normal for me, but sparked some questions from my nurse. I explained to her that "I'm just chillin' and I work out a lot. Worry about it if it's any lower, but this is who I am." She looked at me like I was crazy and sent me back for chemo.

Back down the hall to the infusion center I went. There were a few more patients in the room now, and I could feel all eyes on me as I took my seat. There was a new girl in town, and she was young. Everyone was sizing me up and wondering what kind of cancer I had, I could feel it.

My nurse gave me more Zofran (oral anti-nausea medication) and steroids, then started my first bag of anti-nausea meds. This bag ran thirty minutes and while the slow drip was going, I started to look around and realized just how depressing the infusion center is. Not just the beige, but everyone. They were all old, looked hopeless and helpless...and sick. *What am I doing here? I don't want to be any of those things.*

My wife is an acupuncturist and the most amazing woman you will ever meet in your life. She is a healer and she is a fixer, and (Honey, don't read this!) she's a worrier. That being said, ever since the words breast cancer were spoken to us, she had been feeding me mass amounts of supplements, giving me alkaline water, finding the cleanest foods for me to eat, and making me drink apple cider vinegar shots. She even started making wheatgrass for me to consume twice a day. I was barely able to stomach it all. I mean let's get real, I couldn't.

She kept telling me I was going to be fine during chemo. I was going to handle it great. I "had this." And while I love her so much, I felt so much pressure. Because the truth is, I didn't know that, and neither did she.

I think back to how many hundreds of people said "You're going to beat this" or "You're so strong," but who ACTUALLY knew? Nobody thought I would get cancer, so how would we know if I was going to beat this? I felt like I couldn't let them down, especially my wife. Deep down, I knew that I was about to get my ass handed to me and I was going down hard before I had any sign of coming back up. I felt like a burden. There were parts of me that said, *You might die.* And I felt it driving a wedge between us. The closer we were, the more it would hurt if I left this world.

The pharmacist pulled up a seat next to me during my first bag. She looked me in the eye and slowly and calmly said, "You're fucked." In more words of course. What she did say is that the TCHP regimen was brutal, one of the hardest on the body, yet one of the most effective.

THANK YOU! I finally felt like it might be okay for me to feel like shit during all of this. And for Steph to hear it too was such a breath of fresh air. I wouldn't be crazy or weak if I was crawling across the floor trying to get to the bathroom, or if there were times that my body hurt so bad, I couldn't stand up. It was to be expected. Finally, someone who was honest.

* * *

By bag two, I noticed that the place was filling in a bit. Nobody was less than sixty though. I was starting to feel extremely out of place. I stuck out like a sore thumb. I could feel the eyes on me, every one of them guessing my diagnosis or my drugs, wondering how I got sick so young. Patients don't look each other in the eye in the infusion center. It's too painful. Yet we all want to know each other's stories. *Why are you here?*

By bag three, everyone that had been there for bag one and two were gone. The infusion center was full of people coming in and out, none more than an hour or two. I started to realize just how intense my regimen was. I was four hours in, and all my silent friends had left. *Was I sicker than them?* The infusions started to feel colder and colder as the liquid hit my veins. I could feel it flooding my body and clouding my mind. I was scared. But I was holding it together.

By bag four, I was completely chilled in my veins. This was Taxotere, the one that was going to take my hair from me just fourteen days later. It would continue to be my worst bag every infusion. I could feel that I didn't look right, so I tried not to look at Steph too long.

I can only imagine how hard it is to watch the love of your life get flooded with poison. To watch the light in their eyes slowly dim, only to be replaced by a thick, grey haze. I could feel how I looked but I couldn't stop it. *You're going to have to do better than that*, I thought. I smiled as the next patient sat next to me, sympathy oozing out of their veins and into my general direction as they too, guessed my diagnosis, and wondered how I ended up there.

As they started bag five, I felt a wave of relief. I had seen dozens of patients come and go, not a single person was left that had started the day with me, only my wife and my nurse. I was exhausted and ready to let the chemo ravage my body in my own space.

As the last drip was finishing, my nurse placed a Neulasta shot on my arm to prevent neutropenia, which is a lack of certain white blood cells caused by chemotherapy. The purpose is to stimulate white blood cell growth in the body, which fights infection. It was a small stick-on device that pushed a catheter into my skin that would administer a drug twenty-four hours later at home, so I didn't have to come back to the hospital. I was advised to take a Claritin at the same time that the shot administered to prevent the bone pain that was to accompany the drug. The device would beep, a green light would flash, it would click thirteen times, and then administer the drug over a fifteen-minute period.

A little over eight hours later, I was done. They don't say much to you when you leave other than goodbye. No "good luck." No "here's when you'll feel everything sink in." Nothing. I stood up and felt like I was walking on a cloud. Not a good cloud, like a cloud that I could fall through at any moment without ground below. My eyes were almost as foggy as my brain.

Take me home. I walked to the car without saying a word. I didn't know what the appropriate thing to feel or say was. Silence felt best.

When we got home, I locked myself in the bathroom and looked in the mirror. My eyes were grey with a glossy film that looked a quarter-inch thick over the top. I tried to engage with my kids but every word that was coming at me hit me a few seconds late, so I had a hard time interacting. My parents were at my house. I was trying to process what was happening, and what had just happened. I was also wondering why there were so many people around. It was no time for a social hour. *This blows,* I thought.

I laid in bed to process what was happening and be alone. I was shaking and freezing yet boiling and burning at the same time. I replayed my day at the hospital and the drugs, wondering when my hair would fall out and when the side effects would hit. I even wondered if I would wake up the next day. I had no appetite as I had twenty-nine liters of fluid in me. I was exhausted and nauseous.

I closed my eyes and about ten minutes later, as I was drifting to a more peaceful place, my body jolted. Like you see in the movies when they are using the defibrillator to resuscitate someone. I thought I was having a heart attack. It was violent and shook my whole body from my chest. I'm pretty sure I caught some air off the mattress. It turned out that the drugs were making themselves known and my heart was saying, back off, motherfucker. It will forever be one of the scariest moments of my life. It was a reality check of how brutal these drugs were. To say the least.

As I finally fell asleep that night, I started to picture myself in a glass bowl, the world swirling around me. A year is a long time, and it could be longer.

Would they replace me for missing work? Would people find a better spin instructor? Would my kids start to favor their dad more because he would have more energy and time to be "fun"? Would my friends move on? Would my wife still be attracted to me? Would I have any clients left? What if I lost feeling in my hands and can't do my job? What if the chemo does actually break down my muscles and I can't move? What if people start to forget about my energy, absence revealing that I wasn't needed anyway?

Li?

You're going to have to do better than that, I thought as I drifted off, completely unsure if I would wake up in the morning.

* * *

I've learned that what happens over the next twelve days really does vary by the hour. I got asked a lot "how are you feeling?" and would answer to the best of my ability at the moment. But the thing is, it felt like an impossible question to answer. I found myself getting angry that I even had to. I got defensive. I had a "what's it to you" attitude. There is no way to explain the mental and physical side effects of chemo. People think it's like a hangover, but I'd gladly be hungover for life over having to endure a single round of chemo. Every round of chemo brings added and unexpected side effects. The doctors also don't disclose ninety-five percent of what is going to happen to you. I felt like I deserved a heads up that I would have boils on my ass and a bloody nose 24/7. Apparently they didn't.

* * *

Physical side effects include but are not limited to:
- CONSTIPATION—Nothing like a day of feeling drugged and plugged.
- DIARRHEA—Four times before 7 a.m. every day and then six to twelve times throughout the day. And diarrhea doesn't wait.
- HEADACHES—More like just put my head between two clamps for twelve days and tighten it up.
- NAUSEA—Not the same as your morning sickness, Karen...I'd be pregnant for a decade with that shit over a round of chemo nausea.

e, Don't Send Me Flowers

- HAIR LOSS—Everywhere. I looked like a dildo. Secondly, I got asked a lot if I missed my hair, and to be honest, most days I didn't.
- EYEBROW LOSS—Nobody could tell my facial expressions apart anymore.
- EYELASH LOSS—This one just blows because you can't draw those bad boys on, and you can only refrain from eye contact for so long before it's just awkward.
- SORES ON EYELIDS—They looked like tiny pimples... the new eyelash, if you will. Get on my level. I'm too sexy.
- IDENTITY LOSS—*Who am I?* Okay, just kidding. Oh wait, no I'm not.
- BOILS—On the hips, on the ass, leaving scars, painful to sit, can't even pop for satisfaction. We are talking HUGE, red, pus filled boils.
- MOUTH SORES—The inside of my mouth looked like it was coated in blood and felt like I had stuck a tiny campfire in my mouth. EVERYTHING burned and there were sores all over my mouth.
- BLOODY NOSE—From the dry, cracked craters that NEVER go away, my nose ran red constantly. My white sheets looked tie-dyed from the drippy blood 24/7.
- NASAL DRIP—The nose hairs fall out too, so there was nothing to hold moisture in. I'd be talking with a faucet nose and there was no stopping it. It still happens. I don't even try to stop it anymore. Sometimes it just drips right into my mouth. Other times, I'll lean forward for a minute and let it flow. Self-confidence was at a HIGH. I called it a nose gloss...it never caught on. But nose tampons are a thing.

Lianne Saff

- BLOATING/MOON FACE—Hi, I'm a circle. There's nothing like steroids to boost your self-esteem. Also, 'roid rage is real. Ask my wife. Sorry, honey.
- NEUROPATHY—I needed a constant walking stick. This one freaked me out, and I have an incredibly hard time joking about it. I was no longer stable on my own feet, my ring and pinky fingers were numb, so grabbing objects often required two hands or I would drop or spill them. Even my tongue was numb at one point. When I spoke, it felt like when you hold the tip of your tongue and you are slow to enunciate and/or get any words out that make sense to anyone other than yourself.
- FATIGUE—My poor little body was fighting so hard. When you are pumped with poison, deprived of sleep, and your healthy cells are attacked, it's a new kind of exhaustion. Chances are, if you told me you were tired from work, a long week, or partying all night, I'd give ZERO fucks. I would have given anything to be so tired from such luxurious events.
- BONE PAIN—It's not an ache, it's a straight up pain. Moving made it worse but moving is my sanity so I sucked it up.
- DISCOLORATION OF NAILS—Gross.
- TEMPERATURE CHANGES—An ice-cold bath could feel like a volcano and heat could feel like you were freezing to death. Very confusing.
- HEMORRHOIDS—Nothing like a randomly bleeding butthole to make your diarrhea feels like you are birthing a child out of your butt.
- INSOMNIA—Look, I've had a child that didn't sleep for the first 364 days of her life. She coined the term *insomnia* and then passed it onto me with a side order of anxiety...so I didn't need another layer of this. I'm

just a lucky girl and got hit in the face with this one pretty hard. Here, have some fatigue so you can barely function and then let's keep you awake for good measure. Dope. People said "have you tried weed?" WOW! NOPE!...Of course I thought of that. I'd been given edibles, tinctures, a literal diaper full of bud, pills, vape pens, bath salts, etc. I was a dispensary. But thank you to the 122 of you that suggested it. Thanks to you, not only was I awake at night, but also too high to function. Some might not see that as a problem, but it's not my favorite feeling. I needed my own sleep problems poster in my oncologist's office. Put a picture of my face on an insomnia poster, people would be calling for help left and right, they wouldn't want to look like me when I'm tired. We later did put posters of me up over those damn sleeping animals. I looked extremely haggard, exhausted, and mid-cancer-y just to drive the point home.

- TASTE CHANGES—Chemo damages your taste buds and makes everything taste HORRIBLE. Not to mention, it feels like any food or beverage you're trying to consume is the consistency of cardboard that's been left in the rain for three days. Water, nope. Soup, nope. Your favorite thing is now your least favorite thing. I was being force fed like a baby bird that has lost its mom. Basically, just shove a syringe of your choice down my throat and wash it down with some good old-fashioned Gatorade and call it a day. I would crave something so badly that I absolutely had to have it, but the second it hit my mouth, I would gag and couldn't get it down. The chemo cravings were real. I learned instead to just stop and stare at the lucky item and let it live because there was no way it was going down the hatch.

This resulted in me losing a good eight pounds after each round and then overcompensating the week that I could stomach/taste food again prior to chemo and gaining ten pounds back. One step back and two steps forward. More moon face, please.

- ANEMIA—A deficiency of red blood cells or hemoglobin in the blood, resulting in paleness and weariness. My red blood cells were trying so hard, but chemo kills them. The anemia got worse every round. I watched the point drop after each set of labs, hovering right above blood transfusion, as everyone around me was like "I was anemic once, just take an iron pill!" or "Have you tried adding spinach to your diet?" WOW. *Takes large breath in to calm self* *I know I have chemo brain but I'm not stupid and you aren't a doctor. It's not that easy.* This type of anemia can only be helped by rest and time. If you know me, you know how good I am at rest. If I stop for twelve seconds, I consider it a restful day. This was a BLOW. Recently on date night, I tried to "floss," not my teeth (because that's not sexy on date night), but the dance...because that is sexy. A. I nailed it, but B...20 seconds of flossing caused me to have to stop to catch my breath. Anemia is real. But so was date night. I am constantly lightheaded, breathless, and dizzy. It was getting harder and harder to teach my classes and/or bend over to tie my shoe. I found myself turning the lights off during class and leaning my bodyweight over the podium that holds my computer just to catch a breath and not fall over. It was the only thing keeping me on my feet instead of on the ground. The last thing anybody needs is their instructor on the floor. I'm there to help them, not vice versa.

* * *

6.3.18

Yesterday I was feeling pretty good as far as cancer goes, so I went and got a sweet buzz cut and lived my life.

It's hard to wrap my brain around the fact that my new norm will be laying in misery for 8+ days out of every 21. I can't even put the side effects of this regimen into words...it's literally my worst nightmare.

I'm celebrating every moment that I get to stand up and feel good. Also, I'm so thankful for my wife who is patient with me when I randomly need to lay down and who planned such a fun date for us to give me some normalcy.

Chemo blows...but round one done.

* * *

I was learning to embrace changes in a whole new way, but losing my hair felt bigger than I had anticipated. They say your hair starts to fall out fourteen days after starting Taxol (Taxotere). And it did. But it doesn't just fall to the floor while you are standing still like I imagined. I put my hand on the top of my head, pinched a chunk of hair between my fingers, and gave it a tiny but courageous tug, and there it was. Hundreds of hairs in my hand. It felt like pulling wet grass from the earth. It almost made that same sound also. I thought I would feel something. But I felt numb. Numb must be a feeling because I felt it. I pulled, and pulled, and pulled. Clumps, patches. I looked in the mirror and saw the tiny spots from where I had pulled these lifeless things out of my head.

Over the next few weeks, I started getting a reaction on my scalp. The pain on my head was excruciating from my hair falling out. It's not a common reaction, in fact, I had never heard of it happening and neither had my oncologist. I guess my body was pissed that the hair was leaving. My head was itching so bad that I thought it might bleed. I was up all night, burning, itching, shedding. My sheets were a mess. I went to bed with ice packs on my head for a sliver of relief, but it offered little to none. It felt like my scalp was burning off. I laid awake wondering what was happening to me, why I got all the weird reactions. I clenched my teeth as my body tensed up, and I tried not to itch the sores open. There was no sleep for weeks until it subsided.

There were tiny hairs everywhere, each one serving as a reminder, a torture device. I wanted it gone. The process was taking much longer than I had anticipated. Nobody tells you this stuff. It doesn't fall out in one day. It's over the course of weeks, no matter how much pulling you do. I found myself basically waxing my head with duct tape until my wife had the brilliant idea of using a lint roller. Not only could I press super hard to relieve some of the itch, it was taking hairs with it. Double whammy. Thank you.

It took a good month to go, but I never fully lost it all. I ended up taking a razor to it once a week after that to keep the last standing stragglers short. Better bald than awkwardly having twenty-nine remaining hairs to flap in the breeze. It's a weird feeling putting shaving cream on your head in the shower and trusting you aren't going to nick yourself.

Being bald almost feels dewy or moist. It's cold and very odd, but I grew to love it. I wore a headscarf four times. I wore a wig once. I wore it to work one day and looked in the mirror when I got there and started cracking up. It wasn't me. It was someone else. I was going through something that I couldn't hide with a wig, and to try didn't feel right. So I ripped it off and shoved it in my bag.

Here's the thing about wigs, they all look super put together, a bit too polished. Even the guy at the wig shop couldn't figure out a good style for me. Nothing looked like my hair. He said, "I can't quite figure you out because you seem edgy, but you are also too nice to be too edgy." HA!

So bald it was. This is what I looked like whether I liked it or not. I never put it on again. Not to mention, wigs are extremely tight, and I looked like a stripper. Hats became my thing, but so did the wind on my head.

What I didn't love about being bald is that apparently it was an open invitation for people to comment on my head shape and/or put their hands all over it like it was a pregnant belly. There were so many comments about how it felt like good luck to rub it. I just wanted to scream and ask them what in their right mind made them think they could just come up and touch me and my extremely sensitive scalp.

I also learned later that people love to comment on your hair as it grows back in. Like it wasn't going to come back or something. It really blows their mind. And if you are lucky, it comes back curly and people touch that too and call them *chemo curls*. In reality, I've always had curly hair, so chemo doesn't get credit for my locks. But apparently people weren't paying attention to my looks as much before I looked like an avatar, so the curls are much more noticeable now.

I think people see growing hair as a sign of life. But trust me, I knew I was dying. I don't need the extra comment on how I am now living because I have hair, or how you like it. Six months ago you told me I looked great bald. What mixed messaging. It made me wildly uncomfortable. And please, for the love of God, can we keep our hands to ourselves?

* * *

As my hair left my head, cysts appeared. They were probably the size of a date, right behind my ears and at the base of my skull. Nobody had an answer for this one, which was miserably unhelpful. I was really self-conscious of them because I didn't have hair to hide them and they were massive, hard, sore lumps. These lasted for a few weeks until I discovered castor oil would dissolve them. I never saw them again, and my doctors told me they had never seen that happen from chemo.

Steph took me out for a drink around that time. Let's get something straight. I love a good drink. A hefty G&T, or three, got me through the big D, coming out, and all the shit before it.

It's only three in the afternoon? Let's call it five and pour a stiff one. If you are a parent, you know what I'm saying. If you are in a terrible relationship or job, you know what I'm saying. Hell, maybe you are neither and you know what I'm saying.

I knew I would have to cut back, but what I didn't know is that during chemo, a sip of alcohol would completely offend my taste buds. I took one sip of red wine and almost cried. The acidity burned so bad against the sores in my mouth. So I tried whiskey. Same thing. I tried vodka. I tried it all. It wasn't even a pain you could push through.

If there is ever a time you could use a drink, it's when you have cancer. For the love of God. But sure, take that from me too. (I was crying inside.) One more step away from being "normal." I realized then and there that my social life was going in the shitter for a minute. Not only because I wouldn't be drinking, but because I felt like garbage and it was just the beginning.

30: Round 2

I had stopped trying to cover up that I was sick about two weeks after I started chemo. There was no amount of concealer or wigs or false lashes that could make me look normal. My physical appearance was deteriorating at a rapid pace. Some mornings I would look at myself and just start laughing. I remember one day setting my eyeliner down in defeat. I turned to my wife and said, "Well, this is what I look like." We both started cracking up.

Nothing was going to make me look "normal." We still laugh about this and say it all the time. It's very freeing. This is what I look like—take it or leave it.

There are perks to having a bald head. You save on shampoo and hair appointments. You can literally shower and get out the door without styling anything. But the best part is YOU CAN RUB GLITTER ALL OVER YOUR HEAD!

I taught an event three days after my second round of chemo. It was a large community event for Portland Pride, so in proper Pride fashion, I glittered my whole head. I was like a human disco ball. If you are going to be bald, you might as well have fun with it.

I was still teaching five classes a week, but round two of chemo crushed me. I could feel that my blood counts were getting worse. I was dizzy and breathless if I took too big of a step. I remember I only had to be on stage for twenty minutes at this event. But five minutes in, I wasn't sure if I could do it. I had never experienced that level of dizziness in my life.

Everyone was staring at me, but I wasn't going to let the first time I passed out be with a bald glitter head in front of three hundred people while my favorite song was playing.

You are going to have to do better than that.

I kept going and I knelt to catch my breath while everyone continued to move. I spoke into the mic while doing mountain climbers, gasping for breath.

Between breaths, I said, "Don't quit now because what we don't always realize is that quitting is a privilege. Some people don't have the option to quit."

When I said that, the energy shifted. MY energy shifted. Everyone rose up. I was breathless. I was weak. I faked strong. I was beginning to fake strong more than I'd like to admit. But "quitting is a privilege" became my mantra.

6.24.18

They told me my chemo regimen was one of the most brutal. They also told me that each round gets a little worse.

HOLY ROUND 2

If you ask me how I'm doing, there's a 99.9% chance I won't answer. Not because I don't want to, but because I literally cannot. I don't have words for it. This one has been awful, with a side of laryngitis and a cold taking away my sanity (work). I'm constantly being told what to do, or what not to do, and I just want to live my damn life. Small moments of joy haven't even come daily this round.

Things that feel hard right now:

- Losing my eyelashes
- Hearing about anybody's summer cold
- Not being able to rosé all day, or any day for that matter
- Having no control of my body or my fun

Things that feel good:

- High fives
- Moving, when I'm able
- Getting out of my house
- Random acts/words of kindness
- Not talking about cancer

Thank you again for your constant support. I am so thankful and humbled by the generosity around me. I'm hoping to teach a few classes before round three, keep an eye on the schedule.

* * *

I had adopted the hashtag #watchliannewin. I needed a trail. I had unintentionally started documenting my fight. It was how I was processing. For me, I express myself best through words. Because what is a word if you can't write it or speak it? It's a thought. And thoughts need to breathe too, so I give my thoughts permission to live on paper. I then make them permanent by typing them on my computer for my own eyes and heart to digest. Giving thoughts permission to breathe is therapy.

Every post added an element of performance to my experience. I had an audience. It wasn't about my pain for me. It was about helping people have a better understanding and landing on two feet on the other side. I was giving my pain a purpose. People reached out constantly, so thankful for the lessons and for sharing the truth about cancer from a patient's perspective.

I later learned that people love to watch you fall apart, but that it's not as exciting to watch you put yourself back together. They move onto the next catastrophe, something to distract them from their own pain or discomfort. It's how the human mind works. Social media allows people to check in, then check out. A number of likes makes you feel like they are with you, but then with the scroll of a thumb, they are gone.

But in that moment, I was giving them a taste of my pain, of a different struggle other than their own. I was interesting. I was blunt. I was fighting for my life. They wanted to watch me win, and whether I won or lost, they were watching.

The only thing I was watching at the moment, however, were my flowers from round one dying. I sat and wondered which one of us was going to die first as I watched petals fall to the counter while my hair and eyelashes fell to the floor. We were losing our beauty at the same time. *What would be left of us besides a slimy vase and a naked body filled with poison?*

31: Round 3

Photo by Amy Shick

7.5.2018
*"Only when we are brave enough to explore the darkness
will we discover the infinite power of our light."*
—*Brene Brown* ROUND 3 HERE I COME.

* * *

Let's talk a little more in depth about the question "how are you doing?" when it's aimed at someone going through chemotherapy, or really any hard situation. First, what the fuck kind of question is that? It's selfish and it's not fair and it is impossible to answer. It's also wildly confusing. Let me explain.

This question was asked of me ten to twenty times a day for two years by people that love me and mean well, and by people that were using it for their own selfish knowledge or for something to talk about. I would get so angry that anybody would ask it because I ended up babysitting their emotions about my situation if I even tried to explain a fraction of it. And one of the main things I learned from cancer is that NOBODY benefits from someone feeling bad for you. I didn't need anyone to cry over me. I was crying over myself.

If I could honestly articulate how I was "doing" or "feeling" in any given moment, what would change? Would you pity me? Would you understand? Or would you try to fix it? Would you feel better because you asked? Is this about me or you at this point?

It's hands down the most confusing question in the world, and I vow to never ask it in a situation like this. I will find another way to let people know they are seen and heard. And so, I didn't respond. And I feel like a dick because I'm a people pleaser, and I clearly can see that people had sent me messages asking.

Chemo and cancer are complex. So responding to a seemingly short question created inadequate and loaded answers. Spoken words made it too simple. And if I wrote words, you couldn't hear the tone. So that didn't work either. Responding felt like giving up on what I was fighting for, just so others could "understand." And I refused to give up.

I remember grabbing a coffee around that time. The barista, who was just trying to be friendly, asked how I was doing. I said, "Great!" This clearly threw her off because I didn't look great. She then went on to ask what I was "up to" that day and I replied, "Just headed to chemotherapy!"

And that right there is exactly how you ruin a barista's day. That is also how you stop someone dead in their tracks from asking personal questions. She looked horrified and started backpedaling immediately. I mean, I was bald. It was apparent that life wasn't all brunch and rainbows. I still felt like a dick. I had snapped because I was wary of the questions when clearly, I wasn't great. To the chipper coffee girl, I'm sorry. It wasn't you; it was me.

What if we asked more specific questions like "what's on your heart today?" or "what have you done for yourself today?" or "does your body feel okay?" or "how have you been sleeping?"

Let's do that instead of putting pressure on someone to evaluate every intricacy of their emotional and physical existence at any given moment and funnel it into a combination of words for you. Can anyone even digest and comprehend that?

The truth is, most people can't properly answer the broad "how are you?" question on any given day in the first place.

* * *

I wrote to the general public when I could rather than responding individually. I mean, how do I articulate that I'm spending more time on the floor than not these days, because the ground feels like the only thing stable enough to count on? How do I explain that I needed freedom to be angry without scaring people off? Or how do I describe that I was scared without dumbing down my experience into something palatable?

7.10.2018

I can't imagine what it's like to watch the love of your life go through what I'm going through. I can barely look at myself these days without falling apart. I'm trying to maintain a normal that doesn't exist anymore. The truth is, I cry a lot, I shut down a lot, I need a lot of help, and I don't always say or know what that is. I'm in a lot of pain, emotionally and physically. I have had every imaginable side effect of the chemo and to the drugs prescribed for said side effects. I'm not always happy. I fall asleep by eight. I can't hang like I used to. I'm working half of what I used to, and I'm worried about medical bills. I can't cook right now, I can clean. I ask the same questions over and over because my brain is in a fog.

But her, this woman right here, she takes it all. She so patiently listens, and waits, and cleans, and smiles, and bathes the kids, and works, and orders food because she doesn't cook. She goes head-to-head with the insurance when I want to cuss them out. She makes sure I take my meds on time and gives me a few more that I really wish I didn't have to swallow but am actually pretty thankful for (thank you, honey). She asks the doctors the right questions when I black out, and she holds me when I need a quiet space. She makes me laugh when nothing else does.

@stephworth if I had to choose anyone to have cancer with, it would be you. You are the most incredible woman I know, and I feel so lucky to have you by my side. I'll be fun in a year, I promise. Also, you are gorgeous.

Next time you see this woman and ask her how she's doing, could you also tell her she's doing an amazing job? She's holding it down for all 4 of us.

* * *

My wife was beyond amazing during treatment. She made calls for me, asked questions for me, advocated for me. She made sure I had everything I needed. She also took care of our kids. She pet my bald head as I went to sleep and made sure I knew she thought I was beautiful even though I looked like a mannequin. And all of this after working all day and also working on her startup company. I was resentful at times of her working so much when I was home sick. That was unfortunate but it was completely out of my control. I don't like feeling needy and I don't like asking for help, so it took a lot of effort for me to let her take care of me. But she did, and I'm so thankful.

However, she also had a solution to every problem I had. Every ache, every pain. I needed to do this to fix that, or drink that to help this. And no these weren't gimmicky things like oils or standing on my head for an hour a day. She's a reliable source. But the truth is, I literally couldn't do any more than I was doing most days. I was doing my best and I needed my best to be enough.

I am a strong woman, but I could not down another supplement or take another wheatgrass shot. I could barely swallow water because my mouth was bleeding, and I was so nauseous I couldn't eat. My skin hurt so there was no rubbing anything on anything, and I had a hard time walking most days because my eyesight was so bad and my balance was off.

I was beyond frustrated. I had been frustrated for weeks but I didn't want to hurt her feelings. I mean, can you blame the girl for wanting to keep her wife alive? I felt like I wasn't doing enough. Like I wasn't good enough. Like if I died, it would be because I didn't do that one more thing.

There was one day when I was particularly miserable and bedridden with side effects and barely able to walk to the other room. My wife started telling me I needed to try this or that, or maybe this would work! I looked at her, with tear-stained cheeks, and said, "Honey, I don't need you to fix me. I just need you to tell me I'm doing a good job."

It caught her completely off guard and she stopped breathing for a second. Her brow relaxed and her whole face softened. She said, "Oh honey, I'm so sorry."

I felt bad but I think she felt worse. She didn't realize that I had a whole team of people at the hospital and hundreds of strangers trying to fix me every single day, offering me drugs and solutions and pep talks. I just needed someone to see me where I was and for what I was doing. I needed acknowledgment that she was proud of me. This conversation changed so much about how we interacted through the rest of treatment and still in our marriage to this day. We always take time to stop and remind each other that we are doing a good job.

The thing about cancer is, even if your partner has sat in the same room as you for every appointment, infusion, and surgery, they'll always be in a different chair than you. The perspective of a caregiver is vastly different from that of a patient. I was constantly having to accept that there would always be a great gap between me and those who haven't been through it, including me and my wife.

* * *

It was around this time that I connected with another woman from Seattle who was going through the same treatment as me. I found her one day while I was clicking through breast cancer hashtags on the internet. My situation wasn't just a fluke, and she wasn't the only other one. There were dozens of women. It still wasn't enough to make me feel better about my situation, but enough to know that this shit is happening more than ever. And it's happening in a younger demographic than the pamphlets tell you.

Never in my life did I think a hashtag would save me, but this one did. It was like online friend dating, and it totally worked. You should try it. Meet through hashtags. My friend and I hit it off right away, and I finally felt like someone understood my pain. She was my age and we were a month apart in our regimen. We also had a similar sense of humor and joy for life.

She remained a daily source of strength for me through the rest of treatment. We would have days where we were absolutely miserable. But we also had days that our dark cancer humor ran rampant as we made fun of how we looked, or the fact that we shit our pants on the twenty-foot walk from our front door to our car. It was a breath of fresh air to feel understood in a situation that the world doesn't talk about.

32: Round 4

Over halfway through treatment, I was starting to think about the fact that they were about to amputate my tits. I looked sick by then. I was down a good ten pounds of muscle that I couldn't really afford to lose, and I was bald on every surface. My eyes were a little sunken in, as well as my cheeks, and I was as pale as a ghost. I was spending more and more time wondering if I should write my kids letters in case I died, and less time thinking I was going to beat this thing.

I was lonely, not like bored and I want a friend to hang out with lonely. It was more a deep, painful loneliness. Like standing in the middle of a desert all alone. Nobody understood what I was going through, I'm not even sure if they tried. No fault to them, it's hard enough to make sense of it all being the one going through it. I felt so isolated.

It was the middle of summer, and I couldn't be outside because my skin was so pale. The chemo would make me sunburn in a split second. Not to mention, I had major heat intolerances as a side effect. Seventy-four degrees all of the sudden had me stripping all my clothes off and wondering if I was burning alive. I didn't have the energy to take my kids to the park, and God forbid we try to go to the river. I couldn't take them swimming because I wouldn't have the strength to save them if they needed me, and they couldn't swim on their own yet. All I could do was lie down.

I watched as people went camping, hiking, and boating. I saw their bodies become browned from the sun. I watched as they had summer cocktails and summer romances. As they played games in fields and went to outdoor concerts. I watched from waiting rooms and infusion centers, from my couch and the bathroom floor. I was a screen away, but it felt like I was on another planet. I'd close my eyes and try to picture myself there. I'd try to smell the summer air and feel its tenderness on my skin.

Would I ever get to experience those things again? Would it feel the same? I tried not to become resentful.

You're going to have to do better than that.

7.26.2018

I keep wondering when I'm going to wake up from this...it can't be real. I've lost two of the main things that make up my external femininity. My hair is gone, my lashes are gone, and two months from today...my boobs will be gone. My idea of beauty is in turmoil. I look sick. It's getting harder to look people in the eye, I wonder if they are noticing all the things that are missing. I can no longer hide what I'm going through. Some days I look in the mirror and I cry because I am watching these parts of myself get stripped away...Other days I look in the mirror and I feel so much strength and gratitude for the fight within me and the strength I possess. It is equally beautiful and traumatic.

These things have been a part of me for 33 years...they fed my babies, they got me ZERO dates, we have quite literally had our ups and our downs. They are mine, and while I'm not a boob person, I'm feeling the feels about them before I literally lose feeling in them forever.

No, it's not a free boob job...it's breast cancer and it's an operation to save my life, and its reconstruction, and it's really fucking expensive. It's painful and it's sad, but it's my life. I'm proud to live it.

I am raw. I am in it. And I am trying to articulate all the things I'm feeling and learning along the way. You never know what can help you.

Again, thank you for the support. I cherish every message and gesture more than I can say.

* * *

It's amazing how many people said to me, "At least you get new boobs!" It's also amazing how many times I didn't punch these people in the face.

Comments like this happen all too frequently. First off, it's not free. Everyone must meet an out-of-pocket max and usually miss at least six months of work/income. So if you are anything like me, this "boob job" was going to be more than ten times the price of a regular augmentation when all was said and done. I would just sit there and think, *Do I explain this to them? Is it worth it? Riddle me this, Karen, then tell me how it's free.*

I'm not sure what part of getting your tits literally scraped out to the thinnest layer of skin with an ice cream scooper/scalpel sounds like a boob job, but we need to stop saying this.

IT'S NOT A BOOB JOB.

They take your boobs away from you and throw them in the garbage as far as I know. And they cut the nerves which takes ALL the feeling out of them. FOREVER. And in return, they give you round silicone balls under your skin, that they ever so carefully craft to try to make them look real. Yet if you lose a pound or two, you can see every edge of them. They make noises when you turn a certain way, and if you work out a lot, they sink below your breast line. You will get aroused at the wrong times, if at all. And if you run into a wall, you won't feel a thing. So God forbid you partner tries foreplay and it scares the shit out of you when you realize they have been playing with your nipples and you had no idea because you felt nothing...like, *Yo, how long have you been doing that?*

Not a boob job.

33: Round 5

Well, I wrote my girls letters, all three of them. Just in case.

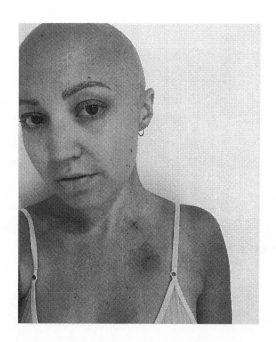

8.20.2018

I cried over spilled milk yesterday. I didn't want to drink it, I wasn't upset about the mess, but I watched myself try to grab the carton and pour it for my daughter and then I watched as my fingers could no longer grip the edges and it slipped out of my hands. My mind and my body are doing different things. Neuropathy. Mindfuck.

THIS IS CHEMO. I am watching it kill my cancer, but I am watching it kill the healthy parts of me too.

My bones are freezing but my skin is on fire. I have sores around my eyes, on my hips, and covering the insides of my nose, constant bleeds. I have moon face/body from the steroids I so badly want to refuse taking. My bones ache 24/7. My head feels like it is stuck between two clamps. I'm exhausted. My fingers, toes, and tip of my tongue are numb...I am losing strength. I have bruises everywhere. My stomach is in knots. I get dizzy when I stand up, I lose my balance when I walk. I am constantly breathless. I am dry heaving if I miss a pill by 10 minutes. I toss and turn all night between hot flashes and nightmares, insomnia. These are the things you don't see via Instagram. This is what days 2-12 look like. This is my life.

I am sad. I am lonely. I am tired. I am the strongest motherfucker I know. I am almost done with phase one.

One more round...Thank you to those who have continued to check on me and offer support. I expect a whole lot of dancing from my friends and the general public on my last day of chemo.

* * *

We have such an amazing community and were able to get out of town after each infusion just to clear our heads. I was home if I wasn't at an infusion center, so home lost its appeal very quickly. I didn't want my home to become a place where I was when I was sick. So our trips, gifted by strangers and friends, were a huge blessing when I felt like I couldn't possibly stare at my bedroom wall for one more minute.

We had been given weekends at a cabin on a farm. We were flown to Scottsdale for some warmth. We went to the mountains and to the beach. Someone even gave us a thousand dollars to go wherever we wanted, and I still do not know who that angel is. And if I'm being totally honest, the trips were way better than flowers.

My favorite moment was when I showed up bald to a Vegas-style pool party in Arizona and people were just staring at me trying to figure out why this seemingly healthy and fashionable chick had Bic'd her head.

The group next to us couldn't stop talking about how gorgeous I was and paying me so much attention. It's not the most comfortable situation to show up in front of hundreds of strangers while you're bald, just knowing they will stare at you. However, the bonus of that situation is I didn't need a bikini wax because I was a hairless cat at that point.

Another guy we were talking to asked if I was sick or if I had shaved my head on purpose. I told him I was sick, and he said, "Good, because if you did that on purpose, I was going to smack you."

I'm sorry, what? No, you would never smack me because I'm too quick, and also you don't hit women. But more importantly, why would it matter if a woman wanted to shave their head?

I was furious and I feel bad for his wife to this day. If she had only heard what he had said, I'm sure she would have been horrified. And if not, that in and of itself would have been a problem.

* * *

I also went to help at my daughter's school around this time. I wore a hat anytime I went to the school because I didn't want to scare the children. I had no idea if they had ever seen a woman this sick before. I was standing in the hall when a couple of fourth grade girls walked by. They had their arms linked and they were going between looking at me and each other, and giggling incessantly. I was just thinking to myself,

Oh here we go. The mean girls. I was oddly self-conscious in the moment.

One of the girls walked up to me and said, "Are you a girl or a boy?"

"I'm a girl," I said.

The girls looked at each other and laughed as they walked away. For a moment, I was taken back to being bullied in high school. My daughter, June, who was five at the time, ran up to me and grabbed my hand. We watched them look back at me as they whispered and laughed.

June yelled, "Hey! That's my mom and she's beautiful!" My heart exploded with pride.

34: Round 6

My LAST ROUND OF CHEMO!!!

Yes, I would still have immunotherapy infusions and, no, I was not cancer or symptom-free. But making it through six rounds of something that you could literally feel ravaging your body and dissolving your cells while still being able to get up and go to work most days felt like a huge feat.

All I wanted was a celebration on my last day of chemo. While the fight was far from over, a large portion of it was. From what I was told, I was going to start feeling better and my hair would start growing back and goddamnit, that was a win.

I begged them to let me have a private room for my final infusion, so we could party instead of sitting in the giant beige unit with my eighty-five-year-old peers. I was told I could not celebrate in the main area because some people in the center would never finish chemo. They were either going to be treated for life or not make it.

Cancer perspective check #687. I was the lucky one here.

I wanted to have more than one visitor sit with me through my final four-hour stint. After this infusion, I was to stay on two of the four drugs for six more months, but they were much less harsh and would only take an hour to administer, so I would likely go alone.

They agreed to let me have a private room as long as I didn't bring latex balloons or confetti cannons. Fine then. *Cancels balloon arch and orders a live band.*

Other than that, it was a go. I didn't ask how many friends I could bring because I didn't want to not be in control, yet again.

For many of my infusions, Steph had dropped me off and left after an hour. I sat through multiple infusions alone. It's not necessarily because I wanted to, but because life had to go on. My wife had to make money because we were both self-employed. Plain and simple, if I wasn't working AND she wasn't working, our bills weren't getting paid. And we had massive bills by then. However, looking back, we would never do it this way again, money comes and goes.

I had dozens of people offer to come and sit with me, but it's hard to explain that you do but also don't want company. It's hard to know how someone will handle seeing you slowly fade into a different reality with each drop of poison, or if they would notice when you needed a break from talking. It's a wildly intimate experience. *Would they notice when they saw life and hope leave my eyes only to be replaced by haze, helplessness, and surrender?*

My dad came with me once, and I felt like I had to hold it together for him the whole time because he was about to lose it. Nobody wants to watch their kid actively fight for their life. And no kid wants their parents to fear their death. But it was exhausting for me to pretend like I was okay when all I wanted to do was have a massive fall apart.

Most people, when uncomfortable, try to make things better by talking or joking. But when you are getting an infusion, it literally slows your brain down. It's exhausting trying to keep up. You could be talking one second and need to barf the next. I often just needed to close my eyes and concentrate on breathing. I guess a part of me felt like I would have to entertain whoever came with me as well, because they would be giving up so many hours of their day.

Chemo is also such a personal experience. I didn't want anyone talking to other people about what it was like, giving them one more reason to feel bad for me or to worry. If my wife couldn't be there, alone was the next best option. I'd get dropped off and have someone pick me up to drive me home. Trust me, you don't want someone with liters of poison in their veins going straight from chemo to getting behind the wheel. My girlfriend had driven me home one round, and it took me four miles to remember one word to make a sentence. She just waited patiently as I fought my own brain to remember something as simple as the word "freedom." And even then, my sentence didn't make sense.

* * *

Despite my thick cynicism, I really had been trying to spread joy and awareness through the trudge. (My nurse on my last day of chemo said, "It's not a journey, it's a trudge." I liked it enough. Thanks, Barb.)

I was alone at my fifth round, and I had asked people on Instagram to send me jokes to keep me busy. As it turns out, people have a lot of jokes up their sleeve. I got more jokes than I could read. I thought to myself, *I wonder if I can get people to send dance videos on my last day of chemo.*

For the next three weeks I pushed the internet once a week to send dance videos on my final day and tag me and #watchliannewin. I wanted to see if people could celebrate life a bit and let their guard down.

I asked for people to send videos of them dancing, whether I knew them or not. What a joy to move your body. But also, how much fun is it to have a mid-day dance party and celebrate? For the love of God, shouldn't we all be doing this daily anyway?

If I learned anything during treatment, okay so I learned hundreds of things, but it's been confirmed that nothing really matters. Regarding the small stuff anyway.

Hair? Nope.

Your summer cold? Nope.

The fight you had with your boyfriend over dinner? Nope.

How little sleep you got? Nope.

LIFE. JOY. YOUR BODY. COMMUNITY. LOVE. HEALTH. Yes, those matter.

We, as people, take ourselves so seriously. It was apparent when everything that used to be important had been overshadowed by my fate. It was honestly a blessing to be pushed back to basics. All I cared about was staying alive and living a joyful life.

I also think that, subconsciously, I wanted to feel like I wasn't alone. The amount of support you need during treatment is insane. And you don't always know what it looks like or how to ask for it, and it doesn't always feel supportive when you get it. But I finally had a clear vision of what I needed—I needed people to dance.

* * *

I arrived at the center early with my wife for my final round. I danced my way down the hall as they led me back to my "suite" (a.k.a. I had a hospital bed instead of a shitty recliner, and they pulled in some wildly uncomfortable chairs for my friends.)

My cancer friend, Sarah, drove down from Seattle to meet me that day and sit with me through my last infusion. She had finished hers just a month prior, so she knew how monumental it was. It's weird to meet someone you feel so close to in person for the first time while you are hooked up to a machine filled with drugs. But we were just at that level. She was my chemo rock, a true gift during such a shitty time, and I thank my lucky stars for her to this day because she made such a huge impact during my trudge. If I had to pick a Breast Bud, it would be her.

As the first bag got started, my wife and her brother opened their computer to show me a video they had made. It was quite possibly one of the best things I had ever seen. They had gotten clips of a bunch of my friends in costume, singing and dancing "We Built This City" by Starship, and made it into a music video.

I'm not sure if the tears running down my face were from laughing or crying but probably both. It was happening! People made a video and they were having so much fun! I was floored.

I checked my phone afterward, and I had hundreds of people tagging me in videos. It was catching on like wildfire. Some had been made prior to this day and people were just waiting for September sixth to post them. Others were spur of the moment. It was the most entertained I had ever been and the most loved I had ever felt. I couldn't believe it.

I honestly thought I'd get about six participants, those six being my closest friends and family. But as time went on, I was being tagged in places across the globe by people I had never even met. Asia, Ireland, NYC, Colorado, Washington, California, Georgia, Florida—the list kept growing. It was one of the most powerful things I had ever felt. I was laughing and crying.

There were costumes and hair flips and rhythm, and some with not so much rhythm, and it didn't even matter. I felt loved and supported and I felt so much joy, not just for me, but because other people were truly having fun and letting go and finding so much joy themselves. It was more than I could have asked for, and it kept me cheery through the moments of the infusion where I wanted to crawl into a hole and cry. I almost forgot I was getting a treatment at one point. Even my dad sent a video doing the Macarena, which is the best because we have always joked that his arms are too short for his body. When it comes time to cross them over his belly, we just lose it with laughter.

My wife. My oh-so-sexy wife made me a video too. The weeks leading up to this infusion she had been exponentially "busy." She was late to come home or had a last minute "therapy" and I was honestly pissed. My weak mind thought that maybe she found someone healthier and hotter and with more hair, but my strong mind knew that wasn't the case. Either way, I knew something was up.

As it turns out, she was making me the best music video of all time complete with back up dancers. It was legit. Like a real, produced music video. You should watch it. Go on YouTube and search "For Lianne." At first, I was mad because I was like, you lied. But then I was like, *Damn, you are hot, and this is incredible. How did you do this?* I was watching her and had no idea her hips could move like that and if I wasn't connected to a machine with a needle and cords inside of me, I would have jumped on her in the infusion center. Sweet baby Jesus, she is good-looking.

On the flip side, I was a little mad that I was lying around sick while she made me this incredible gift. That she had literally been picking up the pieces of me for the last six months, like shattered glass in a dustpan, while I laid there wanting nothing more than for the cancer to be out of my body, and still have the stamina to be in a music video. Being a caretaker is a full-time job, I don't care how independent you are. I envied Steph's health, my friends' health, their freedom.

Chemo resentment is real. You constantly have to check yourself. I wanted to be the hot one in the music video, laughing with friends and dancing and not lying around on a couch bald, dizzy, miserable, alone, and wondering if it was the end.

But that wasn't my path. For one reason or another, I was supposed to be all those things, just not in a music video with friends. Anyway, I digress.

The end of chemo was unfortunately anticlimactic. I think somewhere along the line I had dreamt of a conga line and champagne being poured on my face. We took a photo and quietly left. While I wanted to be a little more stoked to get out of there, I felt sick and I also knew I would have to come back in three weeks for another poke and a different kind of torture. So we all just left with our heads down, maybe walking a little faster than normal. Not wanting to let the doom of the hospital suck me back into its jaws and steal any pride I held at the moment.

Steph, Sarah, and I grabbed a bite to eat, then headed home to celebrate with the kids. I had about thirty minutes of adrenaline left in me before I would be down for the count for the next two weeks, so I soaked it all in.

* * *

9.6.2018

Today I KISSED CHEMO GOODBYE!

Today I felt an immense amount of pain, anxiety, exhaustion, fear...and so much freaking JOY.

I have seen over 300 people, many who I've never met, rise today and FEEL, and get weird, and CONNECT, and let go. And I can honestly say that today, watching a community go global and rise up, has made every ounce of side effect, loneliness, anemia, diarrhea, nausea, hair loss, fatigue, neuropathy, WORTH IT.

To give joy. To feel it. To live in it without boundaries. WHAT A GIFT.

Thank you, Portland. Thank you to the other states and countries who have danced today. It's not about me at all. It's about US. It's beautiful. It's powerful. Keep doing it.

And to my beautiful wife, I am the luckiest. I love you. But if you get famous before me...

I didn't anticipate the emotions that I would have over the next couple of weeks on top of the side effects. Most of the side effects were going to have one last go ravaging my body. They were worse than ever before. I could feel it in every cell, my muscles felt like they were being eaten alive, a tiny bug chewing through them as they were dissolving into nothingness. I felt half disintegrated. Years of strength training, gone in an instant for an incredibly expensive price.

There was nausea, fatigue, and diarrhea. I couldn't eat. I had blisters, boils, night sweats, chills, bone pain. I had anticipated it, but that didn't make it any better. I let it happen, as it was going to happen either way, whether I wanted it to or not.

What I didn't anticipate was the letdown. You know that feeling after a wedding? Like all the planning and the party? And then what? Well, turns out this is nothing like that. Because it was never exciting to begin with. But it was one of the biggest letdowns of my life. Even more than my failed marriage or being questioned in and about my relationships.

I had put my head down and went to work the second I was diagnosed. I shouldn't say work—it was a fucking battle. It was gruesome and unexpected and ugly, the whole bit. I didn't look back. I was going to slay this motherfucker, and I didn't have time or patience to feel bad for myself. I felt a little sad up until then, but nothing could have prepared me for this.

I cried every day after round six for two weeks straight. The kind of crying that you do all day and in the middle of the night in the pillow, so you don't wake your partner. The kind where you choke on your own breath and you gasp for more air. The kind that stains your cheeks and your clothes with salt marks when it dries. The kind that makes your whole body shake and your hands shake until you turn them to fists. The kind that makes you fall to your knees and makes your face sore. I felt it all—relief, anger, grief, fear, joy, confusion.

I started to realize that chemo had been a security blanket for me, while simultaneously making me question if I was actually living in hell. It had been keeping my cancer at bay, shrinking it. Assuring me every single miserable day that it wasn't growing or coming back, for that moment at least. I could rely on chemo when I couldn't rely on anything else. It had been my constant. I kept thinking, Now what? Every emotion was valid and a little too real.

I spent the three weeks between completing chemo and surgery resting. I finally took some time off work. I walked A LOT because it's all I could do. Well, a lot being one walk a day, but it felt like a lot.

My two-mile route now took me well over an hour to complete. I had to stop every thirty feet or so to catch my breath so I wouldn't pass out. I had to cling to the railing by the stairs at the school to climb them. My bones ached deep into the core, my muscles were small and weak. My white blood cell counts were borderline needing a blood transfusion. I felt naked and hollow, like the breeze could knock me over. Tears streamed down my face as every step took what felt like my last breath from my body, the wind feeling like cool water on my bald head.

Most walks, I listened to "O" by Coldplay on repeat. I imagined that if I had to leave this world, that song would be playing as I drifted away. It was playing when I buried myself for the first time in my mind, and every time after that. It is beautiful and tragic, yet hopeful and peaceful.

Two older women passed me, and for the first time I asked myself, *Why me?* I was an athlete that couldn't complete ten steps. I was half dead but somehow completely alive.

I guess it had always been *why not me* until that point. Shit happens to everyone. I never assume I am immune. But it didn't seem fair. I looked at the trees turning for fall. I started to feel like one of them. Stripped bare of all things that made me outwardly beautiful. I was left cold. I wondered if they got scared in the winter. *Would they make a comeback? Would I?*

I realized I had been pushing away that one feeling for the last six months. I was scared. Fear in its most raw form. I had nothing left to give. I had been looking mortality in the mirror every day all while avoiding my own eyes. This was huge.

As tears fell down my face, I sat down and let myself feel all of it. I always say my life is an endless quest to feel it all, but I truly believe that this was the first time in my life that I genuinely did so. I felt the feelings in the air around me, on my skin, in my lungs, in my heart, all the way to my numb fingertips. It's as if I could hear them, see them, taste them, and smell them. I replayed my life over and over. Mistakes I had made, relationships, heartbreak, loss, happiness, closure, triumph.

By the end of it, I landed on one thing. I was confused, more scared of the disease in the moment than I had been during six months of chemo. Why? Because the cancer wasn't gone yet, and even when it was gone, IF it was gone, it could come back. And they sure don't let you forget that. In fact, they pretty much brainwash you into thinking if you don't take everything, they tell you to, it will come back.

9. 23. 2018

I lost the last of my lashes and hair as the trees started to change. I walked every day and wondered if the trees felt the same as I did in the fall. Stripped from one kind of beauty to expose another, something more vulnerable and a little more lonely...scared that they may not come back the same or if at all, yet ready for what's next all the same.

I've always loved the fall, but I relate to it so much more now.

35: I'll take a mastectomy...make it a double

9.25.2018 the day before mastectomy

Photo by Amy Shick

I guess when something tries to kill you, you get rid of it.

I remember before I had kids, I was told my body would never be the same. It would look different, I would have stretch marks, I'd hold on to weight, etc. I've never loved or appreciated my body more than post children, until now anyway.

The thing is your body won't be the same tomorrow either. It's supposed to change as we age, as we grow, have children, get sick. It will never be the same simply because of time, so why are we so obsessed with keeping it that way?

My body is strong, it's resilient, and I'm going to love it even more on the other side...for everything that it's done for me and been put through. And if it looks different, so be it. If I can never feel my boobs again, at least I'm alive. I am honored to live in it and to wear the scars.

Thank you to everyone that helped with the tit send-off today in my classes. I'll miss you hard. The people, not the tits, these guys were duds.

* * *

Pardon me, has anyone seen my tits?
Oh...wait, they're in the trash? *Okay, cool.*

So maybe that is a dumb question at this point as hundreds of people have now seen my tits, and my previous tits, and the tits in between. What I meant to say was, "Hi, my name is Lianne, and someone chopped off my tits when I was thirty-three years old."

Okay, okay, so maybe that's still a bit much. "I got a mastectomy." Is it *got*? Did I go pick one out at the store? I HAD a mastectomy? I received a mastectomy. But technically do I still have it? What's a chest without boobs called if the mastectomy should be in past tense?

It was around this time that my ex sent me a picture of the art my seven-year-old daughter, Harper, had made at school that day. It was a cut out silhouette of a body on construction paper with red, bloody, Frankenstein style stitches all over it. When my ex asked her what it was, she said, "It's mommy."

I felt like I had gotten punched in the gut when he showed me. My heart sat as a lump in my throat. My baby girl was scared, she thought I was dying. She was trying to process it too. I had been very open with my kids, and they seemed as understanding as a five-and seven-year-old could be. But I learned that they were scared too, that I needed to talk to them even more, that they didn't know how to talk to me.

I spent so much time after that moment showing them my body as time went on, explaining every bruise, scar, and side effect. Reminding them that I was alive, that in the grand scheme of things I was okay.

* * *

I was asked multiple times why I was choosing to have both breasts removed. My answer was always simple: my life is way more important than my tits. There was no way in hell I was going to go through all of that just to keep a singular boob. Also, the odds of them matching with one reconstructed and one original were basically zero. And then I would forever have to get a single-sided mammogram, whereas if I had both removed, I would never see another mammogram in my life. On top of that, if the cancer came back on the other side, I would have to do this all over again anyway. Not worth it.

Mastectomy is essentially having your boobs amputated. It's gruesome, inhumane, and a bit barbaric. But sure, bring it on. It's not like they give you any other hopeful options.

I had been to multiple pre-ops, and they explained the procedure the best they could. You don't really get it until you do it, I guess. They were to remove the world's tiniest implants from my body (I had 170cc, which is basically two-thirds of a cup if we were baking boobs), and the remainder of any of my own breast tissue that I had. I assumed what I had left was next to nothing but would soon find out that it actually was one hundred percent next to nothing. I wondered if the surgery would take less time because of my lack of breast mass.

NOPE.

I checked in at 10:30 a.m. on a Wednesday. Of course, because of the cold I came down with five days prior, I had a deep cough that I couldn't kick due to my poor immune system. In true Lianne form, I refused to tell them or postpone.

They gave me my paperwork at check-in, and a wristband with my name, birthdate and a scan code so they could put it all on my tab. I also had a tracker placed on my wrist in case they lost me. Okay so that's not why, but it made me laugh to think about. The device was so that Steph and our family could see from the waiting room what stage of the procedure I was in, and wherever they transferred me within the hospital. There were little screens in the waiting areas listing numbers like flight numbers, along with designated room numbers to go with them. *Who knows where they are going to take me? How many rooms does a mastectomy take?*

They wheeled me to a full-walled cubicle in the middle of the hospital. No windows. I do great with no windows. I am NOT claustrophobic. I was NOT going to panic. I did NOT need a Xanax. (Yes, I did.) They closed the door and I saw footsteps outside. I started to read writing on the window as it was being written. And to me, it read backwards: K S I R L L A F.

Fall Risk. What?

The nurse opened the slider and introduced herself and announced that she was about to pump me with oxycodone, so therefore I was a fall risk. *Fun*, I thought. *Let's go.*

She was sarcastic so we got along great. I felt like I was on *Jeopardy* while she asked me questions for a full forty-five minutes, only I was inevitably going to lose. Some questions were relevant, others were not. I wondered if I would be sent home if I answered one wrong.

There was a tiny Jesus on a cross above my bed. I didn't know if I should be comforted by him or creeped out. I wondered if he had insomnia like the rest of us cancer patients.

I also wanted to ask him why He gave me cancer. He was clearly okay with it. And, if God only gives you what you can handle, why didn't He think I could handle more? I'm tough as shit.

I never understood when people would say "God never gives you more than you can handle" or "Trust in the Lord, he will give you strength." I was having a hard time buying into the Jesus thing because none of it was adding up. I imagine for some people, it gives them a sense of hope and peace to believe. Not only did God give me strength, but He gave me cancer. And if someone gives you cancer, the last thing you do is trust them. I still had some deep-seated issues with Christianity.

After the last few years of my life, feeling like I wasn't accepted in the church because of divorce and same-sex marriage, and having heard that God made me "in His image," it was wildly confusing. *If He made me in His image, then what is the problem here? Aren't we all imperfect? Aren't we all to love and accept one another? And even then, why cancer on top of that?*

Moments later, I see what looked like a walker and a small pair of shuffling feet pass my door and stop. I was thinking there was an old woman who was out for a walk in my unit. *How cute!* Or maybe she was lost. She opened the door and announced that she was there to draw my blood. She was also one hundred and two years old.

Can I run away? NOPE. *Why can't my nurse draw my blood?* Probably because she was still asking me questions like Alex Trebek. I am judging this poor woman, but again, always trust your gut god.

She fumbled over my already swollen and bruised vein for a good twelve minutes while also telling me what a horrible start to the day she was having. *Now would be a good time to NOT talk about how you are not crushing your job. Also, please don't pass out, you've come this far*. She wobbled to my other side, blaming the bed rail for her inability to get to my vein instead of her age, and poked a few more times before she nailed that bad boy. It was a pleasant start to a long few weeks. Also, for the sake of everyone, including her, I hope she retired after that shift.

Next up was Nuclear Medicine. It sounds scarier than it is. A man came and wheeled my bed down a cold and dated white hall with fluorescent lights, through nineteen different doorways, to the elevator. Why I was in a bed and not a wheelchair is beside me, or walking for that matter, but drama, I guess. It was my chariot.

Also, was this guy's only job to wheel people around? I wondered if he knew why everyone was there or if he even cared. *Did he know I was about to lose my breasts?* What a weird job. Every time he wheeled me past someone, I felt their sympathy and I felt my own shame.

He pressed the down arrow on the elevator. I was already on the first floor. This sent my claustrophobic self into an instant panic. There is no fresh air underground. The door opened and he wheeled me down a long brown hall in the basement of the hospital, past the cafeteria (which at this point in starvation smelled like a five star restaurant), turned a corner, and entered through another set of doors to a new hall with an even lower ceiling and less light.

The first face I saw was a girl whose hair I had done for years in the past. She had that look of concern and "I'm sorry" on her face. They must teach that look in school programs that train you to work in hospitals or healthcare settings. At that point, I just wanted to catch up with her. I didn't know how to answer the "how are you doing?" about myself because A, I had no idea how I was doing, and B, couldn't we just catch up like normal people? We all knew I had cancer and was there to hopefully have it removed.

She explained that I was there to have a blue dye injected into my breast that would essentially light up my lymph nodes during surgery to make them easier to find, be removed, and biopsy for residual traces of cancer. Similar to the contrast dye from my MRI.

After explaining, she left the room to go get the doctor who would give me the injection. I quickly realized the moment she left that I was underground, stuck in a bed facing AWAY from the door in a closet they called a room. It was dim, hot, and before I knew it, it was closing in on me. I had no idea where I was or where my wife was or how to get out. I started making an exit strategy. I started counting backward, yoga breathing, wondering, *Is this how I'm going to die?* The seconds felt like hours somehow. Just as I felt myself going black, the door swung open.

The girl must have seen how white I was because she quickly wheeled me to face the door. A thin woman walked in with her. She looked like she had been in the basement for too many years. She explained the procedure again and before I knew it, there was another needle in my body, in my breast to be exact. Just another pinch and burn without my permission.

I was quickly wheeled out of the room by my chauffeur while yelling goodbye and also wondering what could possibly be next. Turns out the hospital runs a tight ship. *Was I turning blue? When did it happen?* We passed the cafeteria, I was still starving. Then, we waited at the elevators while three grown men cut in front of us. I was starting to wonder what the fuck was wrong with people. You have a bald chick in the basement of a hospital, strapped to a bed and you think you need to go in the elevator first? Sure, sir, this is America.

And back I went through all the doors to the fluorescent lights in the weird dingy hall. We rounded a corner and I saw a Physician's Assistant who I knew who worked for another surgeon.

Me: "HEY!"
Her: "HEY! Are you going in?"
Me: "Sure am!"
Her: "Crush it girl, we are all thinking of you!"

I was starting to feel like a celebrity around those parts, and I definitely appreciated the enthusiasm.

* * *

My anesthesiologist came in next. There were so many people that wanted to see me! Just kidding, it's their job. He told me that what he'd be giving me today was, wait for it—drugs. Perfect. He was sarcastic, and it was great. I've never met an anesthesiologist I didn't like. In all my years of hospital drugs, I have yet to meet a dull anesthesiologist. He left on that note and said he would be back to get me all doped up after a quick visit from each surgeon.

My plastic surgeon came in next. The Boob Whisperer. He was small and had what I think was a dry sense of humor. But I also think he was feeling out if he could go there with the jokes yet; kinda like dating. First base was a small joke, but he'd already seen my tits. Bring it buddy, I was about to have my boobs removed. I could hang. The humor was getting dark on my end.

I stood up and opened my gown so he could draw a darling little treasure map on my chest. Dots, dashes, and lines with a sharpie, the fumes from the pen so strong I wasn't sure I'd need additional drugs. I didn't know what the lines and dashes meant, but it looked great to me. Symmetrical. A true artist.

Next up was my breast surgeon. Turns out she wanted to do arts and crafts too. She used a purple sharpie and placed two purple hearts on the side of my chest where she would be removing lymph nodes to be biopsied. They were placed right where my heart would be if my heart was on the right side of my body.

The anesthesiologist came back in with a pep in his step and announced he was ready to give me something to get started. I mean, I would have a pep in my step too if I were getting people high all day. It makes you an instant hospital favorite. I have no idea what time it was, but by the time I turned my head to look at the clock, I was completely baked. I remember saying, "Whoa, this stuff works fast!"

I tried to say a few more things but everything got a little blurry and out of body after that. I felt like I was lying in a bed of angel food cake but also floating at the same time. I don't really remember Steph kissing me, but I do remember being whooshed out of my cubicle. In my mind, it looked like what flying into heaven looks like, but in my case, it was out of cubicle hell. I felt like everyone was staring at me, and I also felt like I was waving like a beauty queen in a parade. It's hard to say what really happened.

The next thing I remember was opening my eyes. My surgical team was right above my face singing, "Just a spoonful of sugar helps the medicine go down." I was in the operating room. It was bright white with contraptions hanging from the ceiling and little blue Smurfs (nurses) buzzing in the background, the sound of clanging scalpels and shuffling feet. There were hums of electricity ringing through the lights above me. I'm not sure if it was the drugs, but the singing was incredibly loud and terrifying to me. It felt like the scary part of a Disney movie where the bad guy has you trapped.

In an effort to get involved, and be cool, and make the situation less creepy, I asked my plastic surgeon to freestyle. I was trying to stay awake. I felt like I really could add something to the song, and just when I was about to sing, I was out. The next thing I knew, apparently four and a half hours had flown by, and I was being woken up.

* * *

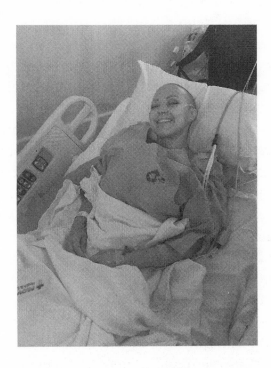

I was fluttering my eyes open, going in and out of consciousness, as I heard steady beeping and hustling all around me. There were voices of panic in the distance and one voice of calm in my ear. I was in a giant blue-grey room with weird paper curtains as room dividers. People were coming in and out so quickly I'm not even sure why they came in the first place.

I heard nurses all around me waking people up. Not all the situations seemed to be going as smoothly as mine. However, it didn't scare me at the moment because I was still fairly high. Looking back, it is a little unsettling. It felt like old videos of soldiers in war movies in the hospitals. Everyone freaking out, wondering where they were, what was left of their bodies, as they were strapped to beds. Somehow, in my drugged state, I wondered how we all ended up here.

How many of these tragedies were planned, and how many were emergencies? Did some people wake up with less than they anticipated? Or did they all go as planned? Whose dreams were going to be shattered more than they anticipated going into the OR? Was it going to be me? I hoped not. I felt an immense relief when I had woken up, despite the pressure of the bandages tightly wound to my chest, keeping me from taking a full breath. I just felt like I might be the lucky one today, losing my breasts and only my breasts.

I felt Steph's hand on mine as she started to come in and out of my vision. The nurses asked me question after question and offered me Jell-O, which was wildly offensive at the time. It's still offensive. Who the fuck wants to be rewarded for getting their boobs chopped off with hospital Jell-O? Nobody. I wanted a gin and tonic and a burger, please.

The next thing I knew, my drug dealer was hanging over the side rail of my bed asking how I was feeling. *FUCKING GREAT! Did I just get my boobs chopped off? I HAVE NO FUCKING IDEA BUT THIS IS GREAT!* (My actual real-time response in my head.)

I gave him a solid (and by solid, I mean I could barely lift my arms and make a fist) fist bump and said, "You crushed it!"

I think this gave him quite a bit of joy as most people don't respond that way. But really, the drugs were great.

There was some confusion about my overnight stay, as they tried to put me in a box without a window and I reserved a suite with a view. I don't know who decided it is okay to put people in a dark hole after such a massive surgery. It probably makes the drug companies more money because they end up prescribing antidepressants. What I do know, is that they were billing my insurance $42k for my stay, so I better get a fucking window. I finally arrived in my suite with a view of a parking lot, and all I could think about was a burrito.

I'll spare the boring details here, but reality is a bitch. And that bitch is fast. The drugs started to wear off and I looked down and saw drains connected to my body. I looked like my cat after he had gotten attacked by a coyote. It is so weird to see tubes coming out of your own body, filled with blood and fluid. The pain is something I am still trying to find words for. They pumped me with as much oxycodone as they could give me, but nothing touched it. Now, don't get me wrong, most people are fine and don't feel pain when they take oxy, I just happened to be immune to it, somewhat like lidocaine.

There was only one position I was allowed to be in. On my back. Getting up was a struggle. My ass was asleep, the painful kind where it almost feels half numb but it hurts. They pounded it into me to stay hydrated, but getting up to pee took nineteen minutes, a wife, a nurse, and every ounce of strength I had. It's amazing how many muscles you use to simply stand up.

It's also amazing how bad it hurt. They had ripped the tissue off my skin, cut my nerves and veins, manipulated my pectoral muscles, and scooped me to nothingness. And that's exactly what it felt like.

* * *

Thankfully, I was released early the next day after a lot of pushing and prodding on my part. Why not be difficult? The social worker from the breast center, whose phone calls I had so skillfully screened for the last five months, popped in right before I was discharged. This woman had also found me twice during infusions and pinned me down for questioning. I wanted nothing to do with her support group. I didn't need one more person who had never had cancer telling me it was going to be okay. I needed her to leave me alone.

She knew I was basically strapped to the bed and that she could catch me. I was trying SO hard not to be a bitch but if I say "I don't want to talk and I don't need your support group, thank you very much," I mean it.

I understand that this probably made me look like I needed it more, but trust a girl here. She handed me two homemade tiny purple pillows to put under my armpits for comfort while sleeping and went on her way. She could clearly tell I was about to bust a stitch if she didn't.

Don't test me, Brenda. But thank you for the ugly pillows that were so helpful in my recovery. I am forever grateful.

* * *

The next three days were absolute hell. I tear up just thinking about it. My breasts were lumpy, my nipples deflated and going in different directions, and I was black, green, and blue. I had tape and gauze all over my chest and my legs, holes and tubes, saran wrap and marker over my chest and torso. I looked in the mirror and my soul felt as numb as my chest, while simultaneously feeling like I had a running chainsaw where my breasts had been.

I was bald, battered, and bruised. Emotionally, I felt nothing. I'm not sure I even knew who or what I was looking at. I had to remind myself that the sea will wreck a ship, just as the chemo and the surgeries wrecked my body. But that doesn't make either any less beautiful.

I had three hairs on my head, two eyelashes total, boils on my ass, open sores on my swollen face, a drip from my nose to my mouth that I couldn't shut off, and I was holding two drains from tubes coming out of either side of my body with blood and warm fluid pooled into the bottom bulb. The only reason I looked like had an expression of any kind is because I had my eyebrows microbladed on before I started chemo like a genius. I had clear tape over my entire chest, and all the markings from the surgeons were still legible. Someone had clearly been there. But I wasn't present when it happened. Everything was gone, forever changed while I slept.

Did they talk about my body when they were operating? Did they feel bad for me? Or was I just another corpse on the table?

I remember the first shower I took after the hospital. I stood facing the water with my eyes closed and let it beat down on my chest, trying to feel anything at all. It was the weirdest experience; you can't imagine what it is like to lose one of your senses until it's gone. But I couldn't feel if the water was hot or cold, and I couldn't feel the pressure. The water could have been off for all I knew or scalding hot. I quickly turned it off before I got upset and crawled back into bed.

I was told I would never regain sensation in my breasts again. It is very odd to not know when you have a nip slip and your tits are hanging out of your bra or your oversized V-neck shirt. Zero sensation was going to be my normal for the rest of my life.

* * *

I had assumed after surgery I would feel immediate mental relief. But I stared and stared and didn't recognize myself. I couldn't decide if my face or my deflated nipples looked more pathetic. I didn't know if I still had cancer. I didn't know if I had a future. I didn't know what I was supposed to be feeling. I didn't know what I was supposed to be doing, what I should share. I didn't know if I should be elated or devastated. I was in so much pain and the oxycodone wasn't working. I had a chest cough so deep that every cough felt like my chest was being ripped apart repeatedly. Each cough brought an ooze of puss and blood into the tubes coming out of my sides. I took shallow breaths for three days just trying to make it to the day I could take Advil. One breath was closer to another minute down.

My kids and wife were home, and my parents were in town. I wanted to be alone. I wanted to be better. I wanted to heal. I wanted to want to celebrate. But that was a simple way of thinking.

I didn't realize how complex and infinite healing would be. Those moments made me realize that it wouldn't be linear, just as it hadn't been since diagnosis. You don't just go through chemo and feel better. You don't wake up from surgery knowing it's gone and just move forward. The mental and physical mindfuck lingers like an annoying fly in your kitchen.

* * *

Six days after my surgery, the PA from my surgeon's office called with my pathology report. It was a Tuesday afternoon, and I was about to take my daily walk/shuffle that I had taken almost every day for the past five months. I had my drains pinned inside my sweatshirt and a beanie on my bald head so nobody would stare with sympathy if they saw me. I knew that day's walk was going to feel like Everest. I am an athlete. This was one of the most humbling experiences of my life. A simple walk was almost impossible, and I never knew what day or symptom would hold me back or let me fly. The fact that I could be so breathless at the top of ten stairs that I had to fold over and hang onto the rail will always haunt me.

I answered the phone after the first ring. I had been waiting for this. I'm not sure I realized that the call could have only gone one of two ways. They would either have good news or bad news. I was alone and I wasn't really prepared for either. Because just as nobody teaches you how to fight for your life, nobody teaches you how to feel after trauma or receiving life-altering news.

She explained that I had a "complete response" to chemotherapy. My lymph nodes were clear. They had gotten clear margins. Basically, I had no cancer left in my body. I was NED—no evidence of disease.

This was the best-case scenario; the chemo had killed it. The chemo along with the sauna, and the fasting, and the supplements, and the two shots of wheatgrass I somehow choked down, and everything else I was doing that I had read about. I instantly started sobbing uncontrollably. I couldn't get a word out, but I was okay with it, because what do you really say in that situation? How do you thank someone who cut your body open a week prior and then proceeded to deliver the best news of your life?

I hung up the phone and immediately started jumping and shaking like a nervous child. I had no idea what was next or what it meant, but I was pretty sure it was good. I immediately called Steph and a couple of friends and for some reason filmed myself and told the whole world that I got another chance at life.

I was smiling and shaking uncontrollably all while realizing how alone I was in my accomplishment, just as I was alone in my fight. People were at work, on vacation. I was alone at home. The same home I was sick in and the same home I fought in, celebrating what my body had done. It's an eerie feeling to be so happy yet alone. To know that I just shared the biggest news of my life, and thirty seconds later my wife would walk in to have a completely different conversation with her patient, that my friend would attend a meeting five minutes later or check out at the grocery store.

And I was home alone, forever changed, every sip of air feeling different.

I will never forget my walk that day. My face was soaked the whole time. I stopped and I sat, and I thanked my body. The world looked so much different. From one phone call. I had felt like I had a giant black box in front of my face for the last six months. I could kind of see around it, but I couldn't move it. I couldn't really see beyond it, and suddenly, it was gone. Everything looked different, even as I write this it still does. It's like another dimension of living, like I got a wide-angle lens for my camera or a new set of colors that nobody else can see. My life turned three-dimensional after being so two-dimensional. I am so thankful. It is so big.

I received over five hundred comments on my post and over nine thousand views. I'm not even sure I know five hundred people; I was just happy to share something real with the world in an era of selfies and influencers. There were so many texts, phone calls, so much celebration.

"You won!"

"You did it!"

But did I? Was I allowed to get that excited? Did I jump the gun? Suddenly, I was sad and self-conscious.

I tried to guard myself and not engage too much. I didn't want to break my own heart. I wanted it to be over. I wanted to crowd surf and ride it out, but something told me there was more to the story. It couldn't be that simple. There was no way, after what I had endured, that it could just be over and good.

Even the PA told me I wasn't allowed to use the words "in remission" for five years, and my oncologist told me twenty.

So what did this news even mean?

* * *

I was able to get my drains removed six days post-op. It was an odd sensation having them snake out a tube that was wrapped around the inside of my chest wall. It wasn't painful, just weird—like a giant worm. It felt like a pinch and a tug and then like they were pulling a hose through the grass, the grass being my body. It almost tickled.

I was so happy to have them removed. Sleeping and maneuvering and showering had felt impossible with drains poking me 24/7. I asked the nurse if I could measure my drains and she mockingly said, "Sure, if you have a tape measure."

Well, lucky me, Betty, I am a woman of many trades and keep one on my keychain! Each tube was sixteen inches long. Mind you, I'm only 5'2" tall so that tube was basically half my height all wrapped up and twirled around the inside of one chest pocket.

Ten days after my mastectomy, I went back for my first post-op. They handed me a paper copy of my pathology report and had the word YAY written on the top. Gold star for me. Good work. Somehow, I felt more excited when I got an A+ on a math test in seventh grade, which felt weird as this was a much bigger accomplishment.

We talked about the fact that I wouldn't get to work out for a solid three months, at least that's what they wanted. The expanders would start to be inflated on a weekly basis. They described what breast exams would look like moving forward, how they were going to watch me like a hawk for five years, the daily chemo pill (Tamoxifen) that I would be starting sooner than later for the next fifteen years. Slowly, any excitement of being cancer-free was fading, and I felt the fear of modern medicine being forced on me. The fear kept rising.

It could come back.
It does come back.
A lot of people don't make it if it comes back.
I still have to have treatment every three weeks.
I still have a port.
I still look like hell.
I still have another surgery or two.
I still have sores everywhere.
I still have to take a pill that causes other cancers.
I will never feel my chest again.

WHAT THE FUCK?!

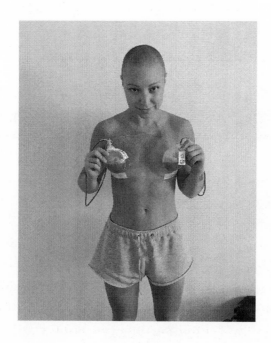

10.16.2018

Healing is not linear.

I read that this morning and it stopped me in my tracks. Think about it. There is so much freedom in that sentence.

I am dealing with the aftermath—a body that's learning to be pushed again, learning to lift my arms up, to grip things and not drop them, to have my brain be able to hold a full conversation without lagging, to not get dizzy every time I stand up. I'm dealing with a mind that goes between being so thankful and so scared. The fact that I have to take a tiny pill every single day for five years to lower my chance of recurrence, that I'm still getting treatment. I feel the need for time and space to process everything that has happened in the last six months. I'm realizing the trauma behind it all, but I also want to move forward and live my life. And then I get stuck in an old routine and old routine doesn't work for me anymore. It's not linear. It doesn't make sense, and that's okay.

The ups and downs of where I'm at are so blatant in my face right now. What just happened? Why can't I feel the joy of a clear pathology report? What was the point of it all? How did I do that? Shouldn't I feel a certain way? I am happy, no I am sad. Why am I still doing it? What's next? This hurts, it must be cancer. Also, thank you, body, for staying with me. I want to hang out! But why do I feel like I can't relate to anyone right now? It's a push and a pull of my heart and my mind. Some might call it a mindfuck, I'm calling it a mindfuck.

Nothing will make you more present than living each day knowing that life will either take a sharp left or a sharp right at any point and it's not always straight ahead. I will forever live my life this way by choice and by circumstance. As turbulent as that is, I am so thankful. What a gift.

It's not supposed to be linear. It's not supposed to make sense. It's not supposed to hurt all the time and it's not supposed to be happy all the time. It's supposed to make you present. That's how you heal. Life man...mindfuck. NONE OF IT IS LINEAR.

36: So wait, he literally whispers to your boobs?

Two days later I found myself back with The Boob Whisperer, also known as the plastic surgeon. He confirmed that he did, in fact, freestyle during my mastectomy. Bless that man.

He left the room so I could undress just to put the robe back on that he would ever so gently open as soon as he walked back in the door. Something about this part of our relationship made me a bit shy. I'm all for dramatic effect, but it seems like it would make much more sense for me to just take my top off, so he doesn't have to leave and it doesn't have to feel like an episode of *The Bachelor* in the fantasy suite. Then, if there are any surprises he can hide it on his face rather than slowly opening the curtain that is my robe to my bare chest and being like "holy shit, what happened?" or "damn, I did a good job." But nobody asked me. I didn't even know what modesty was at this point. I lost that fucker on the freeway in the first mile of this trudge. Anyway, it was suspenseful, so if it keeps people excited, then we will keep wasting our time with the old robe-leave the room—come back in trick.

At that point my boobs looked like a hack job. They were square and lumpy and discolored and misshapen and up to my throat. I only knew because I took one glance to make sure my nipples were there. I was a master at avoiding myself in mirrors by then. I didn't look because I couldn't recognize my own face anymore, let alone my own numb and lumpy chest. There were unpacked black bags under my eyes and even if I wanted to pack them up, I'm not sure I had anything left to put in there. There were blisters and pimples and boils around my eyes and on my legs and my ass. When I looked in the mirror, it was a lot of "who dis?" I was not equipped to answer that question, so I avoided myself at all costs. Head down always, eyes closed if they had to be, anything to not see what I couldn't handle. I wasn't ready to face the girl that I didn't know how to heal.

The plastic surgeon went on to reassure me that, yes, while the expanders suck, they were there to prepare the skin and muscle for the actual implant. I would be getting small amounts of saline injected through the port in the top of my expander every week until I was the size I wanted to be. You read that right, a giant needle to the tit to fill them up. This is where having numb boobs came in handy.

It's amazing how many people reached out to me during that time asking what size I was going to be. I couldn't even believe it. First, it was absolutely nobody's business. Second, it didn't matter and still doesn't matter. Third, I was clearly going for a triple F porn star, tip me over, top heavy. That size. Just kidding. But I did mess with people a little bit. Because people are nosy and have an opinion, and eighty-five percent of people don't understand that again, it's not a boob job. An implant under breast tissue is exponentially different from the same size implant under thin skin.

Lucky for me, I'm small, and I'm not super into boobs. I just wanted to look proportioned and be able to fill out a top. Three fills max. He had filled me to one hundred fifty cc's during surgery. So as far as I knew, I was halfway to my end goal.

During a fill, they find the port with a small magnet on a string that finds the magnet at the top of your expander, and it clicks onto it. For a moment, you could basically put artwork on your tits like you are a refrigerator. They write an X to mark the spot, then insert a large needle to inject a syringe of the sixty cc's of saline straight into the port at the top of the breast.

It didn't hurt, but I did feel pressure as the needle entered the skin, and through the port. As they filled me up, I could feel my chest tighten as the saline drained from the syringe to my breast. It was a very weird sensation, like filling a balloon with cold water inside of your body. They felt hot as the skin stretched and sat high and tight.

HELLLOOOO, boob job from 2003. My tits were in my neck. The week between fills was meant to let your body adjust, stretch, and relax. Until then, the saline sits high. The shape was odd, it looked like I had a sports bra on 24/7, even though the last thing I wanted to wear was a sports bra. I knew if I put one on in the morning, there was a solid chance I wouldn't be able to get it off until the mailman showed up, or my wife got home to help me, because my boobs were rock hard and did not budge. I never did take a full breath with the expanders in. They felt like rocks on my chest.

Somehow, I was still living at the doctor's office. I found myself singing a new tune at each appointment to keep myself from losing it. To the tune of twelve days of Christmas: *On the first day of appointments my surgeon said to me, what size would you like your breasts to be?!*

After my final expander fill, the appointments tapered down to infusions, oncologists, and heart scans. It was still insane, but much more tolerable as I continued to try to find my new normal. I tried to stop and digest the last six months, but I also didn't really understand it. It was still so far from being over that I wondered if it was impossible to process it yet, or if I ever would be able to at all. I started to feel a bit forgotten. Like it was over, and I should have had it all figured out.

11.7.18

People don't talk about life after chemo. "After" cancer. The processing is just beginning and the treatment isn't even close to ending.

Once the pathology is clear, it's a lot of high fives and "you must feel greats." And then everyone moves on as if you had a bad cold. They stop checking in.

Not for us. The truth is life after chemo (for me) has been much harder than life during chemo. At least during chemo, I knew something was killing my cancer. Sure, my energy is a little better and I don't look so terrifying. But what people don't see is the hormone therapy every 21 days, the open sores on my legs and ass from said therapy, the daily chemo pills, the heart scans, the banner across my mind when I see a cleaning solution or a French fry or a stressful situation that says, "DANGER...causes cancer." The extreme anemia. The next surgery dates. The itching all over my body where my hair is trying to come back. The insomnia. The loss of feeling in my body that I will never regain. The face in the mirror of the person I don't recognize anymore, the one who is forever changed by my diagnosis. How hard it is to relate, trying to find a new "normal." The drugs that they want me to take with the list of risks more terrifying than cancer. The scars, the bruises, the bone pain. They don't see the strength it takes to walk up a hill and not run out of breath. People don't see or hear the conversations with doctors discussing what cancer looks like the second time around and that it is, in fact, something that happens a lot. Something that I will never be free from fearing.

They say my risk of recurrence AFTER 20 years will be 1%. My initial chance of getting cancer was .44%...so while that number should be thrilling, it's also debilitating. I will constantly have to remind myself that there is a 99% chance that it won't come back, not that I have double the risk I had before.

So, am I cancer free? No, I don't feel that way. Because right now, somehow, my risk is sitting at 20% recurrence whether it makes sense or not. I'm not sure if those of us that have had it ever will, and I'm honestly ok with that. Just trying to navigate it all and educate people along the way.

37: Like I said, it's a trudge

12.10.2018

Today marked the halfway point in my year of treatment. I'm realizing that while the first part was brutal physically, the second part is proving to try to ruin me mentally. I fought back tears of frustration every second of my infusion today. My physical body is making it look like it's getting easier, but good God what a mindfuck. I feel sad. I feel tired. I feel lonely. I feel anxious. I feel confused. I feel side effects. I feel broken. I feel different. I feel lost. I feel trapped. It's hard to move forward when you have a standing date with a hospital and an IV. It's hard to move on when the daily pill you take to stay alive has a list of side effects longer than you can see.

Today I felt like I was running out of grace and for the first time since diagnosis, I felt extremely angry. I was also widely unimpressed with the condescending tone of my oncologist lecturing me on the drugs that have never touched her own blood.

This sucks. It blows. And yet it has provided some of the most beautiful moments of my life. SO, while today I am mad and lost and all the things, I am grateful. My life is big and if this is what big looks like, I'll take it...it'll pass. But damn.

* * *

We all know about the physical repercussions of cancer and treatment. Well, we do now anyway. But it's amazing to me how much harder the aftermath is—the mental part. It's confusing for people because a few months later, you start to look fine, whatever that means. My eyelashes and hair had started to grow back, and I was working and smiling because I had to. But life slowed down. I had a chance to think about all of the things that I had no choice but to put my head down and just DO, the stuff I was so brave for, the whole trudge if you will. It was traumatic, and it doesn't make sense. And my body is different. Every ache and pain sends me into a panic about another cancer. In fact, I've already had another cancer scare and a wand up my vag to check my ovaries. All clear.

My priorities have shifted. I no longer care about things. I have a hard time empathizing over things that aren't life, death, or injustice.

When you are diagnosed with cancer, your life completely stops. People go on, seemingly zooming around you like screaming kids on a rollercoaster. Meanwhile, you are waiting in line to get on said rollercoaster and that line never moves. People worry about what they ate last night that made them bloated, their ex-boyfriend's new girlfriend, what's happening on TV, how much money they are making, when they will get to the dentist, or how they'll cover their grey hair. They go to work and happy hour and workouts and complain that they are *tired*, over and over again.

And all the while, you just wish all of those people could have a day in your life to show them what tiredness really is and how privileged their *tired* is. You see their posts about being "dead" after a workout while you spent the year wishing you were alive enough to move the way that they have been instead of looking real death in the eyes. You watch them worry and obsess about things that used to worry you but now seem ridiculous. All the while you're longing to get back to a time when you weren't worried about how soon you were going to die, if your kids would remember you, or if your wife would remarry. What you wouldn't give to only worry about being bloated and getting to the dentist or if So-and-so's new girlfriend sucks or not.

When you are going through cancer treatment, you have a purpose. You have to live. Any purpose you had before cancer, or that you thought you would have after cancer disappears. Our one daily purpose is to live. That's it. You are surrounded by people taking care of you, checking in, sending words of affirmation and gifts, offering food, a place to vacation, monetary assistance. There is a buzz around your purpose. Afterward, it's like the line breaks and you only hear crickets.

It's scary to survive. It's lonely to survive when you feel like a part of you has died and nobody noticed. It also hurts to survive. No one is taking care of you anymore, and you just have to figure it out. To be completely honest, there isn't a lot that helps with this. You are just thrown back into life with a second chance and a "good luck see you in three months," expected to carry on like nothing happened. I felt like a rehabbed penguin being released back into the ocean—cold and alone, waddling lopsidedly, confused on whether to stay on land or go in the water.

* * *

I felt exceptionally lost around this time, so I flew down to LA to spend the weekend with one of my girlfriends. I wanted to get away, write, and clear my head. But most of all, I wanted to go see her psychic. I had never seen one before, and I thought, *Why not go when you feel like you might be the most lost you have ever been?* I was open to anything and everything but somehow, I wasn't sure how to put one foot in front of the other.

My girlfriend dropped me off the morning of my reading. I slowly walked up to an iron gate in front of an old house by the beach and was met by an older French woman named Sylvie. She said hello and instantly called me sweetie and walked me into her dining room. My friend had warned me that Sylvie would start reading me right away, but I still wasn't prepared for it.

I asked Sylvie if I could use the restroom before we started. I briefly stopped in front of her 1970s floral shower curtain. I couldn't escape flowers if I tried. They were smothering my peripheral vision. But I looked at myself in the mirror for the first time in nine months, all while avoiding my own eye contact. My hair had just started to grow back in, it was dark and about a quarter-inch long. I had a few eyelashes filling in, and if you didn't know better, you wouldn't have known I'd been sick. I had covered my body up in a mock neck dress and I had enough makeup on to fool someone. I just looked like a girl who had shaved her head for style purposes.

I told myself to relax and to hear this woman out. I was hopeful yet skeptical. But mostly, I just wanted to be hopeful. I think I was nervous that she could also tell me something I didn't want to hear.

I walked back in, and before I could even sit down, she started speaking. She said, "The hard part is over. The battle is over. You don't have to worry anymore." I was so confused. I hadn't said a word to this woman other than my name. She went on to say, "You've been fighting your whole life. Now you just get to enjoy being."

This shook me to my core. I HAD been fighting and doing. *What is "being"?* I wanted that. That sounded incredibly fulfilling. Like something you could be present to do. It almost sounded relaxing.

She told me I needed to write and to speak. I hadn't told her that I had been writing this book for nine months. She told me I would be successful. That I needed to speak about my story, all of it. That I would help a lot of people. That I would travel and write and speak—that was my path.

I was completely floored. *How did she know that I wanted to write and speak?*

She went on and on and toward the end, she asked me what had been hard recently, what I was afraid of. I told her I had been dealing with cancer. She told me that cancer wasn't something I had been "dealing with" at all. That everyone has cancer cells in their body and that mine just went a little crazy. She went on to say that my cancer was gone, forever. She assured me that I had nothing to worry about and that I was going to live to be a "very fun old lady."

Suddenly I was laughing through my tears. I believed everything she told me. I told her I was worried about taking Tamoxifen (the oral chemo pill) and listed my reasons. She said, "Your cancer is not coming back, that's not how you go." I was blown away. I felt free. I didn't know this woman, yet I felt like we knew each other better than anyone I'd ever met.

She kept circling back to writing my story and the theme of change. She kept repeating, "The hard part is over." She said, "For years you have been fighting. It's over. You get to enjoy being now. Just be."

That has never left me. I tried for months to grasp what *being* really was. But I get it now. I am different now. I am not doing, I am being. And when I forget, I go back to that Santa Monica conversation with Sylvie. She changed my life.

* * *

I flew home to my girls, and the next morning my five-year-old crawled into my bed to cuddle like she always does. She started rubbing my fuzzy little head and smiling. She held my face in her tiny, balmy hands, looked me in the eyes, and said, "There you are mommy. You were always there the whole time."

I smiled and kissed her head, and my eyes filled with tears as I realized just how right she was.

38: Hello? Me? Are you there?

Sometimes the healing hurts more than the wound. I wish someone would have told me that because nothing has ever felt more true. I am now almost two years post-diagnosis and I have just begun to process some of these experiences. Over the last few years, I have felt like I was stuck in a video game and couldn't get out. I felt like I needed to jump on a flower or whatever to advance to the next level. Finally, a way flowers could be useful.

It's crazy how normal moments still live and breathe in the middle of chaos and pain. People still go to coffee, fancy dinners, vacations, and concerts, while their friends are battling cancer. They still wash their cars in the midst of a divorce. They laugh about a joke even though they had seen a mass shooting on the news hours before. They go to work after their friend lost a pregnancy.

I watched all of this happen during my divorce and my treatment. We all watch it every day. Humans have a small capacity for sustained discomfort, and so we continue. We continue because it's more comfortable than to sit in it.

I didn't want to become paralyzed by my situation, permanently serious or jaded, letting the emotional battle eat me alive. But I also didn't understand how people could continue to laugh with ease while so much hurt was happening right in front of them.

Life goes on, even if yours stops.

12.11.19

I don't remember the girl before cancer. I get glimpses of what she felt like, I see pictures of what she used to look like, and sometimes I get mad because I so badly want to be her...to be carefree and not be self-conscious about the fact that my tits stay glued to my chest when I lift my arms in the air...to not assume that people wonder why I have weird scars everywhere and my hair is so short and curly...to not feel like I have to explain myself or worry that cancer is going to rob me of time that I so badly want to spend on this earth. I wonder what it would be like to remember what my life used to feel like, I wonder if it's even worth remembering at all. I wonder if my vision will ever return to normal, or my brain for that matter, or if my pinkies will ever work again, if I can reverse the autoimmune disorder it left me with. What it would feel like to get a manicure instead of a blood draw on a regular basis...to be saving for college for my kids instead of a yearly out-of-pocket max. I wonder if my body will ever feel like my own, or if it will always feel like two different people trying to be one...

BUT...then I see photos like this and I am reminded of how much this body has put up with over the last 10 years...stress, abuse, pregnancy, trauma, being stripped of everything the world calls "feminine," and being faced with death in my early thirties. It's mental and physical, the whole thing. This body is resilient as fuck and although it is forever changed, I am thankful I live in it.

It just makes me think...For as much time as we spend wishing things could be different in our bodies, what if we just repeated the things it has carried us through. Would we spend so much time wondering about the what-ifs? Probably not.

* * *

Grief is weird and it shows up in different ways for different situations. Sometimes it is blatantly in your face, and sometimes it sneaks up on you. It shows up as fear, pain, sadness, anger, loneliness, confusion. It shows up when you are the most vulnerable and/or the weakest.

Sometimes you just have to meet yourself in grief; stare at it face-to-face. Let it break you, make you sob, crack you open, and soften you. My grief dismantled who I was as I knew her, my entire being. I was left with a heart and a desire to live and do right by the people around me. My grief broke me, and it was my soul that got to rebuild me. Every. Single. Time. Grief has been my biggest life teacher.

2016 is when I dealt with most of my divorce. My grief showed up as anger, sadness, fear, and pain. 2017 is when I dealt with coming out and navigating a same-sex relationship. My grief showed up as fear, loneliness, and disappointment (despite meeting the love of my life). 2018 was when I dealt with a life-threatening disease and the majority of my cancer treatment. My grief showed up as fear and loneliness. 2019 is when I dealt with much of the physical and mental aftermath of cancer. My grief showed up as pain, anger, and confusion. I held it down like a full-time job for four solid years of my life.

I can't even tell you the amount of people that said either of these sentences to me at the end of each of those years: "I bet you can't wait to kiss this year goodbye" or "I bet you can't wait to shut the door on 20xx."

HOLD UP. WAIT A MINUTE.

I love my life. Even when it was excruciatingly painful, I loved it. You don't get to pick and choose what happens and be thankful for some of it, but not all of it.

How many highs have we experienced from lows? How much joy from pain? How much beauty and learning from tragedy? How dare we decide what other people feel about their experiences? How dare we assume that all hard situations are bad?

We are allowed to be completely shattered, burned, and melted into the ground and let ourselves rebuild into something beautiful. We are allowed to sit in it and not want to rush through it, to let it shape us. I chose to sit in my grief like a stone in water. Letting it rush all around me and smooth me out until it finally moved me to a better place, a different feeling, a new day, or a new year. It wasn't ever going to be a quick fix.

I always responded to these comments with "actually, I loved this year." I would tell them that if they couldn't wait for a certain time period to be over, it clearly made them uncomfortable, so they learned something, and that right there was a gift. I wanted to change the dialogue. I could always dwell on the fact that my life was torn apart, my mental and physical bodies were ravaged, and my dreams for certain years were shattered, my marriage failed, and I was let down by family or friends' reactions. Or I could be thankful that I got three hundred sixty-five chances to wake up each year and make an impact and live a bigger life. I'm not sure why you would want to shut the door on that. The difference is a choice.

There were moments in my life where I didn't have to worry about life getting better, because I knew it would. And I didn't have to worry about it getting worse either, because it was inevitable. And I have never had to worry about life staying the same, because I wouldn't let it.

Our reality changes in minuscule ways every single second. I've always seen each day as a massive opportunity because as far as I know, tomorrow doesn't exist. I am annoying when I wake up, always have been. It's usually way too early, I pop out my retainers and smile at the day and wait patiently for my family to wake up, so I can basically congratulate them for waking up too. And if I didn't think my family would smack me, I'd probably start clapping and whistling too, but this all happens before 7 a.m. so I don't. All that to say, this didn't change when I was in a horrible relationship, or navigating how to be with a woman in a homophobic world, or when I was having a daily stare down with mortality. I was excited about my life every single day, even when it was hard or out of my control. A chance for something better, a chance to feel it all, to connect. A chance to change.

My oncologist and I never saw eye to eye. I never understood why she couldn't back up any of the research or the recommendations with proof. I had been receiving treatment for eleven months and one week, and I was certain that this last infusion was overkill and doing more harm than good. At my final infusion appointment, I showed up with my own research and conclusion as to why I felt I didn't need to finish my final treatment, I had wanted to quit months prior. I dug up the answers that everyone seemed too scared to share. I pushed and I prodded, and I asked all the questions that an oncologist dreads their patients ask. I proved the points and challenged the research.

In the end, she told me I was right and that I no longer needed treatment. That I could leave without a needle to the arm and check in with her in three months. As I was walking down the hall to leave, I heard her call my name. I smiled as I turned around, slightly surprised.

She said, "You were put on this earth to push, you know." She paused. "And you are doing a really good job."

The corners of my mouth curled up to my ears as I said thank you. I turned around, walked out the double doors to the parking lot, tears streaming down my face, and realized that she saw me.

39: There you are

It has now been a little more than two years since my initial diagnosis. I've gone back and forth on whether I should even write this book. If anyone cares, if it would even help a single person, and how to end it—because it never ends.

I've often wondered if this book would fall on blind eyes or deaf ears. I didn't know all the answers to those questions, but I did know that it would help one person—me. I spoke at an event recently and while most people just figure I will speak about cancer when I speak these days, instead I spoke about abuse and how I believe that it was the stress of an unhealthy relationship and coming out that led me to my diagnosis. Nobody knew these huge struggles I had been through; they only knew of the one I publicized, which was my cancer.

I realized as I was telling my story that the reason I was so vocal about cancer in the first place was because I wish I had heard someone else talk about all of these experiences before they happened to me. I often wonder how much more equipped I would have been if these issues weren't so taboo to talk about. If people weren't scared to say the whole truth.

How much could I help people if I spoke up about the struggles in my life? The ones that were at times too scary and lonely to bear. Would it help to share how I decided to start living my own life instead of having others live it for me? What about exploring the feelings that I fought so hard to feel, the things I felt shame over or guilt about because of what society taught me?

We can always learn from other people's experiences. We have all stumbled, tripped, or fallen—walked into situations we weren't prepared for. We all have scrapes, scratches, cracks, and scars to prove it. Yet how often do we open ourselves up to experience the depth of them? We are so quick to bandage them up in an attempt to heal them faster, so nobody sees the pain or shame of a skinned knee or a broken heart.

The healing process is wildly intimate, but if our instinct is always to cover up, or look away, how do we truly overcome hurt? We long to connect and feel understood and have our emotions and experiences validated. But if we don't have the courage to heal in the open air, if we don't leave our wounds open to help others heal their own, how do we truly connect, grow, and experience?

Healing is uncomfortable. It just is. But you feel a hell of a lot less alone if you heal in a vulnerable space. You know what else is uncomfortable? Forgiveness. And just like healing, it's not linear.

I have had to learn to forgive when I was still hurting, when the other party didn't ask for it. Sometimes that other party happened to be myself. Forgiveness isn't always something you just decide to do and then it's done. Sometimes it's a daily choice, a reminder. Sometimes it's two steps forward and two steps back. It's a practice. It can be humbling, and it can be daunting. It's saying thank you for an experience. It's freedom to move on without anger. It's good for the immune system (seriously, Google it.) But no matter what shape it takes or how it feels, it's always part of the healing.

* * *

It's interesting looking back on what I've written, or even where I was a year ago. I've spent the last year dealing with a new diagnosis of Hashimoto's disease, an autoimmune disease that was brought on by the chemotherapy. (Nothing like a sluggish thyroid and some food sensitivities to kick you when you are down.) I have kept my chin up for the most part, but I have been utterly exhausted and at the doctor's office more often than I would have liked.

I was the face of Ulta's breast cancer awareness campaign in 2019 and will be for 2020 as well. I've also been the poster child for many cancer nonprofits, fundraisers, and fashion shows. I've spoken on multiple podcasts and events. I finally realized that I couldn't be everybody's support system or token young, cute cancer girl. I have learned to say no to some of these requests as they have proven to be triggering for me. Cancer changed me, but I want to move on. I don't want it to define me for the rest of my life.

So while I will always speak about my experience, I cannot hold everyone's hand through theirs. This is where I hope this book can help.

* * *

I had a breast reconstruction at the beginning of 2019 that left me with rock hard double D hooters up to my throat, and while I tried to be grateful, I couldn't actually take a full breath because they were literally choking me. They were so wide that they were rubbing my arms raw. I went in for a revision of my initial reconstruction later in the year. I'm happy to report that the girls are much softer and smaller now, but that left me with an incision that took over four months to heal. Needless to say, I was at the doctor every week, yet again.

My hair is curly and messy and large and hilarious and each week I look like a new character. Simon Cowell, Ronald McDonald, a lemon, a mushroom, George Washington, a sheep, Betty Crocker, and my personal favorite...an eighth grade boy who needs a haircut. Bonus points on the mornings that my eyes are red and swollen from the lash serum I keep using to make these post chemo lash stubs grow. Those mornings I look like an eighth grade boy who needs a haircut and is high. Keeping a sense of humor has been crucial through this process because man, it is humbling. Some days I would still prefer to be bald.

I see my oncologist for a whopping seven minutes and $632 bucks every three months plus whatever the lab fees are, so basically a vacation fee, without a vacation. She asks how I'm doing, lectures me on why I should really take Tamoxifen, rolls her eyes like I'm an idiot when I continue to say no, feels up my fake boobs for lumps, and then leaves. Of course, she doesn't leave before scaring me into thinking that my cancer will come back and kill me. She tells me I have a 20% chance of recurrence. But I like to think of it as an 80% chance of non-recurrence. It's a super healthy relationship that we have, and I'm looking forward to seeing her less as time goes on.

I tried to go to therapy per my wife's suggestion, and while EMDR therapy was extremely beneficial after my divorce, I realized that I had already let go of everything cancer related. Maybe *let go* isn't the right phrase, but I've processed it. Neither my therapist nor I could figure out why I was sitting in her chair. It's funny, of everything that has happened in my life, the cancer experience didn't scar me as much, not mentally anyway. I was in a constant state of flow, or maybe it was the drugs, or the surrender. I was present.

Don't get me wrong, I have my moments when I cry because a memory resurfaces, and I can't believe that these things happened to me. Or that I got through them. Or that they were okay to do to someone. The ones that get me the most are the memories alone in the infusion center, or alone and bald, crying on the bathroom floor between fits of dry heaving. But even with that, I have an overwhelming sense of peace in my bones about...well, all of it.

I let myself feel each emotion when it comes up until it passes. I just stare at it and rest in it until it releases, reliving these moments with a clearer head. When the traumas resurface, it's almost as though I'm watching it happen to someone else. I can't believe that it was me. Again, maybe it was the drugs. Or maybe I have changed that much. This feels oddly therapeutic to me, though. I didn't remember a lot right off the bat, but now that the fog is lifting, I see it so much clearer. It's devastating and beautiful and painful and healing all at once. I can honestly say that I am proud of how I have handled each situation.

My relationship with my ex is not perfect, but it's better than it has been. We are in a good place. We can be in the same room, and we always have our kid's best interest at heart. I can only hope that one day we can apologize for hurting each other, and acknowledge what happened, how it got us to where we are now, and move forward. What happened between us made us both a better partner for the spouses we have now, and I am thankful for that.

I've had to accept that he married someone much younger than me, and that she is also allowed to love my kids. That they will feed them processed foods more than I'm comfortable with and provide vacations we may never be able to afford. That my kids will always start sentences with "At daddy's house we have..." or "We went to...this weekend." And I also have to accept that he had to accept that I also married someone that gets to love his kids. It is a very weird thing. But all in all, I am glad he chose who he did.

I still have a few bruises from how my coming out went with my family. I have learned the overwhelming power of reactions and of hesitation. I can only have grace for them and use the experience to shape my own parenting. I hope my kids feel safe to talk to me about who they love, without fear of judgment or of disappointing me. I hope they are comfortable coming to me when they need to get out of a hard situation. I am thankful that my parents and I are in a good place now, and they love our family despite it looking different than they had pictured.

I've realized that while some of my support system and friends disappeared through these trials, the right ones stayed. It still hurts. My relationships with the people who stayed stand strong. And my relationship and bond that I have with all three of my girls is unbreakable. We leave nothing unsaid and sweep nothing under the rug.

* * *

Change is funny. We as humans ask for it all the time, but we want it to look a certain way. And then we aren't satisfied because it's been so curated and insulated with expectations. We get so mad when things happen or change without our blessing, but that isn't how it works. Life changes. Dramatically and drastically. And crazy enough, it doesn't always give you a heads up.

Sometimes, at first glance, the changes life throws at us are not pretty—and other times they're wildly painful. Sometimes it's both. Other times they're amazing and unexpected. That's life. We make resolutions like the course of our lives is one hundred percent up to us, wanting control over every second of it. But that's not living. Living is being. It's opening your arms to everything that comes your way—good or bad—and making the best of it.

Here I am, changed. Mentally, physically, emotionally. And never in a million years did I think that these things would happen to me, nor did I think they would make me better as I was going through them. But I can honestly say, I am so incredibly thankful. For the lessons, for the scars, for what I have learned, and what I will continue to learn. For perspective, for true love. My capacity for growth and empathy and feeling anything and everything has grown exponentially. I never asked for an easy life, I asked for a big one. And here it is.

Have I moved on from any of this? No. Have I gotten over it? No.

There are still days that I can't even look myself in the eyes because I am not ready to deal with what's behind them.

Have I moved forward? Yes. Was any of it okay? No. Am I okay with that? Yes.

Listen, you don't have to move on. It doesn't have to be okay. You don't have to get over it. I didn't heal because time passed. I am healing because of how I work through these massive shifts in the time I am given, how I process it all. I am healing through finding my voice and being completely at peace with being misunderstood at times. I am healing through writing, speaking, and feeling truly seen. I am healing through healthy conversations and relationships.

All these intricacies of my life are a part of who I am. They change shape and emotion and move forward with me, as a part of me. They are written in scars on my chest, the way my eyes see my children, the grey hairs on my head, the numbness of my pinkies, the openness of my heart, and the smile lines around my eyes.

I was so out of control of my own life at certain points that the only thing I could control were my thoughts. And while it was never the easy option, I chose joy every single time. It was my force of stability. It would have been a hell of a lot easier to let the worst of my situations get to me, to be angry and resentful. But that's not inspiring, and it sure as hell isn't fun or fulfilling. I want a fun life. I want a happy life. Being mad is exhausting. Pain is exhausting. If joy is a quick trip out of pain, I'll take it...even if it's a round trip and I have to come back to pain before I can find joy again. It's worth it.

In the end, I think life isn't so much about what happens to us, but more about how we approach those things. Maybe it's about how we happen to life. I will choose, every day, to open my arms and joyfully feel it all to the best of my abilities. To leave myself open when I hurt. I will let it dump rain on my face time and time again as I look up for the sun. And I'll do this for as long as I am given access to this big, beautiful life.

All that said, when the next load hits the fan—please, don't send me flowers.

Acknowledgements

For those that told voted "Yes" that day during chemo on whether or not I should write a book called *Shit You Didn't Think Would Happen To You*—and for the two of you that voted "No", thank you. You didn't know the fire that both of those answers would light in me just by having an opinion. Always answer the polls and always have an opinion, you could inspire someone to do something terrifying. And side note, I only changed the name so it could sit on your coffee table without your kid saying "shit" all day. You're welcome.

To my wife—You once wrote to me: *I am fairly convinced this is not our first time loving each other, and that it won't be our last. In fact, I think we will be together for many more lifetimes, and that's why this love feels like home to me. That's why all the certainty, despite the trying circumstances. That's why all the growth and the lessons, so we can keep expanding. That's why all the silliness and the laughter, because you are my guiding light to who I strive to be.* It's like you read my heart in that letter. Honey, your love and support never cease to amaze me. I could write a whole book on what you mean to me and perhaps that will be my next one. I am thankful for every excruciating moment that led me to you and every beautiful one in between. You are my home. Thank you for choosing me, fighting with me, seeing me, and loving me unconditionally. I love you.

Harper and June—You are the reason my heart beats like it does, the reason I fight like I do, the reason I know the depths of what love is, and the reason I need Botox. You make me better and for that I am thankful. May you always use your voices and fight for what you believe in.

Mom and Dad—For supporting me even when it was hard to understand, being open to change, and for always being a call away. For raising me to be honest in a world that is less than and for loving me unconditionally, thank you. I love you.

Bro—I love you.

To my Ex—Thank you for the lessons and for helping create these two little miracles we call our children.

Sarah—Girl... where do I begin? Thank you for sending me your phone number after two weeks of a bald girl whining to you online. Who knew a cancer bff could come from the internet? I'm not sure I could have gotten through some of that without you.

Juice—I'm so glad we decided not to hate each other. Thank you for always standing by my side through the unexpected and for always making me laugh. Lord knows I need you in my life.

Alex—Thank you for supporting me through literally everything. All those late-night talks on the floor and capp creams when H was a babe solidified this friendship forever.

Jill—For all the confessional nights. And everything else. I adore you and am forever thankful for your support.

Stace, Em, and Shay—You guys were a force when I needed force in my life. Thank you for not telling the world I snuck cigarettes when I was stressed and for watching my girls when I was single and broke. For always holding my laughter and my tears—thank you.

Jessi—Thank you for taking a chance on me and hiring me when Steph wasn't so sure. Your support is everything and the memories we share are unparalleled, especially the NYC ones.

Bethany—Thank you for advocating for real flyers in hospitals. God, I love you. And girl-look at this cover! You are so talented, and your spirit and generosity are unmatched. Thank you for taking on this project with open arms and seeing it through.

Gia—I had no idea how much power this cover photo would have when you asked me to shoot just hours before my mastectomy. There is equal grit and a softness in this photo that is hard to emulate. You captured so much of what keeps me going and who I am. Thank you.

Amy—Who knew you would look back on photos of your own bald head and have so many emotions? Thank you for your time and your gift of capturing what was so hard for me to see in the moment.

Val—Thank you for being the first stranger to believe in the message of this book.

To my friends on divorce team Lianne, coming out team Lianne, and cancer team Lianne—Thank you for showing up, no questions asked. So many moments of those periods were lonely and terrifying. You never needed an explanation; it was just all hands-on deck with a side of good music and a whole lot of joy. I will never be able to fully express my gratitude for your support during those moments.

To those who helped via Go Fund Me, meals, vacations etc.—You know I'm terrible at asking for help. I never thought I'd need to be on the receiving end, but you truly changed my life. I am humbled by your generosity.

To everyone who helped keep my body alive and looking somewhat normal—my surgical teams and their staff. To those who helped keep me going on this book trudge. To those that said the wrong thing. To those that said the right thing. For those that had and continue to have the uncomfortable conversations. To those who came out before me and fought for true love. For those who used their voices and their platforms for change. To everyone who danced and is still dancing. And for those that sent flowers, thank you.

About the Author

Lianne Saffer often describes her life as an endless quest to feel it all. She is a wife, mother, writer, fitness instructor, hair stylist, and advocate for helping people live a loud and authentic life. In her free time, she enjoys listening to her music a little too loud, dancing with her kids, paddle boarding (or doing anything really) with her wife, making jokes that only she thinks are funny, and writing. On any given day you can find Lianne buying yet another houseplant, working out, remodeling her house, or loving on any cat that will let her. She lives in Portland with her wife and two kids.

Saffer believes that we should all use our voices to better each other and create true empathy and understanding. She believes in raising strong women and telling the truth about hard situations. She believes in opening conversations that society has closed and asking questions where you were taught not to. Her goal is to reach and empower as many people as possible with her writing and speaking events in the future. This is her first book.

LIANNESAFFER.COM

INSTAGRAM: @LIANNESAFFER

Made in the USA
Las Vegas, NV
02 April 2021

20675068R00187

INHERIT THE EARTH

From aunt Mildred

Dec - 1975 -

INHERIT THE EARTH

Helen Harding

OLIPHANTS

OLIPHANTS
BLUNDELL HOUSE
GOODWOOD ROAD
LONDON S.E.14

SBN 551 00166 6

Printed by Love & Malcomson Ltd., Brighton Road, Redhill, Surrey, England.

In memory of F. G., who
was always ready to open his home to
visitors from England

1

Norman Blaker scratched the frost from the window pane and stared gloomily out at the swirling snow, already beginning to pile up on the Canadian sidewalks.

"They didn't tell us winter came this early," he commented to his young wife. "Everyone said : 'Go to Canada —the land of opportunity! The land of new beginnings.' That's a laugh! Three weeks in this wonderful 'land of opportunity' and I still haven't found a job."

Janet silently studied the pattern on the dishes she was putting away. True, there was some reason for Norman's bitterness. With the seasonal unemployment that the Canadians talked about, Norman might not get any work until the spring and, as he had said cynically, "by that time we'll starve!"

She knew she must calm him, so she said quietly, "Perhaps it's just a freak storm, darling. After all, the middle of November is rather early for winter to begin . . . although of course Canada *is* a cold country."

"I know, I know, but . . . we thought it was the one solution to our problem. 'Go right away where people do not know you,' we thought, 'where nobody knows you've made a mess of your career because of one mistake. . . .'"

"You *didn't* make a mistake, Norman!"

Norman swung round, took a stride across the room and gripped his wife's shoulders. "You *still* believe I was innocent? You're still sure it wasn't me who played that rotten trick?"

"Of course I'm sure, darling," Janet sighed, soothingly stroking his cheek. "I only wish you'd tell me the full story, but even if you won't, I refuse to believe you could have had anything to do with it. It's just not like you— I've known you nearly ten years, remember, and after four years of being married to you, I should be qualified to judge—just a little!"

The black look fled from Norman's face as he drew her into his arms.

7

"I don't know how I could have endured the past months without your faith in me, Jan. Whatever happens, I shall never forget it."

"And you're going to justify that faith," Janet replied, firmly. "I know it's disappointing not to have found a job of any kind, but you'll get something, you'll see. Meanwhile . . ." As Norman made to break in, she carefully put a hand over his mouth. "No, you are going to hear me out this time. It's silly for us to be so worried when I could easily get a job myself—even if it's only as a copytypist. We've no children to keep me at home. . ."

"That's another thing. . . ."

"Yes, I know we've been disappointed about that, too. But while there are none, and while we're in this difficult situation, I *can* work. We were very fortunate to find this little apartment for such a reasonable rent. Maybe it's not one of the smart, modern ones we had seen photographs of, but it's clean and comfortably furnished, and good enough to start with."

Norman sighed and turned back to the window.

"What are we going to do today, anyway?" he asked resignedly. "Can't look for work on a Sunday."

Janet came and stood beside him without replying immediately. Then, hesitantly, she said, "Look what a lot of people are going into that church opposite." Ignoring the way her husband had stiffened, she continued. "I watched them last Sunday; they seem such a happy, friendly crowd, driving up to the church in their cars, and waving and chatting with everyone."

"Same as Christians the world over," Norman's scowl was back again. "Very pleasant on the outside, but how deep does their religion go? Don't think you're going to get me back to church—not after the way some so-called Christians treated me. . . ."

"Norman," Janet's rebuke was most gentle, "you can't go on bearing grudges for ever. I know we had that unfortunate experience. Perhaps we'll find it's different here. In any case, we haven't made any friends yet—apart from the landlady and her husband. Couldn't we try the church?"

"You really *want* to?" Norman's look held astonishment.

Janet nodded. "You know, dear, it's not the people who matter—it's *God* we worship. Even Christians are human and make mistakes. Let's try again, please," she pleaded.

Still Norman was stubborn. Silently Janet prayed even as she looked at the thin line his lips had formed. "Won't you come along to a service, Norman—just to please me?" 'And to please God,' she added silently.

He looked down at her sweet face framed in dark curls and gradually his own expression became softer. "All right," he murmured as he stooped to kiss her, "just for you—but don't think I'm going to make a regular habit of it."

Her smile was enough reward and within ten minutes they were making their way across the road towards the brick-built church. Even as they walked up the steps, they were conscious of an air of friendliness, and as they reached the open door a tall man with a lean face and small moustache smiled a welcome and held out his hand to them.

"Good morning, sure is nice to see you," was his greeting. "You folks strangers here?"

"We're just over from England," Janet supplied the information. "We've only been in Canada three weeks—we live opposite."

"Why, that's just wonderful," the man beamed. "Here, come along and sign our visitor's book. Then, we'll find you a seat."

Before Norman could hesitate Janet went forward and took hold of the pen the man offered. Quickly she signed her name and handed it to her husband. Norman could do no more than follow her example.

They were greeted just as cordially by the sidesman, given a printed order of service and a hymn-book, and shown to a seat about half way down the church. The form of service was familiar to them both and Janet soon felt at home. When the choir stood up to sing, she held her breath but as the anthem proceeded she gradually relaxed, glancing sideways at her husband. The singing was good; Norman could have no complaints about it and his musical ear would not be offended.

When the time came for the notices to be given out, the

9

minister said, "We are delighted, this morning, to welcome to our church Mr. and Mrs. Norman Blaker, from England. I understand this young couple have only been in our country for three weeks, and we pray that they will be very happy here. We hope they will feel free to join in any of the activities which they see listed on our printed order of service."

At the close of the service, Janet followed Norman quickly from the pew and up the aisle to the door where the minister was shaking hands. She knew her husband would try to avoid speaking to anyone, but she need not have worried. The minister had spotted them and was already extending his hand.

"How lovely to have someone from England," he said. "I spent a couple of years there during the war and just loved your country. Are you here to stay or just on a vacation?"

Despite Norman's black moods, he was by nature courteous and responded to warmth in another's personality. He smiled, somewhat weakly it was true, but Janet knew the first hurdle was over.

"We're hoping to stay and make a new life here," he said. "That is . . . if I can find employment."

"I see," the minister seemed interested. "What kind of work are you looking for?"

Norman hesitated for a brief moment, glanced at Janet, and then said, "Well, I don't mind tackling anything; one can always improve one's position by looking around, but just at present I'd even be glad of a labouring job."

"I see," the minister said again. "Well, I might be able to help—if I hear of anything, I'll let you know."

"I didn't really mean to bother you, but . . ."

"No bother at all," the minister smiled. "We like to help newcomers all we can. I'll be in touch, Mr. Blaker."

Norman stumbled his thanks. "It's very good of you, Mr. ——?"

"McCall is my name—the Rev. Bruce McCall. Now, do we have your address?"

Janet felt it was her turn. "We live just across the street," she said, and supplied the number of the house.

Mr. McCall turned to smile at her and said he'd call to see them one day soon.

10

No word passed between husband and wife as they crossed to the old colonial-style house where their apartment was situated. They climbed the stairs and let themselves into their rooms.

Janet took off her coat and glanced at her husband. He met her look.

"So . . . they're friendly," he remarked. "But we'll see."

"You did enjoy the service, though? The minister can really preach, can't he, and . . . the choir was good, wasn't it?"

Norman nodded. "Yes, I admit that. However, I'm not getting mixed up again with church choirs. The soloist was quite good—nice, pure tones—but what goes on behind the scenes at choir practice?"

"What do you think about the minister's invitation to attend some of the activities?"

Norman spread his hands and shrugged. "You can please yourself. I don't intend to get involved. All right, I'll go to church to worship God on Sundays, if that's what you want, but that's where it will end."

Wisely, Janet decided not to pursue the matter, only too glad to have persuaded her husband thus far.

*　　　*　　　*

The weather did not improve; in fact it became worse. The snow piled up at the sides of the roads where the snow-ploughs had dumped it after clearing operations, and there it stayed, frozen even more solid with each new fall. The landlady assured them the cold weather was here to stay till spring so they might as well make the best of it.

Mrs. Boyle was a poker-faced type of woman, but pleasant enough. Her husband was an invalid, confined completely to the house during the winter, so Janet excused the somewhat blank look on the woman's face each time she bade her a cheery "good morning."

In spite of her husband's protest, Janet found a typing job with a small machinery firm, just ten minutes walk from where they were living, and started work that very week. Meanwhile, Norman tramped from the unemployment bureau to various appointments, but always it was

11

the same story—someone had just been taken on; they were very sorry, and they would keep his name on file. . . .

Although his mood was anything but cheerful, Norman was not one to sulk; rather he gave vent to his feelings by grumbling excessively, or stamping about the rooms, his heavy brows drawn tightly together beneath his thick dark hair. He felt most uncomfortable that his wife was earning while he sat at home, but he saw to it that she came in at lunch-time and in the evenings to a table well laid and a meal prepared.

As she stumbled up the stairs one evening, he opened the living-room door, noticed her faltering steps and went half way to meet her, taking her bag and putting his arm around her shoulders.

"Jan, whatever's the matter—you look washed out?"

Janet gave a weak little laugh. "It's nothing—I've just had a fall."

When she was comfortably settled in the only armchair the apartment boasted, Norman eased the story from her.

"I was so happy to see those huge flakes, and the way the snow was making everything look beautiful, that I forgot to walk carefully. I was tripping along thinking what fun it all was, when I got to the place where the cars swing out from that parking lot at the corner of the street. I hesitated because I'm still uncertain what these Canadian motorists are going to do next. One car started coming out but the driver waved me across, so I started to hurry. The next thing I knew, I was lying flat on the road and looking up at the chrome on the car bumper, listening to the engine revving up. I scrambled up pretty quickly, I can tell you!"

"But are you sure you're not hurt? Why, he might have driven right over you!" Norman was all concern.

Janet laughed and assured him that except for some bruises she felt fine.

"The driver hopped out of his car and helped me brush the snow off my coat. You know, I believe I recognised him as one of the choir in church on Sunday, but I couldn't be sure."

"Oh," Norman's comment was brief and non-committal.

"Well, just be careful how you cross roads in future," he continued sternly. "Go slowly."

"That's the trouble. I'm terrified of crossing these great, wide streets. What with the traffic being on the other side of the road, the quick change of the lights before you can even get half way across, and the hooting of the horns; then the roads are so slippery . . . oh well, we'll get used to it, I suppose."

She began to wonder if she ever would, however, as it became colder and colder. Getting out the fur coat a relative had thoughtfully passed on to her when they left England, Janet bundled herself into it and stepped outside. The radio announcer that morning had said the temperature would rise to about zero (Fahrenheit) during the day but it was now twenty degrees below that, even though the sun was dazzling. After a few yards walk along the street, she grasped her collar even more tightly about her, noticing how her breath had frozen as it touched the tips of the fur.

Her forehead soon felt so cold that she put up her gloved hand to cover it, and bent her head down in an attempt to withstand the wind. Walking along thus, she did not notice anyone coming towards her until, suddenly seeing a man's feet immediately in front of her, she looked up, only stopping just in time to avoid a collision.

"Oh, I'm terribly sorry, I wasn't looking where I was going, I'm . . ." her voice trailed off as she saw the man looking at her intently. She was relieved when he laughed.

"Why that's O.K. Bit chilly, isn't it? Aren't you the girl I nearly ran over the other evening?"

Janet could think of nothing to say, but merely nodded.

"And I saw you in church on Sunday, didn't I?" the man continued.

By this time Janet had found her voice. "Yes, that's right . . . you were in the choir, weren't you?"

"Ah, you noticed me as well? Didn't Mr. McCall say you had only been here three weeks? You came from England, I believe. Say, why don't you and your husband come along to the club tonight?"

"The club?"

"Yes—the O.F.S.L. Club. Couples, single people—any-

13

body's welcome. We meet on the first and third Thursday nights in each month. One of our projects is to publish the church newsletter—there'll be quite a production team there tonight, two or three dozen of us working on it. Come along and see what happens."

"What time does it begin?"

"Sharp at 8.15—see you there." And he was gone.

When Janet told Norman about the invitation, he shrugged and said he wasn't interested but she could go if she liked. However, as she tried to describe the young man who had spoken to her, he grinned suddenly.

"Perhaps I'd better come along, after all," he said slowly. "Can't have young men inviting my wife out, even if it's only to a church club. What did you say it was called?"

Janet told him.

"These Canadians!" he commented. "They always call things by initials; we'll find out what they mean soon enough, I suppose."

"And you really mean you'll come, Norman?"

He sighed. "I suppose I might as well. Gets a bit boring being on my own all day. Might as well be with you when I can, and you seem eager to go."

Giving him a quick hug, Janet set about washing the dishes and doing a few other household chores. She hummed while she worked, trying to still the excitement within her. The people at the church seemed so friendly. Surely Norman would respond, and by so doing find his way back to the God he had served so well in past years.

She sighed as she remembered how some of the people in their church at home had shunned him when they believed he had been mixed up with a theft at the school where he taught. True, the evidence all pointed to his being involved but, although she did not know the full details, she sensed there was some special reason why he didn't deny the accusations. He had even forbidden her to tell anyone that he was a teacher because looking for another teaching post would require references. Better to get some kind of manual job and make good at that, and forget teaching.

14

"Let's pray about it, Norman," Janet had pleaded. "God will guide you to the job He wants you to do."

Norman, however, would have nothing to do with that line of thought. He felt that God had let him down; perhaps he *would* understand why things had happened the way they had, one day, but just at present he couldn't seem to get on very well with praying, and people who had called themselves Christians had disappointed him bitterly. But Janet continued to pray.

*   *   *

They both felt a little shy as they made their way to the side door of the church. Pushing it open, they blinked at the sudden light, and the confusion of people standing about inside. Then Janet spotted the young man whom she had met that morning, and made her way towards him.

His face lit up. "Ah, there you are—your husband, too—that's good. My name's Alex Moore: Let's see, you are . . ."

Norman stepped up and supplied their names, and Alex introduced them to at least a dozen of the people nearby in a matter of two or three minutes. He touched an attractive girl, just a bit older than Janet, on the arm. "Beverley, I'd like you to meet Janet and Norman Blaker—they were in church on Sunday, remember?"

"Why, sure I do—nice to see you both. Grab your sister, Alex, and let her meet Janet and Norman."

Alex's sister added her welcome and turned to her husband, the man who had greeted them at the church door on Sunday morning. "Stan, you've met these folks, haven't you?"

"Sure have. Nice to see you here."

Alex continued the introductions: "Tom over there is Beverley's husband—you must meet him later—he's busy setting up a film we're to see; but here's Pat and Ted . . . Clare, Bill and Marion, Marg and Frank, Bunny and Joe —he's this year's president—Emily and John. . . ."

Bewildered, Janet was almost glad when they were all called to sit down and begin the meeting. The way these Canadians had responded to Alex's introductions and welcomed them both was overwhelming.

15

She was very impressed by the spirit of the meeting. Gay and friendly these people might be, but there was also a deep reverence and sincerity among them which became more and more obvious as the meeting proceeded. The girl whom Alex had introduced as Beverley led a short devotional period as a start to the meeting. Then notices were given out by Joe, and Janet was pleased to see how interested her husband seemed to be in the announcement of a "tally-ho party" to be held just before Christmas. Soon, Tom stepped in to introduce a missionary film.

An hour sped by quickly and Janet began to think the meeting would be coming to a close. Once the film was over, however, and the general discussion which followed it, everyone trooped into another hall where long tables were set out and piles of duplicated sheets put ready for the willing workers.

Noticing their hesitancy, Beverley took hold of Janet's arm. "Come and sit beside me up at this end, both of you. This is the church newsletter, which we send out each month. The sheets have already been duplicated—some of us were busy until midnight last week typing the stencils under Alex's direction (he's the editor). Now, we put the pages together, staple them and mail them off."

Norman was immediately interested and wanted to know how many were sent out.

"Close on three hundred. That's to every church family, ex-members and other interested people. It's some people's only contact with the church they grew up in, or where they were once in membership for a few years."

While they were working, Janet managed to ask Beverley about the name of the club.

The girl laughed. "O.F.S.L.? Sounds like a secret society, doesn't it? It just stands for 'Others First, Self Last.' You see, we all used to belong to the Youth Fellowship. Then most of us got married and we began to feel too old when some of the younger people joined. So a group of us broke away and left the youngsters to run the Fellowship themselves. We felt we wanted to do something different so formed this club, mainly to render any service to the church, or individuals for that matter, that we could."

16

"What else do you do, besides publishing the church newsletter, then?" Norman asked.

"Well, the repair of the church's hymn-books is one of our projects. Then we always decorate the church for Thanksgiving and for Christmas—that's something that'll be coming up soon, too. Oh, and we'll be preparing Christmas hampers for old people." She went on to tell them that they had parties for themselves as well, and urged them to join in the forthcoming tally-ho.

"It would seem that you look *outwards* rather than inwards, all the time, as some Christians do," Norman remarked dryly.

Beverley nodded. "That's the general idea. We enjoy hearing about other places and people—we'd like you to give us an evening, sometime, and tell us about England. Most of us have never been there, but we often dream! Tell you what, why don't the two of you come over to our house after church on Sunday evening? Tom would love to chat with you."

Just then, there was a general cry of welcome as the minister put his head in the door.

"Hello, folks! Glad to see you all working hard! Sorry I couldn't get here earlier." And without any more fuss, he sat down and joined in the work.

The evening rounded off with coffee and cakes, then the benediction. As everyone was putting on their coats, Mr. McCall came up to Norman. "Any news of a job yet?" he inquired.

Norman shook his head and told him that Janet was working, but he had found nothing.

Mr. McCall hesitated, then, turning to include Janet in the conversation, said, "I'd like to call tomorrow evening, if I may, and have a chat. I have a suggestion to make."

Stan tapped the minister on the shoulder. "Pardon me, Mr. McCall. I presume you have a church key? You remember Jack won't be around to lock up tonight?"

The minister nodded. "Yes, I'd thought of that, thanks, Stan. As a matter of fact, I've been to see him this evening. He seems to be making good progress, but must remain in hospital for a number of weeks, I'm afraid. But we'll manage, I daresay."

17

Alex came up at that moment to offer Janet and Norman a lift home.

"That would take you right out of your way, Alex," the minister teased. "These folks live just across the street!"

In the general laughter that followed, Janet and Norman received more "goodbye's" than they could count and, with the assurance that they would see everyone on Sunday, they turned towards home.

*　　　*　　　*

On the following evening, Janet had rushed around the apartment several times tidying this and that, while they waited for the minister's call. At last, the bell rang and Norman went to let him in.

When they were settled and the usual pleasantries over, Mr. McCall said, "I think you said, Norman. you'd be willing to do any kind of work?"

Norman nodded. "I don't like being idle. Anything would be better than wondering what to do with myself all day."

"You may have heard us talking about Jack last night," the minister continued. "He's the church caretaker. A couple of weeks ago, he slipped on a piece of ice and fell heavily. He's fractured his thigh, and you know how long that's likely to take to heal. The members of the O.F.S.L. Club have been most helpful but we need somebody full-time, especially to keep an eye on the heating at this time of the year. I don't know if you've had any experience of this kind of thing, and of course it's only temporary work, but I thought you might be interested."

Janet held her breath. Would Norman accept? Then, she saw the irony of the situation. Norman Blaker—qualified science teacher in a boys' grammar school, organist and choirmaster at one of the largest churches in their home town, being asked to sweep floors and look after church premises. What would he do?

18

2

JANET DID not trust herself to speak after the minister had made the offer of the job to Norman. Silently, she watched as her husband got up and paced across to the window. The clock on the bureau seemed to tick like a trip-hammer, and the slight throbbing of the central heating system punctuated the stillness.

She wondered what McCall was thinking about Norman's hesitation and glanced surreptitiously at him. In a flash of insight, she realised that this kindly gentleman had no doubt met so many people with emotional struggles that he would never be surprised, only sympathetic. She noted his long, slim fingers as he rested his chin on his clasped hands, his strong, regular-featured face in repose, his eyes lowered, his dark head slightly bowed.

At last, the tension was broken. Norman swung round as he spoke.

"All right, Mr. McCall. I'll be your caretaker—just until this Jack is well enough to come back to the job. I've never done anything like it before, but it'll fill a gap. Thanks for the opportunity."

The minister's face, although still serious, brightened. "That's wonderful, Norman. How about coming over to the church first thing in the morning and I can show you all over the premises?"

Norman nodded. "Just one thing, Mr. McCall . . . er . . . I was wondering . . . will you need any references?"

Janet caught her breath on a gasp. She had forgotten, for the moment, about this possibility. Would it mean taking the minister into their confidence?

Bruce McCall looked at Norman keenly for a moment or two, as though endeavouring to read his character. And Norman did not flinch, but gazed straight back at those

19

steady eyes. Evidently the older man was satisfied with what he saw.

"I consider myself a pretty good judge of character," he said at last. Then with an impish grin which immediately made him look younger, "Anyways, we'll take a chance on it! I figure you need work so badly, you'll look after the job and do it well. I'm sure I can count on you."

It was Norman's turn to grin and Janet knew the reason. How often, as a schoolmaster, he himself had encouraged the boys in his charge in just the same manner. Trust a boy, and he'll seldom let you down; let him think you are suspicious, and he'll often disappoint you.

"I'll do my best, sir," was all Norman said, however, unconsciously adopting the attitude and words which might have been used by one of his scholars.

While Janet made coffee and brought out the cakes she had baked in readiness, Norman and the minister discussed salary and hours. Mr. McCall turned to Janet as she set down the tray of cups.

"I should just mention something about hours," he said, including her in the conversation. "I would be grateful if your husband could lock up the church last thing at night; this will mean turning out in the cold again before going to bed and, as you know, there is something going on at the church nearly every night. . . ."

"But living so close to the church, that shouldn't worry us," Janet tried not to sound too eager.

Norman agreed. "I won't mind that, Mr McCall. And anyway, it's only a temporary job."

When the minister at last rose to go, they felt they had made a real friend.

"See you about nine in the morning, then—come straight to the church office, and I'll see you there," Mr. McCall said as he left them.

Norman was silent again as Janet washed the cups. She kept glancing at him, wondering if she should say anything, trying to read his mood.

Suddenly he laughed, and it was a bitter laugh. "Church caretaker—that's a good one. Oh, well, with all the rooms in that large building to look after, I shan't have time to get involved with church activities. I shall have to be behind the scenes; looking after the boiler, setting out chairs

20

for meetings, making sure no-one is making a noise while people are occupied with their prayers behind closed doors. Suits me!"

Janet bit her lip as the tears stung her eyes. This was not the reaction she'd hoped for. A feeling of depression stole over her and she was tempted to make a sharp retort, but thought better of it. She merely sighed, hung up the tea-towel and announced that she was going to have a bath.

Next day, being Saturday, Janet was at home and she anxiously watched from the window as her husband went across the street to the church sharp at nine o'clock. He was much brighter when he returned at lunch-time, and quite talkative about the premises.

"It really is a large building to keep clean," he told her as they ate their meal. "I don't know how Jack has coped, as it is. That new wing at the back of the church—you know, where we had the meeting of the club—was only completed last year. It's the Christian Education wing, and was paid for, apparently, by every member conscientiously tithing! Anyway, according to Mr. McCall, it's already proved its worth, for the young people's activities are flourishing, and the Sunday-school work is being handled in a more effective manner."

"Is it a departmentalised Sunday-school?" Janet ventured to ask.

Norman nodded. "Yes, and they've recently employed some of the more modern methods—to advantage. It means, of course, greater training for the teachers, more equipment and more space for the children to move about. But it does bring religious training more in line with the way subjects are taught in ordinary school. You know, they don't get any religious instruction in the day-schools here," he sounded surprised.

"More need, then, for better Sunday-schools," Janet remarked. "How about the heating system; is it difficult to cope with?"

"No, I think I should be able to manage. It's far more advanced even than the one we had at Harwood Grammar, and I thought that was efficient. But they really know how to use labour-saving devices in this country. Well, time I got moving. With Jack being in hospital for the past ten days, things have piled up and there's plenty to do—dust-

21

ing the pews ready for tomorrow's services, for instance," he added wryly.

"Norman . . . shall I come across and help?" Janet offered.

Her husband shook his head. "No, you've enough to do with the housework here. I can manage. Oh, but you might like to come along to the hospital with me this evening. I thought I'd go to see Jack and get a few tips from him. Mr. McCall thought it might be a good idea, too." Then, with that sudden softening which she loved so much in him, he drew her to him and kissed her lips. "Sorry to have been such a bear, darling. . . . I should be grateful for the job, really—I'll try to make a go of it."

Janet was glad to go with her husband to the hospital that evening. They soon located Jack Simmons in a small room with only one other patient in it. Jack was a small, lean man, probably in his late fifties. His cheeks had a somewhat sunken look, but his eyes were extremely alert beneath a deeply-lined forehead and thin, dark hair. He greeted them heartily.

"I'm right glad to see you and know you'll be carrying on for me until I'm through with this little lot," he indicated the plaster on his left thigh. "Get proper bored sitting here day after day, I can tell you—never done such a thing in my life before. Silly I was not to notice that bit of ice; you get a bit careless after the summer and before the winter sets in properly."

"Yes, it's too bad," agreed Norman. "Still, I'll carry on until you're fit. I just thought you could maybe give me a few tips and tell me something of your routine."

"Well now, there's nothing to it, really. But you must make sure the heating's O.K. this weather, and that the snow is cleared from the sidewalks round that corner and the steps—they can be really tricky with frozen snow on them, you know. And my word, there's plenty who'll complain if those jobs aren't done ready for the Sunday services!"

Norman raised his eyebrows. "They get after you, eh?"

"Oh aye, they do—some of 'em that is; others are real nice and know a body can't do more than he's able. But that Mr. . . ."

Norman lifted his hand in protest. "Perhaps you should

let me find out that sort of thing for myself—no names mentioned, please! Just tell me about the actual work."

Jack needed no second bidding and went into a long rigmarole about where everything was kept, what "not to bother with" and what had to be done "else there'll be a rumpus, no mistake."

Janet noticed with relief that Norman was faintly smiling as they left the ward. But his only comment was, "It seems I've taken on quite a job."

* * *

They were both looking forward to visiting Beverley and Tom the following evening and, after the church service, they were whisked off by Tom in his car, skimming over the frozen roads as easily as though it were summer.

"Don't you get nervous, driving in these conditions?" Norman asked as they went along.

"We get used to it," Tom's replies were usually brief and to the point. "Our cars are fitted with special winter tyres as soon as the cold weather sets in, and we carry bags of sand and other equipment in the trunk to help us get a grip if we should become snow-bound."

"The trunk?" Janet queried.

Tom laughed. "I guess you know it as a 'boot' in England —we have different names for many things here. What do you call the hood of a car, for instance?"

After a little discussion they laughingly realised that in England it was known as the bonnet. Thus, chatting in a friendly, easy manner, they soon drew up at a wooden bungalow, with banks of snow covering the open garden and a freshly-swept path leading to the front door.

As they got out of the car, Beverley opened the door. "Hi!" she called. "How are *you*?" It was a typical cheery Canadian greeting.

They discarded their over-boots on the front door mat and Janet walked through to the bedroom with Beverley.

"I've just got the kids to bed," Beverley chatted on. "It was my handsome husband's turn to be at the church this evening, so he missed out on that chore this time."

Janet smiled to herself. Tom was not what she would have called handsome—just big and comfortable looking,

23

with a pleasant face—but it was obvious that Beverley adored him.

"It's good of you to have us over," she said, a little nervously.

"Not at all—we love to entertain people. Alex Moore is coming along, too; don't know if he'll be bring his current girl-friend or not—you can never tell with Alex. I'm not quite sure who he has in tow at present. Gay old bachelor, that's him!"

"Old?"

"Well, he's thirty-five, like Tom, and we keep telling him it's time he settled down. But I sometimes think he never will."

By the time Janet had taken off her outdoor clothes Alex had, in fact, arrived—alone.

"No girl-friend tonight, Alex?" Beverley queried.

Alex's homely features took on a slight quirk but his face was expressionless as he answered in his breezy, abrupt manner, "No, not tonight—I left them all at home."

"And that's all we'll get from him on that subject," Beverley murmured in an aside to Janet. "He's a close one, is Alex."

If Alex overheard the remark, he ignored it as he said, "That was a good solo of yours this morning, Bev."

"Why thanks, Alex," Beverley's face, which was always attractive, glowed just a little more and her eyes sparkled. "Praise indeed from you!"

"I thought it was good, too, Beverley," Janet was quick to add her comment and was even more surprised when Norman joined in.

"I agree. Whyever don't they give you the solos all the time? You've a far finer voice even than the girl who sang last week."

Beverley flushed and hesitated a moment. "Oh, no," she said then, "that wouldn't do at all—the others must have their chance. Besides, I'm never sure when I can be there with three small children."

It was an informal and extremely pleasant evening, and both Janet and Norman enjoyed the conversation, ranging from a serious discussion of the evening sermon, to some light-hearted banter about the sleighride which was being organised by the O.F.S.L., and which they called a "tally-

24

ho." All three of the Canadians were interested to hear about life in England, and Janet found comfort in talking about it for she had been feeling a few twinges of homesickness during the past week. She was almost sorry when it was time to leave, and Alex drove them home.

*   *   *

The night of the tally-ho was crisp and clear, with the dark sky liberally spread with stars and a full moon adding light to the scene of snow-covered paths and heavily laden trees and bushes. Everyone packed themselves into available cars and drove out of the city to one of the prairie farms. Clambering out of the vehicles, Janet heard Norman beside her gasp at the sheer beauty of the Canadian winter scene.

"What are those lights in the sky?" she asked Beverley who was standing nearby.

"Those are the northern lights," her new friend told her. "Sometimes they even turn red, but those bright green ones are lovely, aren't they?"

"What a wonderful sight!" put in Norman. "It somehow makes the North Pole seem nearer!"

The sounds of bells attracted their attention. Two white horses, impatiently pawing the ground, stood ready harnessed to an over-sized sleigh. Bells and pink rosettes were fastened to their harness. It all seemed to Janet like something out of a storybook.

Soon everyone was aboard, and off they went—about thirty of them—with bells tinkling, horses trotting, the driver cracking his whip and everyone singing the good old-fashioned songs; some known to Janet and Norman, and others obviously of Canadian or American origin.

When one or two of the girls got pushed off the sleigh into great piles of soft snow, there were squeals and hoots of laughter. No harm was done for it merely felt like tumbling into a soft, billowy blanket. Janet wanted the ride to go on and on but Alex, who had been sitting beside her for most of the time, assured her there was more fun to come.

The sleigh took them back to where the cars were parked, and once again they crowded into the vehicles.

Next time they stopped, it was in front of a large house where a middle-aged couple named Marion and Bill lived. Marion was a short but extremely smart little lady with soft, neatly-waved white hair and a face which, even when not actually wreathed in its usual smiles, looked pleasant. Her husband, Bill, was a large, jolly man who said little but laughed a lot and was obviously as much in love with his wife as on the day they were married.

"Come on in, everyone!" Marion called. "Leave your rubbers in the hall and take your coats upstairs, girls. The fellows can hang theirs in the hall. Food's all ready, so don't be long!"

"I'll say it's ready," quipped Bill. "We've been working at it all day!"

Janet's eyes nearly popped when she saw the spread Marion had prepared. There were great, steaming bowls of meat-balls resting on beds of spaghetti, plates of mixed salads of different varieties, an assortment of breads, and several large cakes. Three or four percolators of coffee stood ready on the hot-plate.

"Hello, dearie," Marion made a special point of welcoming Janet. "I'm so glad you could come along to the party. And it's just lovely to know your husband is able to help us out at the church just now, too."

"It's good to be here," Janet returned, deliberately making no comment about Norman's job. "What a lot of cooking you must have been doing."

"Oh no, I haven't done it all. . . ."

"But your husband said . . ."

"Don't take any notice of his jokes," Marion laughed. "At these 'do's' most of the girls contribute something. Fiona there . . ." she indicated a plump, middle-aged, cheerful-looking woman, "brought along the meat-balls, I cooked the spaghetti, Beverley and Peggy made cakes, and Clare has been over helping me with the salads this afternoon."

Janet was conscience-stricken for a moment. "If only I had known, I could have helped."

"We'll give you time to settle in before we ask you to take a turn; don't worry at all. But if you like to help at another party, well then we'll see."

She was such a friendly soul that Janet warmed to her;

for some reason she began to think of her own mother, although really there was little similarity.

The evening finished off with more singing and then, quite suddenly, there was a hush and Tom stood up.

"Friends, we've had a wonderful time tonight, and we do want to show our appreciation to Marion and Bill for their hospitality. . . ." He was interrupted by a burst of clapping. "Before we part, however, shall we spend a few moments thanking the Lord for His goodness and asking Him to prepare our hearts for the services of tomorrow."

Seldom had Janet felt more moved. To round off such an evening of frivolity by changing to a more serious mood and drawing close to God in prayer was, to her mind, a perfect ending.

She commented on this when she and Norman were alone in their own home later. Her happiness was soon shattered, however, when a scowl appeared on his face.

"It was all right, I suppose," was his short reply.

"Surely, Norman, you enjoyed the evening?" Janet was astonished.

"*You* evidently did. You hardly spoke to me all evening —you were too busy talking to Alex!"

Janet stared at him, her mouth dropping open in surprise.

"Whatever do you mean? You surely don't think . . . Why, that's absurd! I was talking to everyone—particularly Marion. And I saw *you* having a chat with several of the girls as well as the fellows."

"Maybe, but this Alex seemed to make a bee-line for you whenever he had the opportunity. Just watch it in future— he seems a bit of a gay lad, that one."

Janet opened her mouth to speak, and then thought better of it. An anxious frown clouded her brow. Norman saw it and softened immediately.

"Sorry, darling," he murmured more gently. "I guess I just felt a bit out of things. Don't let's quarrel over it—it's Christmas next week and we want it to be a happy one.

*　　　*　　　*

Christmas Eve was a glorious day; brilliant sunshine in an equally brilliant blue sky, with the myriad twigs and branches on every tree coated in hoar frost; a veritable fairyland of nature. The frost shone like silver as it sparkled in the sunlight, making the city, busy with last-minute Christmas shoppers, almost beautiful. The glitter of the tinsel in the department stores was nothing compared with nature's own decoration. Janet's homesickness soon fled in this glittering, sparkling land of the "white Christmas."

She made her preparations for the following day in a happy frame of mind. Beverley and Tom had invited them to their home for Christmas dinner; Norman's good humour had returned, and all seemed ready for them to enjoy the festive season.

When she drowsily awoke on Christmas morning, she had that delicious feeling of excitement which she had never lost since childhood. Her thoughts, however, turned to her family in England. She glanced at the clock; just coming up to nine. What would everyone at home be doing, she wondered? Having breakfast? No, for their time would be different. Still very sleepy, she began to make calculations. There must be a difference of six hours between this part of Canada and her home town. That meant it would be three in the afternoon and everyone would be gathering in the lounge to . . . three o'clock—the Queen's speech!

She shot out of bed so quickly that Norman woke with a start. She dashed into the living-room before he could realise what was happening, and began frantically turning the knobs on the radio. Sure enough, in a matter of seconds, Her Majesty was speaking. Janet could, of course, have read the speech later, or probably heard a recording. But in that split second that her mind had cleared, she had known that this was the one thing she could do on this important day that would be the same as her family was doing—and at exactly the same time. She felt the invisible link that families experience at Christmas-time the world over.

When the speech ended and the first strains of the National Anthem sounded, there was a lump in her throat. Before the tears which were misting her eyes spilled over she was aware that Norman was standing in the door-way. Quickly he came to her and gathered her into his arms as she sobbed out her homesick heart.

"I know," he comforted. "It's times like this that you remember all you've left behind, isn't it—Mum, Dad and the family? And you did it for me—you didn't really want to come. It's been tough, I know, but thank you, darling. I'm sure everything is going to work out all right for us."

Numbly Janet nodded. 'Pray God, it will,' she thought silently.

The National Anthem gave place to Christmas carols and the homesick, couple silently listened, their arms around each other, their hearts beating as one in a moment of understanding.

Then, the breathless quiet was shattered by the sharp, insistent ringing of the telephone. Reluctantly, Janet stretched out a hand to pick up the receiver as she was nearest to it. She started as she recognised the voice at the other end. Placing her hand over the mouthpiece she gazed anxiously at Norman.

"It's Alex Moore," she mouthed to her husband.

His frown was immediate. "Whatever does *he* want on Christmas morning?"

3

"Hi!" CAME Alex's breezy voice over the telephone. "Just called to wish you and Norman a Merry Christmas. What are you folks doing?"

Briefly Janet explained that they had been listening to the Queen's speech and would later be going to dinner with Bev and Tom. Then she went on, "Merry Christmas yourself, Alex. Are you spending it with your sister?"

"Sure thing. We've been up since the early hours, too, seeing what the kids have in their stockings—Peg and Stan have three girls, you know. But what I really called for was about New Year's Eve. Have you any plans?"

"Why no, Alex, we hadn't really thought about it."

"It's a big event here, you know, and January first is a holiday. Someone in our crowd usually has a house-party and this year Peg's giving it. She thought you and Norman might like to come along."

"That's very kind of her—I'll speak to Norman about it and let you know—and thanks a lot for thinking of us."

"That's O.K. Have yourself a good time today. Cheerio for now. Probably see you at the service this morning."

Janet passed on the invitation to Norman as soon as she had rung off. He grinned. "These Canadians are always throwing parties," he commented.

"Well, I suppose New Year's Eve is rather special."

"Umm. It would be rather nice to do something, wouldn't it? No need to ask if you would like to go."

"And if you're honest, darling you would, too—at least you always used to like getting together with a happy crowd of people of like minds to have a good chat, with a bit of fun thrown in. . . ."

"Yes, with people of 'like minds.' Trouble is, I don't really know my own mind these days—I don't seem to think the way I used to anymore."

Janet put her arms around her husband. "I know, but basically you're still the same wonderful person you always were, and you'll come out on top. You're just in a muddle for the present."

He gave no answer, for he knew she had hit on the truth.

After the Christmas morning service at the church, Janet quickly exchanged greetings with the various people she had begun to know, thanked Peg and Stan for their invitation, and promised Bev they would join her within a couple of hours. Then she hurried back to her home while Norman waited until everyone had left before locking up the church. She needed just a few minutes alone; a brief period in which she could draw near to the One who had sent His Son to bring peace. And she prayed that Norman might find that same peace of mind.

The day was crisp and clear, although cold, but Janet and Norman decided to walk over to Bev and Tom's home; it was not very far. As they stepped out along the snow-packed sidewalks they frequently had to stand aside for a child eagerly trying out a new sledge, or for proud young parents pulling their offspring along on conveyances with runners, the streets not being suitable for wheeled prams during the winter. At the street corners, any large enough piece of ground had been flooded and allowed to freeze, making perfect skating rinks for the children to try out new ice-skates, and they were certainly making the most of the bright sunshine to do so.

They turned into the main street which ran through the city. Loudspeakers outside the store on the corner which had been playing recorded carols during the past few weeks rang out with "Joy to the world, the Lord has come!"

"Doesn't that sound nice, Norman?"

"Umm, not bad—a bit tinny this canned music, but it does add to the festive atmosphere, I suppose. They must have set up some automatic device for the recording machine to keep going throughout today—the store's not open, of course."

"The whole city seems to have been singing one big carol for weeks, with Christmas music pouring out of stores and cafés on every street," remarked Janet.

"The music in the church was good the past two Sundays, wasn't it?"

Janet could hardly believe her ears. Norman rarely had anything good to say about the church. "But you didn't come in to any of the services—how did you hear the music?"

"Oh, I listened from the vestry at the back. Wanted to hear what this choir could do at Christmas-time. Not bad at all, really."

"I think *you* could train them even better, and you're certainly a finer organist," his wife told him quietly.

Norman looked at her sharply. "I'm not getting mixed up with *that* again; choir directing is a thankless task, trying to keep the peace between soloists, and struggling to get some kind of musical response out of a lot of wooden people. Whatever you do, don't mention my past work in the church choir here—promise."

"All right, I promise. But this choir's so good, I wondered if you would enjoy being in the tenor section; they're a bit short on that side."

"No, I wouldn't. Alex Moore seems to be able to hold his own all right there, with the support of those other two chaps."

Janet said little else during the remainder of the walk.

Nowadays, it seemed that Norman's irritability was so quickly roused. Would he become worse? Surely, something would happen to turn him back to the easygoing, dependable man she had married.

Nothing could have lifted the nostalgic feeling in Janet's heart more than the happy day they spent with Bev and Tom, and their three children. Paul, the eldest, was a serious-looking boy and just beginning to realise that, at nine years old, he was growing up and capable of looking after his mischievous six-year-old brother, Gene, while his mother coped with little fair-haired Gail, who was just three.

"Your little girl is sweet, Beverley," Janet remarked as she helped her new friend with the washing-up after a traditional Christmas dinner.

"She's a poppet, isn't she?" readily agreed the mother. "I just love her. I guess I should be a bit more modest about my children, but I'm afraid I do think they're rather special."

"I envy you," Janet tried to make her tone light, but she bit off the words just before her voice trembled.

Beverley touched her hand in sympathy. "I'm sure, in God's good time, you'll be similarly blessed, my dear," she said softly. It was one of those intimate moments which were becoming frequent in the friendship springing up between the two girls, for they had enjoyed several heart-to-heart talks during the past few weeks.

Later, they all gathered around the piano, Beverley playing (reasonably well, as Norman afterwards remarked to Janet) and all of them joining in the well-loved carols, singing whatever parts they wished in the harmonies, while the children's voices rose in shrill trebles above their elders'.

It was when the children were in bed and they were enjoying a final cup of coffee that Beverley remarked to Janet, "You should join the choir, Jan. Sounds as though you have a nice voice, from what I could hear."

Janet glanced quickly at Norman, and he replied for her.

"Not a bad idea, Beverley. I know she'd like to; she's no soloist but she can hold a tune well."

"Well, thank *you*," Janet laughed, relieved beyond measure at the effort her husband must have exerted to agree to Beverley's suggestion.

"Are you musical, Norm?" Tom asked suddenly. "You seemed to be doing O.K. with the harmonies yourself, I thought."

Norman looked at him sharply, and hesitated; then he said quickly and breezily, "I leave that to my wife. No choir for me, thanks."

"Well, come along next week, Jan," Beverley went on with her persuasion. "I'll introduce you to Blair Andrews, the organist. He's a bit of a 'fuddy-duddy' and scathingly sarcastic if anyone strikes too bad a discord, but I believe his bark is worse than his bite. Anyway, we've learned to ignore his remarks, and he's a good musician. He'll probably want to give you a voice-test, and then . . ."

She was interrupted by a shrill little voice from the direction of the bedrooms. "Mummy, I can't go to sleep."

"I'll see to her," and Tom immediately rose and went to his small daughter. But she was not to be put off.

"I want Mummy!"

Soon, all adults were gathered around the little one's bed. She was not upset, but still flushed with the excitement of the day.

"What is it you want, honey?" asked Bev.

"I want to hear you sing about the baby Jesus again," piped the wee mite.

Beverley's face was tender as, very softly. she sang the children's favourite carol for what must have been the twentieth time during the past few days: "Away in a manger, no crib for a bed . . ."

Before the carol was ended, the little girl had closed her eyes, her lashes long and dark over her petal-like cheeks. Janet felt Norman's hand take her own in yet another moment of deep understanding; it set the seal to her happy Christmas Day.

*　　　*　　　*

The New Year's Eve party with Peg and Stan, and their new friends, was a gay and cheerful affair.

It was not a large crowd; Bev and Tom were there, and of course Alex. Then Marion and Bill arrived, and finally Clare. Clare seemed to be a special friend to everyone, although to no-one in particular. Tall, dark and very striking, she had a vibrant personality. Her sister, Pat, with her husband, John, had also joined them.

Not one of the friends was particularly boisterous or could be called the "life and soul of the party"; but everyone enjoyed being there. Most of them had grown up together and their friendship had matured at the same pace as their years. Each respected the other and took pleasure in the contribution every person had to make to the fun. Various games were organised by Stan, as host, and even Janet lost the wallflower feeling she had often experienced in her younger years. She noticed also that, although Norman obviously avoided having too much to do with Alex, he seemed glad they had been invited to share their friends' New Year celebrations.

'How could we help but enjoy ourselves, though,' Janet thought to herself, 'with Peggy giving everyone the kind of welcome that makes them feel they are really important.'

Peggy was rather different from her brother, Alex. A vivacious, outgoing personality. she kept up a steady flow of chatter, jumping in at once whenever it seemed that a lull in the conversation might cause boredom.

"There should have been more of us," she explained briskly. "I phoned the organist and asked him if he would care to bring his sister along and join us. You can imagine what the answer was!"

Clare laughed. "Too true. I don't know what you choir-members do to Blair, but once the music side of any occasion is over, he hops off before anyone can even say 'Hi' to him. And he drags Mary Jane off, too, which is a pity."

Beverley laughed. "But she never seems to want to go anywhere without him. Honestly, she just idolises Blair—there never was such a musician, in her eyes. No wonder she's never got married; no man could hope to compete!"

"Don't you be too sure about Mary Jane not wanting to go anywhere without Blair," put in Marion wisely. "It's my opinion that girl would've loved to come along to this party. But she seems swamped by her brother, somehow. Whenever I've spoken to her, I've found her the sweetest girl. Since their parents died, she's devoted herself entirely to looking after Blair."

"We'll have to keep asking her out—without her brother —and help her enjoy herself more," Pat joined in. "Why don't you have a try, Alex? You're usually the one to champion the 'lame dogs.' She could do with a bit of the Moore charm!"

It was said in good part and everyone laughed, but Janet sensed that Alex was embarrassed. She felt it was her turn to jump in with a remark to turn the conversation in another direction.

"You've made me curious to meet this organist," she said. "Do you think he'll accept me into the choir, Beverley?"

"Why sure, he will," Beverley assured her.

Peggy bounced back into the conversation. "You're joining the choir, Jan? That's wonderful! We'll look forward to seeing you up there. You and Norm both seem one of our crowd now. I keep meaning to ask you, too, Norm—how do you find the job at the church?"

"Trust my wife to ask an embarrassing question," Stan laughed. "You shouldn't put him on the spot, Peg. If he didn't care for the job, how would he answer you? Say, tell me though, you two. I hope you don't mind the way we shorten your names to Jan and Norm. We all do it here, as you've no doubt noticed."

"We don't mind," Norman said pleasantly. "In fact, it's quite a change—a new name, for a new life, in a new country!"

Janet beamed into his eyes, unnoticed by the others as they laughed.

"But I will answer your question. Peggy—or should I say, Peg?" Norman continued. "I don't mind the job at the church, for it's a change and better than doing nothing, or rather tramping around to interviews. Besides, it's only temporary. And if I may add my small bit to the conversation about your organist—I often hear him practising, you know. He's quite good. But I agree, he's a very close character. I can never get two words out of him."

Tom had not been saying a great deal; just observing Norman quietly. Now he asked, almost casually, "What work did you do in England, Norm?"

Norman hesitated barely a minute. Then, as though he had prepared himself for this inevitable question, Janet heard him saying, "Oh, I mucked about in a science lab. here and there—nothing very special. I thought I might be

35

able to find something more interesting in Canada, but I've seen nothing yet."

Tom and Stan exchanged glances but, before anyone else could speak, Peggy announced that the food was ready.

Alex had offered to drive Janet and Norman back to the church for the watch-night service and as they made themselves comfortable in his car he asked, "Have you folks seen many of the decorations about the city?" When they told him they hadn't, he turned the car round and headed in the opposite direction. "We're in plenty of time, so we'll go the long way round," he told them.

Soon they were slowing down, and drove at a walking pace past houses gay with the lights of Christmas. Not only were there trees lit up in nearly every front window, but many of the trees growing in the gardens had also been hung with lights and the porches and rooftops were outlined with strings of twinkling red, blue, green and yellow. On the gently-sloping roofs of some single-storied dwellings, Christmas scenes had been set up, softly flood-lit in various hues. There were Santas in sleighs, reindeer, snowmen, groups of carol-singers and many other motifs. Returning towards the heart of the city, they saw lights strung right across the wide streets and in front of some of the more important buildings, gigantic Christmas trees towered glittering to the sky.

Janet's eyes were sparkling as brightly as the decorations by the time they reached the church.

"Wasn't that kind of him, Norman?" she whispered excitedly as they went in to the service together. "Fancy going to all that bother!"

Norman looked down at her shining face and didn't reply.

After the service, she stood beside him as he waited to lock up the church. As the last car pulled away he put his arm around her. "Happy New Year, darling. May it bring us much joy."

*　　　*　　　*

The following week, Janet went along to the choir practice and when Beverley saw her she led her towards the organist. He was a tall man, in his early forties, obviously very short-sighted judging from his thick glasses, with fair, wavy hair and a slightly sardonic expression. He greeted Janet somewhat vaguely, and asked her to remain after the practice so that he might give her a test. She enjoyed the evening and was somewhat relieved at the end of the try-out when Blair Andrews pronounced that she would "do" for the soprano section. As she was obviously not of solo quality, he seemed little interested in her.

Norman was waiting for her when the interview was over, and Alex was also standing around. They both sounded pleased to know she had passed the test.

"I was just wondering . . ." Alex continued, a little hesitantly, "I believe you're a typist, Jan?"

Janet nodded.

"What with Christmas and New Year celebrations," Alex went on, "it's not been easy to get enough people together to do the typing for the church newsletter. Could you help me? There's a typewriter here in the church office, and I thought of coming along tomorrow evening to get some of the stencils done."

As always, Janet looked to her husband. He was scowling, and Alex had noticed. "You don't mind, do you, Norm?" he asked quickly.

"Oh, she can do it if she likes," Norman replied ungraciously. "I shall have to be over here myself seeing to the heating in readiness for the weekend, so she'd be alone at home."

"All right, then, Alex," Janet cut in hastily. "I'll help you out. I'm used to typing stencils, and shall enjoy it. Norman can come along and give us moral support."

Norman merely grunted.

The church felt eerie the following evening as Janet entered, and there was a hollow atmosphere about the place. She had, however, seen a light in the office so made her way upstairs.

Sure enough, Alex was already seated at the desk tapping at the keys of the typewriter with two fingers. He looked up and grinned as she opened the door.

"Not much good at this, I'm afraid," he remarked. "Glad you're here—where's Norm?"

"He's coming later. Just writing a few letters home."

37

She took off her coat and sat down in the chair Alex had vacated.

He perched on the edge of the desk and regarded her silently for a few moments. She met his gaze unwaveringly, wondering what was going on in his mind. True to form, his question was abrupt and to the point.

"He doesn't like me much, does he?"

Janet caught her breath. "It's not that he doesn't like you, Alex. It's just that . . . oh, I don't know how to explain . . . I think he just gets a bit jealous if any other man is too friendly with me—silly isn't it?"

"Umm. Understandable, I guess. I'd be jealous if I were in his position . . ." He broke off as they heard stealthy footsteps coming up the stairs.

The door opened and in walked a strange-looking man whom Janet had noticed about the church on several occasions. He was quite short, rather shabbily dressed, and his eyes were over-bright, almost wild looking, while his straight, dark hair stuck out at the back of his head.

"Hi there, Ben," Alex greeted him. "What are you doing here tonight?"

"Saw the light on as I passed, Mr. Moore," the man's speech was just a little slurred. "I thought there must be some meeting on I didn't know about and that I should be at."

"No, not tonight, Ben," Alex told him. "We're just doing a bit of work here. Jan, I'd like you to meet Ben Tullett. He's one of our church members," he winked at Janet from behind the little man's back.

Janet kept her expression serious. "Pleased to meet you, Ben."

"I've seen you," the man told her. "You're out from England, ain't you? I heard of that place. One of me pals come from there. Leastways, he's not me pal now, since I got converted. I was a bad 'un, you know, missus. Drunk every night—but I got saved, praise the Lord."

"That's wonderful, Ben. I'm glad."

"Yes, and it's a changed man I am, missus. I live a blessed life now, and the reverend here—Mr. McCall—he's a good man."

"He is that, Ben."

"And where's your blessed husband then, missus?"

38

"I'm right behind you," cut in Norman's voice.

Ben swung around; they had not heard Norman coming up the stairs.

"Oh, there you are, mister. I know you, don't I?"

"Yes, Ben, we meet here nearly every night, don't we? You're fond of this church building, aren't you?"

"Ah, it's a blessed place, mister. I just love to be within its walls."

"Better be getting along home now, hadn't you?" suggested Alex.

"Yea, I'll go, Mr. Moore," and Ben, without looking back, shuffled his way out of the office and down the stairs.

Norman watched him from the hallway until he had left the building.

"Strange character," he remarked as he came back into the office.

"Oh, there's no harm in him," Alex observed. "Just a bit retarded; he's been coming to the church for about three years. He was a bit of a bad lot, I understand, but he's O.K. now."

They dismissed the strange little man from their minds and got on with the work. The two men had little to say to each other although Alex made one or two attempts to draw Norman out. Eventually he gave up and addressed himself mainly to Janet, talking quite a bit about the newsletter and the work it entailed.

"Sorry to have kept you so late," Alex apologised as they locked up, later. "But you've been a great help, Jan."

"You're very welcome, Alex. Glad to help. It's Saturday tomorrow so I needn't get up early. No work tomorrow."

Norman laughed. "Hark at her—no work! She'll be rushing around like a mad thing, doing the washing, dusting, sweeping, and then out to the shops."

"No good me dropping in for a chat tomorrow, then," laughed Alex.

"No good at all," Norman snapped out the words, turned and marched off across the street. Janet said a final word of goodbye to Alex and followed, sighing a little.

*　　　*　　　*

Coming in from her shopping trip the next day, Janet

met their landlady waiting for her in the hall. The woman's face held an even straighter look than usual.

"Hi, Mrs. Blaker. Your husband's got a visitor. And I'm a bit worried. There seems to be some sort of argument going on up there. I showed the young gentleman up and he didn't get too warm a welcome. I can tell you. Their voices have been raised ever since—at least, your husband's has."

Janet frowned. "I wonder who that can be. Thanks for the warning, Mrs. Boyle. I'll go and see what's happening."

She went up the stairs as quickly as two heavy shopping bags would allow. Her husband's angry voice reached her from behind the closed door on the landing.

"You young fool—I told you never to contact me again, and to forget the whole affair. And now you come here— here of all places. Whatever are you thinking of?"

"I had to come, Mr. Blaker," Janet recognised the voice immediately. It belonged to one of the boys Norman had taught in school back in England. "I needed your help. Besides, the university here is one of the best for my studies— you know that, as well as I do."

"I suppose so," Norman's voice had become resigned. "But for goodness sake, keep your mouth shut. No-one here knows anything about what went wrong in England, so . . ."

Janet decided it was time to make her presence known. She made a great noise of putting down her bags and opening the door.

She forced a smile to her face. "Why hello, Peter, what a great surprise! Welcome to our new home!"

4

JANET WAS fully aware that Norman made himself smile as he turned to her.

"Hello, darling. Yes, it is a surprise, isn't it? Fancy young Peter turning up in this way. He tells me he has a place at the university here. It's a marvellous opportunity for him in the scientific studies he's so keen on—and so good at."

The nineteen-year-old boy before her rose and shook hands, a dull flush creeping from his neck and over his otherwise pale features, to where fair hair was carefully combed back from his forehead. His deep blue eyes did not seem quite able to meet hers. 'He looks so young and vulnerable to have left home and come to a new country,' she thought, somewhat maternally.

The thought prompted her questions : "Are you alone, Peter? And where are you staying? Do you know anyone here? When did you arrive?"

Norman laughed. "One question at a time, dear. Give the lad a chance. He only arrived last night."

"I have digs in a nice house out near the university, Mrs. Blaker. My landlady seems a friendly, homely kind of woman and I think I shall be happy there. . . ."

"Just like home, eh?"

Peter shifted from one foot to the other. "Well . . . she's not quite like Mum, of course, but then who could be? But . . . well . . . no, it's not like home—there's no father there to . . . gosh ! Mrs. Blaker, you know what I mean . . . you know how it was with my father."

Janet put her hand lightly on the boy's shoulder, forcing him to look straight at her. "Yes, Peter, I know; you felt he was far more strict than most fathers, and you longed to break free?"

"That's just it, Mrs. Blaker. So when I had this opportunity—why I just had to take it—especially as Mr. Blaker was here. I thought there'd be *someone* I could turn to if I got in a fix, as it were."

Janet met her husband's eyes but for once she found it difficult to plumb the depths of the look in them. She could not tell what he would have her say, so she took her own initiative.

"Well, Peter, you'll soon make friends out at the university, I'm sure. It will be a new life, but I know you can make it a good one. I expect you may be lonely from time to time; so whenever you want to, you know you're very welcome to come along here and join us in a meal."

Norman's head was turned away so she did not know

41

what reaction her words had. "In any case," she continued, "you can have supper with us this evening."

"We're due at the hospital to see Jack at seven, remember," her husband put in suddenly.

"So we are. Perhaps Peter would like to come along; it's only for a short visit, after all. Then afterwards we can take him down-town and show him the city on a Saturday night. It's not too cold today."

Puzzled at Norman's lack of enthusiasm over the arrival of one of his ex-scholars, Janet set about to make Peter feel the warmth of welcome he so obviously needed. Very few words passed between her husband and the boy; that in itself was strange, she thought, for part of Norman's success as a teacher had been that the boys always felt they could talk to him. She could only assume that the scandal which had shocked the school made her husband feel embarrassed before any of the boys—yes, it was understandable, she realised.

They found Jack Simmons looking very much better and declaring he would soon be discharged from the hospital. He was, in fact, getting about a little now, with the aid of a stick, and the ward sister spoke well of his progress.

He was interested in meeting Peter, and the lad, obviously disappointed that Norman had so little to say to him, opened up and chatted at length with the older man.

"Ah, I've often wanted to go back to the old country myself," Jack remarked. "I was but a few years younger than you, my lad, when my parents decided to emigrate. So I can still remember the old place. Lancashire—that's where I come from, and many's the time I've wanted to go back there, see them tall chimneys in the industrial towns, smell the smoke in the air—sounds strange, but that's how I feel."

"Why don't you go then, Mr. Simmons?" Peter inquired. "I expect you'd find the place changed a lot, but you'd probably enjoy the visit."

"Now that's quite a good idea, young man. Perhaps I will at that. I've been saving up for years, hoping to make a visit to the old country. Now I've someone to take my place for a few months at the church—why, I might just as well make up my mind to go. I know my missus would like to see the place; she's heard so much about it. What d'you say, Norman? Can you carry on for a while longer?"

42

Norman grimaced. "Might just as well, Jack. No other job seems to have come my way so far."

"I've got a sister there, too; living in Birmingham now, she is," Jack went on. "I'd like to go and see her. She never came out here with us, but got married when we left. Got a grown-up family now."

Janet caught her breath, and Norman's scowl was black. Neither said anything for a while, nor did they dare look at Peter who was shifting uncomfortably in his seat. When Norman finally spoke, it was almost with an air of resignation.

"Well, I'll carry on, Jack, if you really want to go."

"I'll think it over and see if there's any chance of getting a couple of seats in a plane soon—my, but the missus will just love to fly," Jack added with a chuckle.

Later, when they had left the hospital, Peter turned to them all apologies. "Gosh! I'm sorry, Mr. Blaker. Birmingham of all places—and I was the one to suggest he paid a visit home!"

Norman, though worried, was at all times fair. "It's not your fault, Peter. You weren't to know. Besides, Birmingham's a big place and we lived a few miles outside, remember. It's a million-to-one chance he'll meet anyone we know."

As soon as they had seen Peter on to his bus back to the university, however, Norman lapsed into silence. Standing beside the stove, waiting for milk to boil for their evening drink, Janet knew she must say something.

"Norman . . . couldn't you persuade Jack not to go? I thought you might say something when he mentioned Birmingham, but you put up no resistance at all—it was so unlike you."

Norman sighed, coming close to her and standing, hands in pockets, looking thoughtfully down at the stove. "I can't explain it, Jan. I just suddenly felt, 'What's the use? If the past is going to catch up with me, let it.' Somehow, I just felt all the fight go out of me. First, Peter turns up, then Jack says he's going to Birmingham. . . . Oh, I don't know! We'll just have to hope for the best."

Janet took the saucepan off the stove and turned to face her husband. Putting her hands up on his shoulders and looking deep into his eyes, she said, "We must *pray* for the best, darling—only then will things come right."

Norman smiled, rather crookedly, but said nothing, only stooping to kiss her lightly.

*   *   *

It must have been seeing someone from their home town, thought Janet, that made her homesickness so acute during the next few weeks. She was constantly thinking of England, wondering what her parents were doing, realising that spring would soon be showing the first signs of arriving.

She had never felt completely at ease with Betty, the girl with whom she worked. Betty was a little older than herself and, although a true Canadian, she lacked the spontaneous warmth which had endeared so many of her new friends to Janet.

Simply as a means of trying to make conversation one day, Janet remarked, "Half way through February, and snow still piled up wherever you look. I had a letter from my mother this morning and she tells me there are snowdrops out in our garden at home, and even the odd crocus —spring often comes quite early in England."

Betty looked at her sharply, then blurted out, "Can't you talk about anything else but what happens in England? You're in Canada now—not the 'old country.' I'm fed up with you boasting about what happens over there, and how much better this or that is. . . ."

Janet gasped; this was indeed a surprise. "But, I . . ."

The girl was not to be put off. "If England is such a wonderful place," she continued, "why did you leave it? And if it's so much better than Canada, why don't you go back there?"

So shocked was Janet by this time, that she could find no words with which to answer the girl. Silently she bent her head over her work, knowing that if she did attempt to answer, the tears would flow; she had never felt so homesick.

Norman could tell that something had upset her as soon as she arrived home that evening. When she explained, his comfort was all she could have wished. At his best, her husband was one of the kindest, most sympathetic men she knew.

44

"Peter dropped in to see me at the church earlier today," he told her suddenly. "He was talking about going out for a run on the skis."

"Why, wherever could we ski here? It's all so flat, just like a vast, open plain," Janet remarked, a trifle bitterly.

"He says that the river-banks are great fun for skiing. Oh, it's nothing like the runs we had in the Lake District or Scotland, but he says it's enjoyable. He's been out a few times with some of the chaps from the university; he wants us to go along with him sometime. He says he can borrow some skis for us. How about it?"

Janet brightened immediately, and they were soon making plans over the telephone with Peter.

The following Saturday afternoon saw the three of them fastening on their skis and gingerly testing them out. Their confidence soon returned, and they slid their ways between the scrub oak and poplar which lined the banks of the river outside the city. It was little more than cross-country skiing, with an occasional slope, but there was a lot of pleasure in gliding over the thickly-packed snow, in and out among the trees, pausing to watch the small wood animals scurrying in the undergrowth and then following their trails across the snow.

Janet revelled in the blue of the sky reflected on to the white surface, making it appear even more dazzling. Everything seemed so peaceful here, so still and clean-looking. The city had, during the past month, lost the fresh appeal of newly-fallen snow, as the mounds piled higher and higher, becoming more dirty each day with the dust of the traffic. Here, however, all still looked pure and virgin-white.

Eventually, they came to the river-bank itself. Peter immediately took off, whizzing down the slope and far out on to the frozen river. Janet stood, uncertain.

"All right, love?" inquired Norman, looking back before following the boy.

"Is it safe to go out on to the river?" she asked. "You hear about thin ice and . . ."

Norman laughed. "There's no thin ice here, Jan. It's a foot thick at least, and will be for weeks. Come on—it's quite safe."

As indeed it proved to be. In fact, Janet would hardly

45

have realised she was skiing on the actual river itself, had she not known it was there. Relaxing, she'd moved on to the slope, knees slightly bent, ski-poles behind her, and swooped downwards after her husband. She caught up with him as he brought his skis to a halt, looking up at him with flushed face and sparkling eyes. Her homesickness had fled.

* * *

"Norman, will you mind if I go out without you next Friday?" Janet asked breathlessly as she hurried up to their apartment after choir practice.

Norman's eyebrows shot up, quizzically. "Explain!" he demanded with an amused look.

"It seems that, once a year, the choir go to visit an old folks' home on the other side of the city. They sing to them, then get the old people to join in a few hymns; the minister goes along, too, and gives them a message. I believe there's also an opportunity of seeing over the place and of chatting with the folk while we have refreshments. It should be fun."

"And I suppose everyone will go by car?"

"Yes. Bev's asked me to go along with her in their car. She's a good driver.

"It sounds like a good example of practical Christianity. Of course I don't mind you going; it'll make a change from spending an evening with a morose husband," he remarked, rather cynically.

She perched on the arm of his chair and gently rested her cheek against his. "There's no need to add that," she told him quietly. "It's a difficult time for you, I know, but never forget—I'm in it with you—whatever happens."

He patted her cheek and sighed. "Without you, I couldn't go on," he said. "But I want you to have a happy time when you can, so go along with Bev. I promised young Peter I'd visit him one evening and look around the university, so I'll make it next Friday."

Norman had, in fact, already left by the time Janet was ready to join the choir members the following Friday. She was putting on her coat when the telephone rang. It was Bev.

"Jan, I'm terribly sorry. I shan't be able to make it tonight. I have a shocking cold—I couldn't sing a note even if I came, and it wouldn't be fair to take my germs among the old people. I thought I'd let you know, as I offered you a ride. I'm so sorry."

"That's O.K., Bev, I'm only too sorry you won't be there. I shall miss you. But I expect someone else will fit me into their car."

"Oh yes, there'll be plenty of others. I've phoned Blair and given my apologies, but you might explain to the others; he's sure to forget it."

Janet passed on Bev's message while everyone waited for last-minute arrangements to be made. Immediately, Alex came up to her.

"You were supposed to be riding in Bev's car, weren't you?"

Janet nodded.

"Well, there's room in mine. I only have Geoff . . ." he indicated a tall, dark man carrying the white stick of the blind, ". . . and Eric, who acts as his guide, as you know. So I shall welcome more company."

Janet enjoyed the evening as much for the conversations she had with the old people, as the actual singing.

One old man, interested because she had so recently come from England, was anxious to tell how different he had found Canada when he had first emigrated. It was hard work on the farm, he told her, but harder still when he had done a spell in a lumber camp, away in British Columbia, within the shadow of the Rockies.

"Do you know," he fixed her with an earnest stare, his pale blue eyes sombre, "even in the summer, some of them mountain streams are real ice-cold. I've knowed a man tumble into one and the impact of that tremendous cold upon his body was so great—my, it had terrible effects; made a great gash in his skin! Ah, those years with the lumber—they were bad."

"It was better on the farm, then?" Janet asked.

"Ah yes, but 'twas rough, too. No neighbours, to speak of, and miles to the nearest village. No churches to go to on the Sabbath, either—just a little shack. Why, when I was baptised, it was in the river. Ah, you look surprised, but our Lord was baptised in a river, remember."

Janet recounted some of the conversation while they

47

drove home, turning around and chatting with Eric and Geoff, who was a great listener. Eric added his bit.

"Yes, it was hard on the farms, in the early days," he said. "My parents farmed out in the mid-lake area, and many's the time we had to dig ourselves out of the farmhouse on a winter morning. But my two sisters and I never once missed school. Whatever the weather, my Dad would bundle us into the sleigh, harness the horses and drive us the couple of miles to school. In the summer, we rode the horses there ourselves, in the saddle, but in the winter our Mum would wrap scarves around us until you could just see the tips of our noses showing from the blankets in the sleigh. Why, sometimes we were the only kids at school and Dad . . ."

He broke off at an exclamation from Alex. A second later, the car stopped with a suddenness that threw Janet against the dashboard.

"Sorry," Alex put out his hand to steady her. "I've taken the wrong turning. It's such a dark night, I couldn't be sure if I had reached the junction or not—and I haven't. We're stuck fast in a snowdrift."

"What can we do?" Janet was all concern.

"I'll see if I can give it a shove, and I have some sand in the trunk which may help."

"I'll give you a hand, Alex," Eric immediately offered.

"Oh no, you stay there, Eric, and make sure Geoff doesn't get into any mischief." As always, Alex turned the situation into a joke. "Jan can help me, if she will."

Janet was out of the car quickly and adding her small strength to pushing the vehicle. It was no good; nothing seemed to shift it.

"Why not let Eric help?" she asked.

Alex shook his head. "He had a bad heart attack last winter; it wouldn't do. I've known stronger men collapse in this type of weather."

"What can we do, then?"

"The only thing is to walk back to the garage we saw at the last corner. . . ."

"I'll go, Alex. It would be better for you to stay with the car, in case someone comes along to give you a hand. And if you keep trying with the sand while I'm gone it might help."

"It's at least a mile, Jan, and the snow's piled high all the way. D'you think you can make it?"

"I'll try," she called, already on her way.

The next half-hour was one of the worst Janet could remember. Temperatures had struck low that evening—well below zero. The wind was gusty, and a light flurry of snow was falling. With the night being dark, it was difficult to see just how deep the snow was in places and she stumbled countless times in her effort to hurry. Once, she even fell headlong, but the snow was soft and she felt no injury. She was only too glad she was wearing warm clothing, although her face stung with the cold and by the time she reached the garage she felt like an iceberg!

As she staggered into the warmth of the place, the man on duty quickly sized up the situation; he was used to such calls of emergency. It was not long before she was driving back with him to the spot where she had left Alex and the two men in the snow-bound car.

She said little as the man from the garage helped Alex and, with the aid of steel grids, bags of sand and a tow-chain, moved the car back on to the road. By the time she was once more sitting beside Alex on their way now safely back to the city, the exhaustion of that long walk in the cold had brought on a heavy feeling.

Alex did not speak either, until he had deposited the two men at their separate homes. They were, in fact, nearing the church when he finally voiced his thoughts.

"I don't know what I'd have done without you tonight, Jan. I hope you're not too worn out?" His tone was full of concern.

"No, I shall be all right, once I've had a good rest, Alex. It was all I could do in the circumstances. . . ."

"Not every girl would have done it, though," persisted Alex. "Thanks, anyway . . ." he stopped the car and turned to her. "I'm not very good at expressing my feelings but . . ." he put his arm along the back of the car seat and leaned towards her. She stiffened, but in that moment his arms were around her and his lips had met hers. She was so surprised she had no chance to resist.

The next moment, the car door was wrenched open, she felt herself pulled from Alex's grasp and the voice of her husband rasped in her ear.

49

"So, this is the way you go out with the choir, is it? Riding in Bev's car, are you? I might have known!"

5

Janet scrambled out of Alex's car and confronted her husband.

"Norman, please, you've got it all wrong—it can all be explained quite simply, can't it, Alex?" She turned to the other man, who had slowly stepped out from his side of the car.

"Just showing a bit of gratitude—that's all; nothing in it, I assure you." But Alex's voice lacked the confidence which would have averted Norman's anger.

"Showing gratitude? For what, may I ask?"

"Norman," broke in Janet, "it's far too cold to stand out here arguing, and I'm . . . I'm . . ." she swayed and would have fallen had not Alex steadied her. Immediately Norman sprang forward, pushed Alex away and grasped Janet's arm himself.

"I can look after my wife, thanks all the same. What have you been doing to her to get her in this state? She's worn out!"

"You'd better ask her yourself—it's obvious you won't take *my* explanation," and without another word Alex swung back into the car, started it up and was gone.

"You'd better get indoors," Norman said grimly and piloted his wife towards the house and up the stairs to their apartment.

Janet sank into the armchair, too exhausted for words. The tension of the night's events gave way to great sobs which shook her shoulders. Instead of soothing her, Norman busied himself in the kitchen, making hot drinks, clattering about with cups and saucers, his lips set in a grim line, his eyes glittering angrily.

When the drinks were ready, he handed one to Janet without a word.

"Thanks," she mustered her strength. "Norman, please listen to me. . . ."

"I don't want to hear about it tonight. You're in no fit state for anything other than rest. I'll hear your explanation in the morning—and it had better be a good one. To think—I can't even trust my own wife, now!"

"But, Norman . . ."

"All right, so maybe it wasn't *your* fault. Maybe it was all Alex's. There's another of your professing Christians—making up to another man's wife when his back's turned! No, I won't hear more now. Have your drink and get to bed."

It took Janet a very long time to get to sleep, despite her tiredness. As a result she awoke late to find that Norman had already left the apartment and gone across to the church. She did not see him until lunch-time.

When he came in, it was obvious that much of the anger had gone, to be replaced by a rather grim silence. Mid-way through the meal, the telephone rang and Norman answered it. It was Bev.

"Hi," came her voice over the wire as Janet took the receiver from her husband. "I called earlier but Norm said you were still sleeping. You must have had a tiring time last night—what happened?"

"Why, Bev, it was all so unexpected. You see, I rode in Alex's car and, coming home, he took the wrong turning and landed in a snowdrift, so . . ." she went on to explain about her long walk to get help. By the time she had finished talking to her friend, Norman had risen and was standing looking out of the window, a deep frown still on his forehead.

"So," he began immediately she put the receiver down. "That's how it was?"

"I told you it could be simply explained."

"Umm. When Bev phoned earlier, she told me about the last-minute change in plans, so I know why you went in Alex's car. *But*, it still does not alter the fact that you were letting him kiss you. You didn't put up much resistance, did you?"

51

"I know it seems strange, Norman, but it all happened so quickly. . . ."

"Well, you'd better make sure it doesn't happen 'so quickly' again. You've been far too friendly with that character all along—and I don't like it!"

Janet bit her lip. She knew it was no use trying to make her husband see any reason when he was in this kind of mood. Besides, she had been startled by her own feelings, although she supposed it was because Norman had been so bad-tempered lately that it was a relief to be with someone who wasn't so easily upset. But she was a little disappointed in Alex for leaving her to face the music, and driving off in the way he had.

The atmosphere between husband and wife remained cool and Janet went to do her weekend shopping with a heavy heart.

She was wandering through one of the large department stores, trying to find some diversion for her mind in the gaily arranged display of goods, when a voice sounded in her ear.

"Hi!" came Marion's unmistakable tones. "So glad I met you. I was just thinking a cup of coffee might be a good idea."

At that moment, Janet thought it about the worst idea possible; she still felt so tired, and she dreaded having to make polite conversation. But how could she refuse?

Marion chatted in a general way, while they were waiting to be served at the coffee bar. Then, shifting on her tall stool a little, she looked keenly at Janet and asked, in the kindest way possible, "Something upsetting you, dearie?"

Janet's sigh was more like a shudder and she nodded her head, keeping her eyes on her coffee so that her companion would not see the tears filling them.

Marion put her hand on Janet's arm. "Now, you just tell me about it, if you'd like to; and if you'd rather not, why then I'll quite understand."

Suddenly, Janet knew this was exactly what she needed. Gulping hard, she poured out the tale—even to the embrace with Alex.

When she had finished, she dabbed surreptiously at her eyes and drank down her coffee, holding the cup with a trembling hand.

Marion was quiet for a while. When she spoke, it was in her usual sweet and motherly tones. "Now, I've known Alex for a long time," she said, "and I'll admit he likes the girls. But he'd never—no, never—do anything mean like making up to a married girl. I'm sure Norman has absolutely nothing to worry about. But it seems to me that your husband is just a little unsure of himself at present?"

Janet nodded but didn't offer Marion any explanation.

"Well now, I guess that's what's making him so possessive and morose," the older woman went on. "So, although *you* know, and I'm sure Alex knows, there's nothing in it, perhaps it might be better not to be too friendly with him for a bit. Simply pass the time of day and treat him as one of the crowd, but ride in someone else's car if you're going anywhere and don't give Norman any more cause for suspicion."

At last, Janet smiled and looked up into Marion's eyes. "Thanks for your help," she whispered.

"I'm afraid I've not done anything, really, only listened. . . ."

"And that's just what I needed. Times like this, I miss my mum. I can't write and tell her these things for she'd only worry."

"Well, while you're here, just look on me as your mum," Marion laughed. "I'll adopt you—along with my other daughter! There, now, don't forget—anytime you need a motherly chat, just call on me!"

*　　　*　　　*

During the next few weeks, the whole church became more of a hive of activity than usual. The annual gift day was scheduled for the last week in March, and this year the minister had rallied them with the challenge of paying off the last remaining debts on the new Christian Education wing.

The girls in the O.F.S.L. Club had planned to put on what they called a "silver tea," and Janet was, of course, eager to help. At a meeting in Bev's home one evening, various duties were delegated and Janet was asked if, as well as helping Pat and Clare make sandwiches, she would like to serve on the great day.

"Yes, I'll do whatever I can to help," was her response. "As long as I know what's expected of me."

"Just put on your prettiest dress and your new spring hat, and hand round the trays of sandwiches and dainties," Bex told her. Janet smiled to herself, glad that she was now quickly able to understand the different phrases her Canadian friends used. She'd even tried to make a few of the tiny fancy cakes termed "dainties" which were a feature of any party occasion, and Norman had enjoyed them.

"We'll ask the minister's wife to be the first to pour . . ." Peggy was saying.

The query must have shown on Janet's face. "Don't you have these silver teas in England?" Clare asked kindly, and when Janet shook her head, the others, all trying to speak at once, explained that it was an honour to be asked to pour tea from the silver teapot and as usual the minister's wife was to be given the privilege for part of the time. Janet gathered that it would be quite an elaborate occasion and became excited about the part she would play.

When she arrived at the hall that had been hired on the day of the silver tea, she saw that Marion was sitting just inside the door beside a table on which reposed a large silver bowl. This, Janet learned, was for the receiving of gifts—silver at least!

She took off her coat, satisfied because she had put on one of the smart, silk dresses she had brought from England and a straw hat. Soon she was in the throes of the afternoon's excitement, handing round sandwiches to the big crowd of people who had turned up. She suddenly thought of Marion sitting by the door and decided she might like a sandwich.

Moving near to her, she offered her tray.

"Why thanks, dearie. Just what I needed. Isn't it a marvellous turnout? I do hope we manage to raise a lot of money; it will all go into the funds, of course, and Monday's the gift day for anyone who isn't able to get here to make their donation this afternoon."

So engrossed were they in looking about at the different people that, momentarily, Marion forgot to keep her eyes on the bowl. Suddenly, Janet saw her shoot her hand forward and noticed she had taken a tight hold on the bowl.

Then she saw Ben Tullett sidling away from the table, a sheepish grin on his face.

"What's the matter, Marion? Surely Ben wouldn't put his hand *into* the bowl?"

"I don't know—I just don't know. I'm sure we should trust people but I'm never certain what to make of that character. There have been things missing from the church, that have never been traced; things like scarves, a pair of snow-boots, one or two cups from the church kitchen. And it's only been happening since Ben has been with us. So we're a little suspicious of him. I don't think he'd take money, but he might fancy the silver bowl—that seems to be the way his mind works."

"Shall I get Norman to take what money there is here, then, and put it in the church safe, Marion? Mr. McCall has entrusted the spare key with him over this weekend because of the gift day. He'll be leaving soon because he's a few jobs to do at the church before this evening."

"That might be a good idea, Jan. Yes. O.K., have him come along and collect the money right now. Then I can add the rest to it when we're through. People have been so generous; there must be close on a hundred dollars here."

Norman readily agreed to take the money back to the church, so put it carefully in his pocket and was soon off down the street.

"How are you getting on with him now, dear?" Marion inquired when he had left.

Janet shrugged. "Oh, he's still very cool, which is most unlike him. He usually gets over his moods as quickly as they come. But I've taken your advice and kept out of Alex's way. Tell you the truth, I was a bit put out that he left me to do the explaining to Norman."

"That's just like Alex," Marion told her. "He'll never argue. I've heard him quote, more than once, 'Convince a man against his will, he's of the same opinion still.' I wonder if he's offered Norman an apology since?"

"I don't think so. I haven't seen them speak to each other since that night."

When Janet arrived home, she was surprised to find Norman talking with Jack Simmons in their living-room.

"Why, Jack, how wonderful to see you better and out of

55

hospital! Pity you couldn't get to this afternoon's tea, though."

"Ah yes," replied the man, "although those sort of posh occasions are not really in my line. Besides, I only got out yesterday. And I'm off next week."

"Off?"

"Yeah—off to the old country. My missus was that pleased when I told her your husband would carry on while we were gone, that she went ahead and made in-quiries. And what d'you think? There were just two cancel-lations on a flight leaving next Tuesday! So, of course, we took 'em. We'll only be gone four weeks; but that's better than nothing—and besides we couldn't afford more. My, but I'm looking forward to it, I don't mind telling you."

Janet caught Norman's eye, but said brightly, "Well, I hope you enjoy yourself, Jack. Give our regards to your wife and wish her a happy trip, won't you?"

"I will that, and I'll give your love to the old country—what part did you say you came from?"

Norman cut in quickly. "From the Midlands, Jack. Now, I would be grateful," he continued, deftly changing the subject, "if you could tell me what's expected of me with the warmer weather coming along. You were explaining about the boilers. . . ."

Janet left the two men, went into the kitchen and began to make preparations for their evening meal. It wasn't until Jack had left and they had finished eating that Norman suddenly said, "Goodness, I've just remembered—I didn't put that money away in the church safe. I'll go across and do it right now. Care to come with me and give me a hand with a few last-minute chores?"

"Of course," Janet was only too glad of this faint over-ture of friendliness from her husband.

As they entered the building, the melodious tones of the organ could be heard.

"That must be Blair practising for tomorrow," re-marked Janet. "That's the anthem we're singing. Oh, and there's Geoff going over his solo part—don't you think he has a wonderful voice, Norman?"

Norman agreed. "Strange, how very often a blind per-son is exceptionally musical. What Geoff lacks in sight, he really makes up for with his voice."

They put the money away and went through to the

church, just in time to hear Blair say, "I haven't got that book up here at the organ, Geoff. Wait just a moment and I'll fetch it; then we can run through your solo for the following Sunday. Oh, hello, Mrs. Blaker . . . Mr. Blaker. How did the tea go? Take plenty of money?"

Janet was a little surprised that he should show such an interest, but answered in an equally friendly manner. "Oh yes, it was all very worthwhile. We estimate we took close on a hundred dollars; we've just put it away in the safe, out of harm's way!" she laughed.

"Can't be too careful," remarked Geoff. "It'll be good to get those debts wiped off."

Blair left them chatting to go and find his music and when he returned he was holding his hand up, a bundle of keys in it.

"I guess you dropped these, Mr. Blaker. I found them just outside the church office."

Norman started. "Good gracious!" he exclaimed. "How jolly careless of me. Good thing you found them, Mr. Andrews. Thanks a lot. But don't let us disturb you. We've got some dusting to do and we'll work quietly here."

"That's O.K.," the organist assured them. "Geoff just wants to go through his solo."

As promised, Norman and Janet worked quietly but it was not long before they had paused, enraptured with the rich baritone voice ringing out the gospel message. Geoff was singing, "The Stranger of Galilee."

" 'In fancy I stood by the shore one day . . .' " he sang. Janet touched Norman on the arm and they both sat and listened. She caught her breath as the baritone quietly sang the words, " 'I saw how the man who was blind from birth . . .' " then the voice opened out into a great crescendo, ringing with the clear, firm conviction of one who really understands and feels the words . . . " 'in a moment was made to see.' "

Janet was never sure when it happened but by the time Geoff had reached the last verse, with its message: " 'O friend, won't you love Him for ever, so kind and gracious is He? Accept Him today as your Saviour, this Stranger of Galilee,' " Norman was grasping her hand tightly between both of his own and his expression was more at peace than it had been for weeks.

They did not speak to each other, however, but silently finished their task. Then they left Geoff and Blair still practising, put away their cleaning materials and went out of the church's side door.

Norman was closing it behind him, when a slight shuffling made them look round. "Anyone there?" called Norman.

"Only me, mister," came Ben's slurring voice. "I just bin listening to that man singing; my but he's got a beautiful voice, hasn't he?"

"Did you come in for anything special, Ben?" asked Norman.

"No, mister, just to feel the peace of these blessed walls around me—that's all. It's the Sabbath tomorrow, y'know. Ah, but I love the Sabbath."

"That's good, Ben," Janet said. "Going home, now?"

"Yeah, I'm going," said the little man and he shuffled off.

"Just a minute," called another voice from inside the church. "Wait for me—I've been looking for you two everywhere," and Peter stepped out from the shadows of the hallway. "I thought you might be down by the boilers, but it's all dark there."

"Didn't see you at the tea, Peter." Janet remarked in greeting.

"No, I didn't really like to come. I don't know many of the people yet. . . ."

"You should come along to more of the meetings in the week and get to know them," she persisted.

"Well, I can't really, with the amount of studying I have to do. It's as much as I can manage to get here to morning services on Sundays. . . ."

"Oh yes, and don't forget you're coming to lunch tomorrow."

"Thanks, Mrs. Blaker, that's what I wanted to see you about. I've been asked out for a drive tomorrow afternoon by one of the chaps at the university and wondered if you'd think it awfully rude of me if I didn't come, after all, but scooted off back to his place immediately after the service?"

"No, of course not, Peter. I understand. Come next week, if you'd like to—it's up to you."

*　　　*　　　*

It was after the morning service that Marion caught Janet by the arm and handed her a small bag. "Here's the rest of yesterday's takings, Jan," she said. "Do you mind getting Norman to put it away with the rest? I *must* rush as Bill's waiting."

Janet found her husband, handed over the bag and left him to put it in the safe while she went across to their home to prepare the lunch.

She was busily making gravy when she heard Norman running up the stairs and looked up inquiringly as he burst into their rooms.

"Jan—Jan, darling, whatever are we going to do?"

Janet, seeing his ashen face and staring eyes, rushed to her husband and gripped him by the arms. "Norman! Tell me—what's happened? You look as though you've seen a ghost!"

"I feel as though I have. How can I tell you? Jan—that money we put away in the safe yesterday—it's gone!"

Janet drew back, her own face losing all vestige of colour. "Oh no!" she gasped. "Not again—no, Norman, it can't have happened *again*."

"It *has* happened again," his voice came out almost with a sob.

6

JANET PUT her arms right round her husband. "Darling, at least I was with you when you put the money away. I have proof this time of your innocence. But who *could* have taken it?"

He stared at her with a long, searching look. Then he spoke. "It may not be quite the mystery we imagine. As long as I know you're behind me, I may be able to handle this one a little differently."

Janet suddenly let go of her husband. "Norman, I've just remembered. At the tea, Marion and I were talking and, for a brief moment, we were so busy looking about that we weren't watching the bowl with the money in it. Then, suddenly, Marion spotted Ben putting his hand out towards it. She grabbed it pretty quickly but he had a funny look on his face. That's why she got you to take the money to the safe. And, you know, Ben was in the church yesterday."

Norman looked at her intently for what seemed ages. Then very deliberately he said, "So was Peter."

She gasped. "But, Norman, you know Peter . . ."

"Exactly, I know Peter—no, don't ask me any more because I'm not going into details. You can think what you like, but keep your thoughts to yourself. Just now, we must get in touch with Mr. McCall and tell him everything we know. Perhaps we should keep quiet about Peter being there yesterday. Maybe there'll be another way. . . ."

Lunch was forgotten and very soon Mr. McCall was sitting in their living-room with them, talking over what had happened. Then they went across to the church, turned out the contents of the safe, looked in every possible place; there was no trace of the cash. Nor were there any signs of a break-in from outside.

"There's nothing further we can do at this stage," the Minister said wearily. "It's not really a large enough amount to notify the police—at least not just yet. Leave matters with me. I'll say something at this evening's service.

He did not, however, mention the disappearance of the money until after his sermon. Then he said, in his calm manner, "I know you will be extremely shocked to learn that the money taken at yesterday's tea is missing from the safe, where it was locked away last evening. . . ."

There were stifled gasps from everyone in the congregation, and a few exclamations of, "Oh no!"

"I am sure," the minister continued, "that no blame can be attached to anyone here. Although how a thief could get in, unlock the safe, take the money and lock it up again without leaving any trace, is extremely mysterious. Just in case, however, someone in the congregation *did* yield to temptation, I am appealing to him, or her, to return that sum of money. And this is how I ask you to do it.

"As you know, tomorrow is our gift day. I shall be in my

60

vestry throughout the day, as arranged, to receive any monetary gifts you care to make. You can give those gifts to me in envelopes, which I shall place in a suitable receptacle. Those envelopes will not be opened until the following day, when an accounting will be made. If the person who took the money from the takings of the tea cares to place it in an envelope and hand it to me as their contribution towards the gift day, that will be sufficient. We shall ask no further questions; we shall be only too grateful that person has found the courage to make amends for his mistake. Above all, remember, if this is a theft, that person is robbing God. *But* that same God is a loving Father who will forgive to the utmost if anyone truly repents. . . . Now, in place of a hymn, we shall pray and I have asked the organist to play quietly as we leave the sanctuary. . . ."

The well-known hymn which Mr. McCall had asked Blair to play as the congregation filed slowly out of their pews was, "Come to the Saviour now, He gently calleth Thee; in true repentance bow, before Him bend the knee."

"How appropriate," Janet whispered to Norman as she waited with him until everyone had left. "That music was just what was needed. If the guilty person was in church, surely they couldn't resist its appeal."

"If he *was* here tonight," Norman remarked grimly.

She looked at him sharply. 'Surely he cannot suspect Peter,' she thought. 'Although it does seem strange he rushed off this morning without coming to lunch as arranged; and he *was* at the church last night.'

The money was not returned on gift day. But, as Norman kept reminding Janet, the thief may not have heard the minister's appeal on Sunday evening.

It wasn't until the following weekend that they saw Peter again. He had phoned to ask if he could come to lunch on that Sunday and while they were eating he opened the topic which was uppermost in their minds.

"Isn't that dreadful about the money? I heard everyone talking about it this morning. Have you any ideas about who could have taken it?" he asked, almost naïvely.

Janet held her breath and watched Norman.

Her husband turned to the boy, searching his eyes intently. "No, I've no idea at all, Peter. It's all very strange. Can *you* offer any suggestions?"

Peter flushed. He cast his eyes down, and played with the food on his plate. "No, Mr. Blaker. I don't know anything about it at all—I swear I don't. . . ."

Norman quickly put his hand on the boy's arm. "That's O.K., Peter, I believe you. But I think someone must have been watching the church pretty closely last Saturday night and slipped in when we weren't looking. But I can't think how they got the safe open."

So the weeks went by and the mystery was not solved—nor was the money returned.

* * *

As Easter approached, the city began to take on a completely different appearance. Janet and Norman soon learned that spring in western Canada meant the disappearance of snow, ice and frost, and the break-up of the rivers. They lived fairly near a bend in the river which ran through the city and one morning their landlady called upstairs to them excitedly, "River's breaking up—just been down to the bridge and my word what a noise! You should go and see it."

Always eager to learn something new about the country, Janet and Norman hurried to the bridge and stood watching. With a great roar, the ice-mass cracked here and there; soon the great chunks began to move downstream. The movement gained momentum and while some lumps of ice piled up on the side, others began to flow freely. Then patches of clear blue water appeared, and into those small patches a few members of the local boating club had put their canoes and were now chasing the ice-chunks down the river.

"They're crazy!" gasped Janet. "It must be dangerous."

Her husband grinned. "Yes, I should think so. But some fellows will do anything for a bit of excitement. I only hope young Peter keeps away from it—you know what a dare-devil he is."

His hopes were ill-founded, however, for it was during that evening the telephone rang and they learned that Peter was in hospital, having joined his university friends in their race down the river, and fallen into the ice-cold water.

62

They were told that his leg had been badly crushed and the doctors were worried about the possibility of pneumonia, as he had been in the water some time before his friends had realised what had happened.

Janet and Norman immediately hurried to the hospital. He was just regaining consciousness.

"Sorry to have worried you, Mr. Blaker," he said weakly. "Guess I should have been more careful."

"You should," Norman hammered out the words. "I've warned you many times not to be foolhardy. . . ."

"Norman," gently interposed Janet, "he's probably learned his lesson. Don't nag him now—he's not fit."

Norman gave her a sudden smile, then looked back at his ex-scholar with a grin. "Good thing my wife's here to stand up for you, lad," he remarked. "Just take care, in future. As it is, this will interrupt your studies. . . ."

"I know, Mr. Blaker," the boy said ruefully, "but I'll get my books brought up when I feel more like it. *I won't let you down,*" he added pointedly.

Janet frowned. Just what did Peter mean by that last remark? He was not under Norman's tuition now. How could he let him down? It was just another mysterious link in the chain of events which her husband did not want to explain to her yet.

With the advent of spring, Janet was glad to see Canadians shedding fur coats and donning brightly-coloured cottons, lighter shoes and gay hats. A few flowers began to appear as the snows melted. But also, as the snows melted, the streets became muddy pools through which the vividly-coloured cars splashed, to arrive at their destination looking a dirty grey with even the windows splattered with mud.

One evening, as she and Norman crossed the street from the church, a loud honking could be heard overhead. Alex happened to be standing beside his car, talking to Clare. He looked up, then spotted Janet and Norman, and directed their eyes upwards, also.

"The geese have come back—spring is here," he announced, and they were just in time to see a flock of those beautiful birds wing by on the last stage of their long flight from the south.

"That's one of the most beautful sounds at this time of

year," Alex explained. He made as though he would continue the conversation, but Norman turned abruptly and began to cross the street. Alex had evidently, however, made up his mind at last to put matters right. He strode after him, while Janet waited anxiously.

"Don't you think it's about time we called a truce?" she heard Alex ask her husband. "I'm sure Jan has explained about that night; I promise you, it won't happen again. Can't we at least be on speaking terms?"

Norman stopped, looked at him casually at first, then grinned a trifle crookedly. "I suppose we might as well," he said reluctantly. "You must admit, however, it looked pretty suspicious."

"Yes, I guess it did," agreed Alex. "You want to take more care of your wife, you know!" It was said light-heartedly again, but Norman's frown came back for a brief moment. "Oh come on, shake on it, and I'll promise to direct my attentions elsewhere in future," Alex said.

"Just do that," and Norman shook his hand, then turned and went indoors, with Janet following.

*   *   *

The streets were dry by Easter Sunday, and everyone was out in spring clothes. The church was packed, although Norman remarked somewhat cynically that the ladies were probably only there to show off their new Easter bonnets.

There was a flurry of excitement among the ladies of the choir for Evelyn, Marion's daughter, was to be married in a couple of weeks' time and a "shower" had been arranged for her. Janet was greatly puzzled as to just what a shower was, but Bev soon enlightened her. It was to be a surprise party for the bride-to-be at which they would all give her a little gift. "Shower her with presents, as it were," Bev remarked.

The party would be at Bev's home and Janet went along early to help her friend with the preparations. The children were being kept busy in the garden with Tom, so as they worked, Bev and Janet talked.

"It really is nice to see the kids with their dad," Bev remarked. "You know, he's always so busy round at the church that some weeks they hardly see him at all."

"But he does a wonderful work there, Bev," Janet said. "What with being Sunday-school Superintendant, one of the leading lights in the O.F.S.L. Club, on the board of deacons. . . ."

"Exactly . . . and umpteen other committees. Believe me, Jan, it's quite a problem to us. He's a wonderful husband, and I never cease to thank God for such a blessing, but I often wish he was home more often."

"I know what you mean. It was a bit different for me, but when Norman . . ." she broke off, suddenly realising she had been going to mention Norman's school and organist activities in England.

"Yes?" queried Bev.

"Oh nothing—forget it, please."

"You know, Jan, I've often thought there's something strange about Norman. Neither of you say much about what your jobs were in England; you always evade the question. Norman's just not the type only to do a care-taking job—he's way above that. So what . . ."

Janet looked at Bev with appeal in her eyes. "Please, Bev, don't ask about it. Someday perhaps I'll be able to tell you more, but not now." And with that her friend had to be content.

The others soon began to arrive; the usual crowd—Peg, Clare, Pat, Fiona, and one or two more. Then they sat waiting, and finally Marion drove up with Evelyn.

"Surprise, surprise!" chorused the girls already assembled, and Evelyn's face dutifully registered surprise, although Janet was sure she must have suspected she was to be given a party.

Evelyn was, however, radiantly happy and Marion beamed at everyone, pleased in the knowledge that her girl had found a good, upright Christian man with whom to share her life. Janet did not know the young man very well, for he was away at a Bible college, but she had often talked with Evelyn and liked her. The girl took after her father in features, but also possessed her mother's charm and sympathetic interest in other people.

She was duly led to a specially prepared chair of honour, which had been draped with a white sheet and decorated with pink bows. Confetti was shaken over her, a beautiful corsage of roses was pinned to her dress and the presents, carefully arranged in a decorated box, were brought in and placed before her.

The main entertainment of the evening was in watching the bride-to-be open each gift, express thanks, lay aside the ribbon-bows and wind the string into a ball. When all had been opened, the string was formed into a large circle, first slipping Evelyn's engagement ring on it, and the unmarried girls stood holding the piece nearest to them.

Janet watched them, in particular the organist's sister, Mary Jane; Bev had confided that she was very glad to have got the girl along to the party as she was so shy.

Music was played, the ring was slid around the circle, and when the music stopped whoever held the ring in her hand was, tradition said, destined to be the next bride. There was much girlish giggling but when the music did stop it was Mary Jane who held the ring.

Her plain features took on an embarrassed expression and she blushed violently. "Oh no, that's most unlikely," she laughed. "I'm too much of a mouse!"

"Don't you be so sure, my girl," put in Evelyn. "I'm no great beauty, and I'm getting married. You never know what may happen!"

In the general teasing atmosphere, refreshments were handed around, but they were all to remember that party and wonder if it had, in fact, been a prediction.

*　　　*　　　*

The mystery of the missing money, although pushed into the background of everyone's minds during the Easter celebrations and the excitement of the wedding, was still a source of concern.

The O.F.S.L. Club members decided that something must be done to replace the cash and at the meeting held towards the end of April, they discussed plans.

Another tea was suggested. Mr. McCall said no, perhaps they should do something different this time. After all, it was awkward enough asking people to give twice. Shouldn't the donors receive something for their money this time?

"I know," Tom announced suddenly. "We'll have a car wash!"

"Splendid idea, Tom!" exclaimed the minister. "Just the

job with the dirty roads we've had lately. When would you suggest? The Saturday before the 24th May long weekend? Then everyone can have clean cars to go to the lake."

Janet gave Bev a nudge. "Explain, please!" she demanded. "What's a car wash?"

Quickly Bev whispered to both her and Norman. "We hire a suitable parking lot, advertise that cars can be washed at so much a time on that particular date, the money to go to the church, and people bring their cars along. A group of us do the work, so there's no expense—we make a hundred per cent profit!"

"Grand idea," agreed Norman. "We can help, can't we, Jan?"

Janet nodded. 'Anything to get that money,' she thought. When the discussion was over, Joe, as President, rose.

"Friends, I think we have come up with a worthwhile programme, and I do hope you'll all support it. The fact still remains, however, that someone has that missing money. I believe you feel, as I do, that we should never be satisfied until the mystery is solved. At present, however, we can do nothing—except pray; let us pray that the person, whoever he or she may be, will have the courage to own up and return what belongs to the service of God. We believe it will be better for that person's soul if this error is confessed. So let us pray. . . ."

The meeting finished thus. It was inevitable that as they drunk their coffee, they should gather in groups and discuss the missing money, turning the matter over again and again as to who could possibly have done such a thing.

They were so busy in their conversation that no-one noticed the church door open. Then a well-known voice hailed them. "Hi there, everyone. Here I am—back from the old country, fighting fit and ready to take up the reins again."

There stood Jack Simmons, certainly looking well and beaming all over his face.

"Why, hi there, Jack," came from a dozen voices. They were soon showering him with questions about his trip which he answered in high spirits, obviously proud to be the centre of attention for a few minutes and making the most of it.

There was a sudden lull in the conversation. Then, very

quietly, the man asked, "Any news of the missing money yet? Has anyone owned up?"

"No, as a matter of fact, we were just talking about it," the minister told him. "It's still a complete mystery."

"Maybe not," Jack nodded his head knowingly then, looking directly at Norman stared at him until everyone's eyes turned in that direction. "Perhaps I've got a line to go on. What do we know about the man who's been doing my job for the past few months? That's what I want to ask you. What references did you have before you agreed to let him have the run of the place while I was in hospital?"

One big gasp seemed to go around the room. The minister immediately spoke up. "There were no references, Jack," he said very quietly. "I needed none—I know a good man who can be trusted, when I meet one."

"You didn't know him very well this time, Mr. McCall. I found out a thing or two over there in the old country. That man's a fraud! Why did he leave England? You never bothered to ask him, did you?"

The minister put up a restraining hand, but Norman jumped to his feet, his eyes blazing. When he spoke, however, his voice was fully controlled.

"Let the man speak, Mr. McCall. Maybe everyone should hear this, and judge for yourselves. Go on, Jack. Just what have you to say?"

"Simply this—you were chucked out of the school where you were science teacher to the top class of lads—my nephew among them—because a large sum of money was missing from the Head's office. It was cash which had been raised to build a new swimming pool at the school. All the evidence pointed to you—and you never denied it; in fact, at the trial you pleaded guilty and went to prison on a six-months' sentence."

Janet's heart was pounding and she sat on the edge of her chair, looking only at Norman, her face flushed.

"Everything you say is correct, Jack. Have you any more to add?" Norman's eyes blazed but his tone was still under control.

"No, that's all—except that the Head threw you out. So you come here and pulled the wool over our eyes. There's the culprit, friends," the caretaker pointed an accusing finger at Norman. "He's the one you should question. He's the one who steals money. Ask *him* where the missing hundred dollars is!"

Janet felt the tension mounting. Once before she had lived through a scene very similar to this—and everyone had turned against Norman then. But how would *this* group of Christian friends react? She prayed, how she prayed!

7

NORMAN CONTINUED standing, looking around at the group. Almost it seemed, thought Janet, that it was they who were on trial and not her husband, as he looked at them one by one, trying to read their reaction. The minister made to speak, but Norman was ahead of him.

"You've heard what Jack has said," he began. "It looks bad, I know, and I admit that what he has told you is the truth. I spent four months in prison, and two months out on parole. Then Janet and I came here to start a new life. More than that I'm not prepared to say. . . ."

"And we have no wish for you to explain further, Norman," Mr. McCall interrupted. "What is past, is your own affair—between you and God alone. We can only judge, if judge we dare, as we ourselves have found you. Speaking for myself, I have always considered you a thoroughly decent sort of fellow who would never do anything mean or spiteful, thoroughly frank and honest, and a conscientious worker. We have all grown extremely fond of Janet and yourself during the months you have been here and I am only too sorry that our caretaker has told us what he has in such an unfortunate manner."

"Thank you, sir," Norman seemed again almost like one of his own ex-scholars. "It is just like you to believe the best in a man. But there's still this case of the missing hundred dollars. If any of you believe that because of what happened in England, I'm the obvious guilty one here . . ."

"Of course you're not!" All heads turned as Alex came out with his exclamation in an almost disgusted tone, and several eyebrows were raised. He had spoken so spontaneously that now he looked thoroughly embarrassed, and hardly knew how to qualify his statement. So he rather feebly added, "He's not the type."

The minister smiled; he knew Alex so well. "Thank you, Alex, I'm sure you voice the opinion of us all. I'm going to suggest that we set aside our coffee-cups and spend a few moments quietly together, rather than dispersing now to go our various ways and gossip about the matter. So, if you'll all be seated . . ."

Automatically, Norman looked around for Janet and she was by his side in a moment, her head held high and almost defiantly, and her eyes fixed on his with a look of deep and trusting love. She sat down as close as she could to her husband and slipped her hand in his, not caring who noticed. Alex, watching her, felt almost envious of Norman. 'What it must be to have a wife like that,' he thought.

Jack was looking extremely uncomfortable by this time and quietly obeyed when Mc McCall motioned him to a chair. Several people heard the minister say in a low tone to him, "Those were harsh accusations, Jack, and I shall be glad if you will say no more at present. You and I will have a talk tomorrow."

Then, picking up his Bible, he told the group. "I am going to read a few verses of Scripture, recalling some of our Lord's words : 'Judge not, that ye be not judged. For with what judgment ye judge, ye shall be judged . . . Jesus stood down, and with His finger wrote on the ground, as though He heard them not. So when they continued asking Him, He lifted up Himself, and said unto them, He that is without sin among you, let him first cast a stone at her. . . . And why beholdest thou the mote that is in Thy brother's eye, but considerest not the beam that is in thine own eye?"

Closing the Bible, the minister invited them to pray : "O Thou who knowest the secret thoughts of each one of us, and who lookest not on a man's appearance but on his heart, cleanse us from any unkind thoughts which we may have and fill us with Thy Spirit—the spirit of love, compassion and understanding. We are so quick to cast stones,

Lord; help us to look within and see whether we have any right to condemn another, even though all evidence may persuade us that way. We pray again about the matter which is causing us so much concern, that the one who has had this lapse may be given courage to own up and be fully restored into fellowship with us and, more important, with Thee; for we believe that he or she will even now be suffering agonies of spirit because of what has been done. Set a seal upon our lips, O Lord, that we may not be tempted to pass on the information we have heard tonight, nor gossip about suspicions. Be with us now as we separate and go to our homes; comfort and sustain our two friends, Norman and Janet, and may nothing mar the bond of friendship which we have in this group. We ask this in our Saviour's name, who gave His life for His friends. Amen."

There was absolute stillness for two or three minutes, and the atmosphere was keen with the sense of prayer. Janet was sure that even Norman must be aware of how his friends were praying. She gripped his hand even more tightly and he placed his other one over hers; his head was bowed low and his shoulders drooped dejectedly.

Then Jack moved, creeping out of the room with a shamefaced expression and not daring to meet anyone's eyes. Janet watched him, then saw Tom motion to Bev. They both stood up and, coming to where she and Norman sat, Tom gripped Norman's shoulder, murmuring, "God bless you, Norm," and Bev impulsively dropped a kiss on Janet's forehead. Then they left without another word.

One by one, the members of the club rose from their seats to go home; but there was not a single person who left that room without first coming across to Norman, shaking him by the hand or muttering a few words. At last there was no-one left but the minister.

He stood up and held out his own hand to Norman.

"I'm truly sorry for what has happened, Norman. Jack's never been one of the most tactful people. If only I could have forestalled him—it was most unfortunate."

Norman stood up, eying the minister keenly. "I hardly know what to say, Mr. McCall. When Jack made those accusations, I thought it was all up—we'd have to move on and try to start a new life somewhere else. But the way they all reacted . . . it was because of what you said, of course, and I just don't know how to thank you."

Mr. McCall shook his head. "No, Norman, don't give me the credit. These are Christian friends, and they think a lot of you; I know they do, for one or two have spoken to me about you and your wife. . . ."

Norman looked round at Janet and put his arm about her shoulders. "Poor Jan, what she's been through for me!"

Janet could not trust herself to speak, only smiled up at her husband tremulously.

"Yes, Norman, you and Janet are among friends here and if any of us can do anything at all to help, you've only to ask. That, after all, is what friends are for."

"That wasn't the way it was at our home church in England," Norman put in bitterly. "There, everyone was horrified because of what had happened. They considered I wasn't fit to continue with—the—the various activities at the church. My wife was shunned and everywhere people were whispering in corners."

Janet found her voice. "Norman, you know why it was. The church secretary, Mr. Sears, who was also Head of the school, completely turned against you. His opinions were always respected and so everyone followed his lead. Even those who didn't really want to believe you were in the wrong seemed forced to in the end, especially when you pleaded guilty at the trial."

"But didn't anybody stand by you, Norman, even though they thought you were guilty?" the minister was clearly aghast.

Norman shrugged. "It was quite a wealthy church and somehow it wasn't quite the thing to mix with a jail-bird."

Janet put in, "Let's be fair, darling, one or two friends were kind and rose to your defence on several occasions—I heard them."

Norman nodded. "Yes, that's true. But it seemed as though everyone was against me. If it hadn't been for our families and you, Jan, life would have been unbearable."

"And there was an added reason for that, too," put in Janet, quietly.

Norman silenced her with a look. Then swiftly he softened. "Perhaps, though, Mr. McCall has a right to hear everything."

72

The minister put a restraining hand on his arm. "No, Norman. I've no right. If it would help, then I'm willing to listen. If not, then I shall respect your silence. It is obvious to me that your wife does not believe you were guilty and I'm sure she should know. Why you should plead so at the trial is your own business. . . ."

"And even I don't know the reason," murmured Janet.

The minister started, and turned to look at her. "Then there's absolutely no reason at all why I should know, my dear," he said understandingly. "Now, Norman, let's be practical for a moment. We'd already agreed that when Jack returned you might want to relinquish the job here at the church. I've been wondering if we should ask him whether he would like you to continue because, with the new wing, the work is really too much for one. In the circumstances, you probably won't want to work alongside him?"

Norman thought for a few moments. "No, I think it would be better not to. Trouble is, if this rumour gets about the city, my chances of finding any other work are pretty slim. And I thought, with the spring coming, I'd stand a better chance!"

"Well, you've a month's pay still to come—in lieu of notice, if you see what I mean. So take your time and call on me for references whenever necessary. No, don't look startled. I shall merely speak as I have found you. I believe Jack said you were a teacher? Well now, Stan is on the local education board; he may be able to help."

"I hesitate to take favours," Norman's reply was quick.

Mr. McCall put his hand on Norman's shoulder. "Norman, let me be frank. You don't seem able to accept friendship very well. It's understandable in the circumstances, but you must learn to let people help you when they really want to."

Norman was quiet for a few moments. "You're right, Mr. McCall. Somehow, you seem to understand me so well. Why you should stand up for me the way you did tonight —yes, I know, it's what a Christian should do. But it was almost as if you didn't believe what Jack said."

"I had to believe what Jack said," replied the minister, "because he probably gave plain facts. But I don't have to believe that you really were guilty. I've never yet been proved wrong in my judgment of a character, and I'm convinced you're trustworthy. Besides," and he smiled suddenly, "Mr. Walter Turner was a very good friend of mine when I was in England during the war."

Both Janet and Norman gasped. "Mr. Turner! You know Mr. Turner—the maths teacher at the school?" Norman said, his eyes lighting up. "Then . . . you mean . . ."

"Yes, Norman," Mr. McCall admitted, "Walter wrote to me about you. We always exchange letters once a year at the festive season, and this Christmas he mentioned that he thought you were probably attending my church. He said he was a little concerned about you, although he didn't go into details, and hoped I would be able to show you friendship. I replied, reassuring him and he wrote back again. At the time, I must admit, I thought the wording strange, for he said, 'That young man is thoroughly trustworthy and a very fine character, I am convinced, whatever anyone else may say about him.' So you see, you do still have someone in England who thinks highly of you."

"And yet," Norman began and Janet knew only too well what was coming, "Walter Turner would not call himself a professing Christian. Makes you think, doesn't it?"

Mr. McCall sighed. "Yes, it's one of the tragedies of church life that so often there is back-biting and malice where there should be love and understanding. Well, I must be off now. I'll leave you to lock up, Norman. Come across and see me in the morning.

*   *   *

When Norman did arrive in the minister's office the following morning, it was to find Jack there already. He felt rather sorry for the man; he had obviously realised fully the harm he had done but as yet he was not big enough to admit it, and although at the minister's quiet insistence he begged Norman's pardon, it was obvious he still held the same opinion.

If Jack was unrepentant, however, their other friends made up for it. Numerous telephone calls assured both

74

Janet and Norman that they were being remembered in prayer, and there were a number of invitations for them to visit. They did not feel able to accept many of these, although they did go round to Bev and Tom's home after church the following Sunday evening. They came away feeling almost cheerful because of the way their friends had made them realise that nothing could mar their friendship.

Norman began his trudge around the city again in search of work and managed, with the help of a reference from Mr. McCall, to find a few weeks' temporary work, doing holiday relief in one of the railway offices. It meant a certain amount of shift-work and consequently Janet was alone on one or two evenings. She was, therefore, only too glad to go to see Marion at her home one evening.

"Bill's working in the garden," indicated the older woman. "Look what a big yard we have!"

Janet smiled as she looked out at the park-like expanse of grass and trees; in Canada, anything from a ten-foot square lawn to a hundred-foot garden was called a yard. She stood watching Bill tying up the plants. The windows were open and the soft air fell comfortingly on her face. The lilac was just beginning to burst its buds and there were a few tulips struggling to show their colours after the long, hard winter. It had seemed such a long time to wait for spring, and now it had come her heart still felt chilled.

Bill looked up, saw her at the window, and waved cheerily, his round face breaking into a friendly grin. She waved back.

"It must be a lot of work," she remarked as Marion came in with a coffee-pot in her hand.

"Yes, but he loves doing it. So now we can have a nice, cosy little chat over a cup of coffee."

Janet sank into one of the comfortable armchairs in Marion's living-room and looked about at the tastefully decorated home which had been built up over the years.

"My, I love your place, Marion. My dream is to make a home for Norman like this one of these days."

"And you will, dearie, I'm sure of it," replied Marion smilingly. "Let me pour this coffee first, and then, before Bill comes in to interrupt, there's just something I want to say. . . ."

She handed Janet her cup, then the cream and sugar,

and, lastly, a plate of cookies. Taking her own cup in her hand, she began very gently. "How is Norman, dear?"

Janet smiled. "Well, you know, I think he's changing a little. I know we often say that all things work together for good, and this seems to be what's happening. If Jack had not said what he did that awful evening, Norman would never have discovered that there are people about with a true Christian spirit. You see, it wasn't so in our home church—at least, not with most of the folk there, although some were all right. And it's made Norman bitter about the church. I think now, however, he may find his Christian Faith again. I've been praying that something would happen—although I didn't expect it to be quite so startling!"

"Umm. That reminds me of a sermon Mr. McCall once preached with the theme, 'Be careful, God may answer your prayers.' I don't expect you'd have wanted Jack to come out with that information for the world, but God is working through his tactlessness."

"I think Norman still has a long way to go," Janet said with a sigh. "But I really believe this is a beginning."

Marion put down her cup, then almost apologetically she said, "Jan, I want to say something, and I hope you'll forgive me. You remember back in the winter, when we had coffee together down-town, you agreed that Norman was just that little bit unsure of himself at the time? Well, it's obvious to me now why that was. But I wonder if that incident with Alex worsened matters so much, sort of made him unsure of you as well, that . . . oh dear, I just don't know how to put it. . . ."

Janet stared at her. "You mean, you think Norman *may* have taken that money, because of the way he was feeling at the time?"

Marion's eyes brimmed with tears. "Oh dear, I don't know, Jan. It was just a thought, that it might have been possible. . . ."

"No, Marion, it could *not* be possible. Why, I was with him when he put the money in the safe that Saturday evening."

"And on the Sunday morning, when I handed you the rest of the takings?"

Janet gasped. "Goodness, I had never thought of that!
76

Oh, Marion, surely not—no, I absolutely refuse to think it."

Marion put out her hand quickly. "I'm sure you're right, Jan dear, and I wish I hadn't mentioned it, but I thought if anyone could help him, if he did have a lapse, you would be the one. I do hope I've not upset you?"

Janet shook her head. "No, it's O.K., Marion. It was an understandable thought, I guess. But, you see, I know my husband. What's more, I don't even believe he was guilty of what happened in England, but he won't tell me the details."

"Well, you just keep right on believing in your husband, dearie. I'm sure that'll be the way he'll find his true self again."

*   *   *

All arrangements were soon made for the car wash which had been discussed on the fateful evening at the O.F.S.L. Club, and Janet and Norman were pleased when Joe telephoned to ask them to help.

"It's jolly hard, to go about among them all as though nothing had happened," Norman admitted to his wife, "but it's the only way, of course, to prove I'm innocent of stealing that hundred dollars. Besides, they've all been so very decent."

"Norman . . ." Janet began awkwardly. "Have you any idea at all who might have taken it? Sometimes I think you know. . . ."

Norman shook his head and his eyes held their usual frank, steadfast gaze as he looked at her. "No, I just don't know, and I've given up thinking about it. I know what it's like to be wrongly accused. I'm certainly not going to start suspecting people myself."

So they joined their friends at the parking lot, facing them with cheerfulness and endeavouring not to show their anxiety.

There was soon quite a line-up of mud-splashed cars to be cleaned but, with two helpers to each car, they soon emerged gleaming from the showering hoses. Their owners were enthusiastic in their thanks, remarking that they wanted clean cars to drive down to the lake the following weekend. Fortunately, it was a warm, sunny day with a clear blue sky, and showed every promise of remaining that way for a few days.

Janet and Norman were busy on an enormous roadster when, looking up, Janet exclaimed, "Norman look, Peter's out of hospital!"

Norman stopped, put down his leather and held out his hand to the lad.

"Glad to see you about, Peter," he said. "Feeling better?"

"Yes, thanks," Peter replied, rather half-heartedly.

"What's up, then? You look pretty glum," remarked Norman.

"I've just heard what happened when Jack came back from England."

Norman sighed. "I thought no-one was supposed to gossip about that. Oh well, I suppose it was inevitable. Yes, Peter, apparently his nephew is Tony Jones—need I say more?"

"Tony Jones! The fellow who told my father he saw you coming away from the office the afternoon the money was missing?"

"The same," Norman told him grimly.

Peter's face was the colour of a beetroot. "Gosh! Of all the people to be related to Jack! I wonder how much more he told him?"

"Don't worry," Norman's voice was so low Janet could hardly hear his words as she continued to polish the car. "If he had heard more, he would have said. I'm sure he doesn't suspect the truth. But I'd keep away from him, if I were you—can't be too careful."

"I think I'll keep away from everyone for a while," Peter murmured in reply. "Term's nearly finished, so I'll take a trip out west for a spell."

"Yes, do that," Norman advised. "Got enough money?"

Peter flushed. "Yes, thanks; Dad's been quite generous."

Almost as though he meant to start west at that moment, Peter turned and, with only a brief wave in Janet's direction, walked quickly down the street.

It was not until the evening that Janet could bring herself to voice what was in her mind.

"Norman," she began hesitantly. "I know you don't

78

want to tell me the truth of what happened at the school, but assure me on one point, please?"

Norman looked up from the book he was reading. "Depends what it is."

"Was Peter involved?"

8

NORMAN CONTINUED staring at his book for what seemed to Janet an eternity. Thinking he could not have heard her, she began again, "Norman . . ."

"Yes, all right, I heard you," Norman cut in, rather irritably. "You asked if Peter was involved in what happened in England. Well, he knows the truth of the matter —that's all I'm going to say."

Janet looked at her husband aghast. "What! You mean, you told that boy all about it, and yet you've absolutely refused to let *me* know—me, your own wife!" It was not often that Janet was really annoyed but now she felt the heat of anger sweep over her in a rush.

Norman started when he saw her blazing eyes. "Oh come on, Jan, don't get so worked up. Stands to reason, doesn't it? Peter's the Head's son—he'd be bound to find out."

"And yet I always had the impression that Mr. Sears didn't know the truth," Janet was still flaming as she flung the remark at him.

It was obvious her husband did not know what to reply. She waited, letting the moments tick by. Eventually he spoke again. "No, that's right, too, the Head didn't know the truth. But it so happened that Peter . . . er . . . found out—that's all. He was sworn to secrecy, of course. . . ."

"Even from me!"

"Yes, my dear, even from you. Now let's forget it. I promise you, really I do, you'll know everything one day."

With that his wife had to be content. She continued to

seethe inwardly, however, and the natural sweetness of her face was marred for several days by a grim expression. So unlike herself did she appear, in fact, that the girl she worked with remarked upon it.

"Whatever's the matter with *you*, for goodness sake? Homesick again?"

Janet shook her head wearily. "No, Betty, not that. I've got something on my mind that's bothering me, that's all."

Betty studied her work-mate silently for several minutes. When she spoke, her words did nothing to ease the burden on Janet's heart.

"Worried about your husband, no doubt? People do surprise you, don't they—even when you've been married to them for a year or two. I don't suppose you ever suspected he'd turn thief when you married him."

The hot colour rose to Janet's cheeks and she stared at Betty unbelievingly. "Who have *you* been talking to?" she pounded out the question.

"Oh, just one of the members of the church you go to. I met her in the grocer's. The caretaker's wife told her what they'd found out about your husband. No wonder you both got out of England the way you did—skipped the country properly, didn't you?"

"No, we did not 'skip the country,' as you so sweetly put it," Janet continued to glare at the girl. "We faced up to things and eventually, when all was cleared, we left home for a new country, to try and build a new life for ourselves."

" 'When all was cleared . . .' You mean when your husband had served his term of imprisonment. Quite a man you've got there, haven't you?"

"Yes, I have," Janet snapped. "And one of these days, Betty, you'll regret those words. Because, sometime, you're going to find out just how fine the man I have married is." And with that she turned back to her work, thumping the keys of her typewriter with increased fervour.

She might have known the rumour would get around. Jack's wife was no more tactful than he, and couldn't help gossiping with her friends. None of the club members, Janet felt sure, would spread the news of what had happened that night when Jack had returned. The minister's words on that occasion had sealed their lips.

She said nothing to Norman about the incident at the office and he interpreted her silence as a continuance of her resentment because he refused to confide in her. They were both almost relieved when the door-bell rang. Going down to answer the call, Janet found Alex on the step, a large cardboard box in one hand and what looked like a record player in the other.

"Why hello, Alex," she greeted. "Do come in . . . and upstairs."

She led the way. "Norman . . ." she called as she opened the door to their living-room. "Here's Alex, and he looks like the proverbial donkey—well loaded."

Norman came through from the kitchen and eyed Alex suspiciously. "Good to see you, Alex, but what's all this?"

Alex deposited his burdens on the carpet, cleared his throat, put the fingers of his hands together nervously and looked down at his feet. Eventually, he began. "Well, it's just that : . . Well, I know Jan enjoys good music and, from one or two remarks you've let drop, Norman, I think you do also, so I brought along my record player and a few long-plays. Thought it might cheer you both up—I guess you need it right now . . ." he tailed off rather helplessly, looking so embarrassed that Janet longed to put her arms around him and thank him.

Instead, she gripped her husband's hand and said, "That's just wonderful of you, Alex. We've only the radio to give us music and we do miss going to symphony concerts. There's not many of them here." Then she hesitated and glanced at Norman, feeling his fingers tremble.

When he spoke, the words came out almost breathlessly. "You couldn't have done anything better for us, Alex . . . what records have you got?" Even Janet was amazed at his eagerness.

Together, the three of them went through the selection of discs, Janet and Norman exclaiming in delight at Beethoven concertos, Mozart and Tchaikovsky symphonies, Rossini overtures and Handel oratorios, as well as a few of lighter music from Gilbert and Sullivan to homely ballads.

It was not long before the Tchaikovsky 6th Symphony was filling the room with its poignant melody. Quietly Janet went to the kitchen to make coffee and put together a few sandwiches to serve their unexpected guest. Glancing through the open swing door, she paused in her preparations and watched her husband's rapt expression. It was a very long time since she had seen him like that. Would Alex's thoughtful gesture be yet another link in helping him find himself?

Her sensitive nature knew better than to bring out the refreshments before the symphony was over. As the last notes died away, however, she wheeled in the trolley.

Norman turned to her, his eyes bright with the thrill of the music. "It's come back, Jan! I thought the music had gone out of me, but it's still there."

It was Janet's turn to look thrilled. Quietly, and not minding that Alex was there, she dropped a light kiss on her husband's forehead. "I always knew it would be all right, darling," she said softly. "But Alex will be wondering what you're talking about . . ." she warned, realising that Norman had completely forgotten their visitor's presence. He turned to him, trying to form words, but Alex merely waved aside any remark he might have made.

"That's O.K. Don't mind me. I didn't realise the music would mean so much to you, Norm, or I'd have brought the records along sooner."

"It was good of you to bring them now—especially at this particular time," Norman remarked.

"Well," Alex began, then went on in his rather tactless manner. "I wasn't really thinking of you so much, Norm; it was your wife—she's been looking so despondent this last week that I thought she needed a bit of cheering up. . . ."

Norman's scowl was beginning to form again, so Janet interrupted quickly. "Oh come on, Alex, don't be so self-effacing. You know very well you thought Norman would enjoy the music, too—you said so when you arrived. And another thing—it was you who spoke up for him that dreadful evening at the club."

"Oh well . . ." Alex began uncomfortably.

"Yes, that's right," Norman took up the subject. "And I've never thanked you, Alex. After the way I had treated you, that was jolly decent."

Alex had by this time decided, as always, to be light-hearted about the whole affair. "Think nothing of it," he said breezily. "I guess you'd do the same for me. Now let

82

me tell you the other reason I came. This is the long weekend—we celebrate the 24th May here, rather than having the Monday off at Whitsun. Bev and Tom and their three kids will be away down at the lake where they have a summer cottage. Stan and Peg and the girls are going along with them to help them get it ready for the season. They won't need me down there as well, so I was wondering if you'd both like to come out for a run on Monday, and I'll show you something of the Prairies? After all, you've been living in the middle of them for six months now and it's about time you really saw them."

"Isn't it just flat, open space, though?" asked Janet hesitantly, playing for time a little in order to give Norman an opportunity to think about the invitation. "Is there anything to see?"

Alex laughed. "Why don't you come along and find out?"

"Well, as long as you'd rather not take out one of your girlfriends, Alex," Janet said. "When we first came here people said you always had someone in tow, but we've seen little evidence of it so far."

"Oh, I've been concentrating on one or two girls I've met away from the church and taking them out during the winter. I didn't really care for any of them very much, however. I guess all the best ones have already been snatched up!" he remarked with a grin at Norman.

Norman suddenly realised just then, as Janet did, that Alex genuinely wanted their company. "O.K., Alex, thanks. It'll do us both good—clear away some of the city cobwebs. We'll look forward to it."

"Right then," Alex rose to leave them. "And you've planned to come to the club wind-up the following week, I take it?"

Janet and Norman laughed, and it was Janet who said, "Yes, but we're not really sure what a wind-up is, Alex."

"Just another excuse for a party," he explained. "This time of the year all the activities are finishing up before closing down for the summer. Lots of people have cottages by one of the lakes which they open up for the summer and spend as much time as possible there, so the city's pretty empty. So we have parties to 'wind-up' the season, so to speak."

"And the club party is next week?" Norman asked.

83

"Yes, and a proper banquet it will be, too. Tom's in charge of entertainment, so it's sure to be fun. Peg and the rest of the girls are doing the food—you'll probably be roped in to help, Jan. Then the choir wind-up will be a bit later, but that's not such an elaborate affair. Usually, it's just a few refreshments after practice, but pleasant enough."

"Doesn't the choir operate during the summer then, Alex?" Janet asked.

"Oh yes, but nothing ambitious. Well, see you early Monday morning, if not before," and Alex was off.

*   *   *

"It seems hard to realise," remarked Janet as she settled herself in the back seat of Alex's car the following Monday morning, while her husband slid into the front seat beside the driver, "that only a few months ago we could hardly walk outside the door without being frozen stiff! And now, we're being roasted!"

"Yes, that's Canada for you. And it'll get hotter. In June, July and the beginning of August the temperatures rocket up into the eighties, I guess—and higher still on very hot days."

"It doesn't go above ninety though, surely?" Norman wanted to know.

"I've known it as much as a hundred!" comforted Alex. "But that's not often, of course. Then, the evenings are usually better. Lots of people sleep in their basements in the hot weather as it's cooler down there."

"I've noticed that in many homes here, the folk have made their basements into quite decent rooms," Norman was obviously in the mood for talking.

Janet sat back while the two men chatted together in front. She was not feeling particularly interested in the scenery. The eternal flatness seemed to mock her, and everywhere looked dry, hard and brown as they left the city behind. Soon, however, the vast prairie began to take on a fresh, clean appearance as though some great hand had just washed it, although in actual fact there had been little rain for weeks.

Then, gradually, a few gentle undulations appeared,

making the scene more interesting and before long one or two minor hills broke the monotony. Clean, neat-looking and orderly farms perched on top of a hill or nestled against the gentle slope of another. Each farmstead was a compact unit, with brightly coloured red and white buildings beneath green roofs, clustered together and surrounded by a very necessary shelterbelt of trees. A tethered cow standing at the entrance to one of the farms paused in his chewing to turn and gaze at them as they sped by.

The rich black soil which had so recently been turned over and seeded, the intense blue of the sky and the brilliant green of the grass made such a picture of peace that the cares seemed to slip from Janet's heart and she relaxed against the back of the seat, watching the clouds.

Now she realised fully the beauty of this great rolling prairie-land. Here, where the flat land met the sky on every horizon, with little to interrupt the view, there was a magnificent expanse of sky. Never before had she been so aware of the immensity of that great blue space across which the clouds chased each other, and every now and then blotted out the sun so that the road was sometimes in shadow but more often in sunshine. What patterns those clouds formed !

"You're quiet back there," Norman interrupted her thoughts.

"Just being happy with the beauty of the sky," Janet said, smiling.

"Yes, it's amazing, isn't it?" Norman agreed. "You know, Alex, we thought we'd come to a vast, barren land throughout the winter. How different it all looks now !"

"I thought you'd enjoy it," Alex told them. "I was speaking with Tom just before he went off for the weekend and he said it would be a good idea to take you both down to the lake in a couple of weeks' time and see their place. That'll be something rather different from this. . . ."

Janet broke in, excitedly. "Alex, did you see that bright orange and black bird fly right across in front of the car? What was it?"

"An oriole," Alex informed them. "Let's stop a minute and you'll see more wild life."

He turned off on to a rough cart-track and stopped the car. Leaning out of the window, he looked skywards, then his eyes dropped to the ground. "Did you notice that meadow lark?" Janet and Norman shook their heads. "It was singing up high and then swooped down—it's probably got a nest somewhere on the ground. Look, there's a red-winged blackbird. . . ."

"What's that chirping I can hear?" Janet wanted to know.

Alex listened for a minute. "Only a cricket, I guess." Then he began to quote:

> " 'In intervals of dreams I hear
>   The cricket from the droughty ground;
>   The grasshoppers spin into mine ear
>   A small innumerable sound.' "

Norman looked at their companion quickly. "Don't tell me you also like poetry? You're a surprising chap; we're always finding out something new about you."

"Oh, I read quite a bit of poetry. You'll find a book of it in the glove compartment there," Alex remarked casually. He started up the car again and backed out on to the highway. Norman had found the book and was turning over the pages.

"You can read to me as we drive along if you like," Alex continued. "These long, straight roads can become monotonous and it helps to keep me awake!"

"That's more in Jan's line," laughed Norman and handed the book back to his wife.

"The one I was quoting is quite near the beginning—it's called *Heat* and is by a Canadian poet, Archibald Lampman."

Janet found the poem and began to read:

> "From plains that reel to southward, dim,
>   The road runs by me white and bare;
>   Up the steep hill it seems to swim
>   Beyond, and melt into the glare."

They all three enjoyed that day on the Prairies, as they stopped at midday in one of the regular picnic sites dotted along the highway and enjoyed the lunch Janet had prepared, lingered to take photographs of the small white prairie churches and tall, colourful grain elevators which stood, sentinel-like as symbols of the Prairies. They drove homewards with the sunset.

*　　　*　　　*

It was, in fact, nearly three weeks later when they eventually went with Alex to the lake where Bev and Tom, with their children, were again spending the weekend. They drove for over seventy miles and the scenery was much flatter, although there was much of interest to notice and Alex was an excellent guide.

"See that old stone fort," he pointed out as they sped along. "That's where one of the famous battles between the Indians and the Hudson's Bay men took place. Horrible massacre, it was."

"How long ago?" Norman asked.

"Oh, about eighty years or so," Alex said.

"Is that all?" Janet was amazed.

Alex reminded her how relatively young in history the country was compared with Britain.

They drove up to the little wooden cottage beside a lake ringed with evergreens, poplar and birch, and liberally dotted with islands, their rocky promontories often housing a solitary cottage-home similar to that of their friends. As far as their eyes could see, there stretched miles of unspoilt natural beauty; rocks, trees, and lakes leading one from the other. 'Much as it must have been when the French explorers discovered this great west land,' Janet thought.

The children ran down to meet the car and were soon clamouring around the adults.

"Hi there!" Bev's gay voice rang out while Tom added his welcome from a ladder where he was just finishing painting round the edge of the roof.

"Isn't it hot?" Bev cried. "I hope you've brought your swimsuits. I thought we could have a dip before lunch— there's a nice sandy beach down there, and we have a small boat which the boys love. Paul's learned to handle it very well and Tom's quite pleased with him."

It wasn't long before they were all changed ready for swimming, and they walked down between the trees to the lakeshore. The two boys, however, were much more keen to take the boat out. Alex, who surprisingly could not swim, agreed to go with them.

"Make sure you have your life-jackets done up properly," Tom advised, as the three of them pushed off from the shore.

The others struck out into deeper water while Bev played on the edge with little Gail.

"This is wonderful!" exclaimed Janet as she came up from a dive. "The water is so clear."

Tom scooped up a palmful and drank. "And it's pure, too. Try some."

Janet was a little dubious but, following Norman's example, eventually did so. Bev laughed, calling out, "If Tom says it's O.K., it sure is. It's part of his job to test water and air about the city to see it's pure."

Janet noticed Tom gazing out to where the boat was. "Are they O.K., Tom?"

"I think so; Paul's pretty capable, and they should be all right with Alex."

The swim exhilarated them and, laughingly, they came out of the water and flopped down on the rocks. Suddenly, young Gene's piping voice reached them across the water.

"Daddy, Daddy, come quick, the boat's . . ." his voice ended in a wail.

Looking up, they were just in time to see the small dinghy roll over on its side. Alex was flung well clear, and so was Paul, but Gene had been sitting on the up-side and, obviously remembering his father's training, sat quite still.

Tom sprang up in a flash and began to sprint for the water. "O.K., son, sit tight. I'm coming."

Norman was beside him. "You get the two youngsters. I'll go for Alex," he panted as they plunged into the lake together.

Breathlessly the two girls and little Gail watched as the men struck out. The child began to whimper and Bev put her arm around her. Janet dug her nails into her palms. The boat had been a fair distance from the shore, and Alex could not swim. Tom had reached his older son now and was making his way back to the shore with him. But of Alex there was no sign!

9

Tom reached the lakeshore and laid young Paul down on the rocks. He was all right but was crying a little.

"O.K., Bev," Janet said quickly, "I'll look after Gail while you see to Paul."

"Good girl," remarked Tom briefly. "I'll go back for Gene now. How's Norm getting on?" and he turned to look out over the water.

Norman was by the boat and they saw young Gene pointing excitedly. The next moment Norman had dived and it was merely a matter of seconds before he re-emerged with Alex safely in tow. Tom immediately set out again towards the boat. By the time Norman had got back to the shore, Tom had the boat righted, and both he and the small boy were pushing back towards the anxious onlookers.

Although Alex was only slight of build, Norman was panting heavily as he laid him down. Bev was managing both Paul and Gail all right by now so Janet went to help her husband, rubbing Alex's white and limp limbs briskly. She was relieved to see that he was breathing and had not completely lost consciousness.

When Tom had tied up the boat and carried Gene up on to the rocks, Bev ran back to the cottage for blankets and more towels. She was back in a trice and very soon had both Paul and Alex wrapped up comfortably. Alex soon began to breathe normally and by the time Janet and Bev had made a large pot of tea he was rousing himself. They motioned him not to speak for a while, as they sat in the sun on the rocks, watching him anxiously. Carefully, Norman helped him to swallow a few mouthfuls of tea and the colour began to come back into his cheeks.

"Sorry to give everyone such a fright," he gulped eventually. "I guess I'm not used to boats. I must have moved at the wrong time, or something, and I went right under the boat. . . ."

"You rocked it, Uncle Alex," explained Gene knowingly. "Daddy always tells us not to do that. You have to be careful in boats. And you didn't have your life-jacket done up properly. . . ."

"Aw, Gene, Uncle Alex knows all that," interrupted his more mature brother scornfully. "It was just an accident. But we're O.K. now."

"Yes, son. everyone's O.K. now," said his father seriously. "So what do you suggest we do about it?"

Paul looked up at his parents who were watching anxiously, no doubt wondering if their teaching had found its home. It had. "I guess we'd better thank our Heavenly Father for protecting us," the boy said frankly.

Bev and Tom looked at each other, well satisfied. In the the silence which followed, even the baby of the family was quiet while Tom prayed in thanksgiving for their safety.

Later, while they sat inside the cottage eating lunch, with Alex resting on a couch, Tom brought up the subject of Norman's work.

"How's the job going, Norm?" he inquired kindly.

Norman shrugged. "It's O.K., but I'd rather be helping round at the church really. I felt more useful. This is just a dreary office job. But there's only another two weeks of it, and then I'll be looking for something else."

"Well, I was wondering about that," Tom continued. "You see, I meet quite a few people and I've heard that they're needing an assistant in the science laboratory out at the university. It's not too important a job, especially for someone of your experience—I understand you taught science to top-grade boys?" As Norman nodded briefly, Tom went on, "I'll speak to the man in charge about you, if you're interested."

"That's good of you, Tom," Norman said slowly, "but do you honestly think they're likely to employ someone with my reputation?"

"They needn't know," announced Tom.

Janet gasped. "But, Tom, how can you keep it from them? The rumour's sure to get about."

"Maybe, but they'll take my word for it that you're thoroughly honest and trustworthy. Stan's well known out there, too, and he'll put in a good word for you. They know we wouldn't recommend anyone who was not up to standard."

Norman stared at Tom, hardly believing his ears. "But you've nothing to prove that I'm trustworthy. Why, for all you know, Jack might be right. There's been no actual proof that I didn't take the money from the church."

"Only that of your own character which belies any meanness at all. A chap who strikes out to save another from drowning without a second's hesitation, isn't likely to steal a mere hundred dollars from a church."

"Especially when the chap he saves is someone he's not too sure about," put in Alex meaningly.

Bev and Tom looked puzzled and Janet interposed. "Don't bring that up, Alex—that's past and gone." Then turning to her husband, she spoke gently. "Darling, this is a wonderful opportunity. Will you let Tom speak for you?"

Norman looked down into her eyes and read the expression of hope there. He turned back to Tom. "O.K., Tom, and thanks a lot. You won't be sorry, I assure you. As to me going in to rescue Alex . . ." he went on quietly, "someone once rescued me in that way, and I've always wanted to do the same for someone else. I'm glad I was able to be useful." He looked down at his plate, toying with his food as he spoke.

Janet's eyes held astonishment. "Norman, you never told me. Who was it and when?"

Norman glanced at her, then at each of the others in turn, seeming to wonder how much he should add. "I was only in my early teens—before I knew you, Jan. It was on a school outing, and it was . . . Mr. Sears who rescued me."

"Oh no!" Janet gasped, and her face grew white.

"Say, isn't that the name of the man you said was your church secretary and the Head at the school?" Tom asked incredulously.

"The same," nodded Norman.

"And Peter's father," breathed Janet.

"Peter's father?" repeated Bev. "Well that explains a lot. I wondered why Norman didn't seem very pleased to see him when he first arrived from England. I don't blame you —you certainly didn't want to be reminded so vividly of your trouble over there."

"So he saved your life once, only to ruin your career later by his self-righteous attitude?" remarked Tom. "Well, it seems you folks are due for some better times, and if I can do something to help you both, it'll make me very happy. Incidentally, speaking of Peter, I understand from the university staff that he's quite a bright boy."

Norman looked up quickly. "Who told you?"

"His science lecturer. Seems way ahead of all the others in the class. Must be the excellent teaching he had in England!"

Norman shook his head. "No, it's Peter himself. He was the best student I ever had. I'm glad to hear the university think he's good too."

Alex seemed to have recovered from his watery adventure by the time they were due to leave the lake, but Tom made him promise to visit the doctor before going to work in the morning. He didn't, however, feel like driving home so Norman took over the wheel.

It was the first time Norman had actually driven in Canada, although he had obtained a licence soon after arriving in the country. Janet kept glancing at him as he manoeuvred the big Canadian car and realised how much he was enjoying this thrill of once again having a vehicle under his control. Suddenly, life looked more hopeful than it had for a very long time, and she wondered if their future was to be as clear and uncluttered as the scenery stretching away into the distance before them.

*   *   *

One by one the activities at the church came to a temporary standstill for the summer. The club party had been its usual success, and soon many members were going their various ways wishing everyone happy holidays. The choir held its wind-up at the beginning of June and by that time there seemed an impatient air of expectancy everywhere.

Janet found herself sitting beside Mary Jane Andrews while they ate the refreshments she had helped Bev prepare for the choir party.

"Your brother couldn't stay for the party then, Mary Jane?" she turned to the quiet girl.

Mary Jane shrugged. "Yes of course he could have, if he'd wanted. And he should have, as he's the choir leader.

I don't know what's got into him lately. He hardly says a civil word—just snaps my head off at the least little thing." She sighed. "A fine summer I look like having."

Janet touched her hand sympathetically. "I would imagine he was a difficult man to live with," she said. "If you're ever fed up, just give me a ring, or come on over and see me. I shan't get away for the summer—we can't afford it—and with Bev away at the lake I shall be feeling lonely."

The girl's face lit up. "Thanks—maybe I'll take you up on that."

The little bit of kindness Janet had been able to show seemed to have cheered Mary Jane up and she looked almost pretty as she smiled her thanks. Alex had drawn near and heard the last part of their conversation.

"If you're not doing anything on 1st July, I'm taking Janet and Norm down to see Bev and Tom again, and you're welcome to come along too," he invited.

Mary Jane shook her head. "No good, I'm afraid, Alex, thanks all the same. Blair would be furious if I left him for a full day out."

"Do you always have to do just what he wants, though?" Janet wanted to know.

"It's the surest way to peace and quietness," Mary Jane said resignedly.

Later, Alex remarked to Janet, "You know, that's the first time I've ever heard Mary Jane say anything against her brother. He must have been hard to get on with lately for her to make those remarks."

Norman's job finished at the end of the month and, as the 1st July was Dominion Day and a holiday, they took the trip with Alex. This time, the day at Bev and Tom's cottage was without incident. Tom and Norman had a long talk about the job at the university, while the others sunbathed, and Janet was pleased to see her husband relaxed and happy.

They arrived home to find Jack Simmons wandering aimlessly around outside the church. When he saw them, he waved and beckoned Janet and Norman over. Alex drove off as they walked across to talk to the caretaker.

Janet felt a trifle reserved with the man these days but

she was relieved to see her husband make an effort to greet Jack fairly cordially.

"Hi there, Jack! Surely you haven't been working to-day—it's a holiday."

"Yeah, I know, Norm, I know," Jack's tones were dull. "But I couldn't enjoy no holiday all the while I kep' remembering what I'd done to you."

Norman put his hand on the man's shoulder. "Let's forget it, Jack. You did it on impulse, and I'm sure you had the good of the church at heart."

"Well, you must admit, it looked pretty queer," the care-taker began to defend himself. "And you did go to prison. . . ."

Norman winced. "Yes, I did, Jack. But let's forget it. You know, I was thinking," he squared his shoulders and took a deep breath, "I haven't any more work for a couple of months now, until the term begins at the university, How'd you like me to come over and give you a hand for a few days a week? This is a big building for one man to look after."

Jack gazed at him, admiration replacing the previous look of distrust. "Would you really do that, Norm? I'd be right glad, if you would. Let bygones be bygones, eh?"

"As you say, Jack. It's over and done with."

"'Cept they haven't found the culprit yet."

"Any ideas, Jack?" Janet put in.

The man shook his head. "None, more's the pity. From what I can hear, things seemed to point to Ben Tullett being the guilty party, but no-one can't get any sense out of him, and I don't somehow think he'd have the sense to get into the safe so cleverly. One thing I am sure of now, though—it weren't your husband who took the money!"

Norman was obviously amused. "How can you be sure?"

"Oh I don't know," Jack shrugged. "You're just not the type," he echoed Alex's words of that fateful evening.

"Well thanks, Jack. Tell you what—I'll come over in the morning and see Mr. McCall, to make sure it's O.K., with him for me to help you. Then we'll think out a working arrangement."

Janet and Norman walked thoughtfully back to their rooms. Once indoors, Janet turned to Norman.

"That's amazing, isn't it? I suppose Jack was so completely influenced by the attitude of the O.F.S.L. Club members and by what the minister said, that he's caught their spirit."

"Yes," agreed Norman, "and I think it was probably only because he's so easily influenced that he came back from England and let out those accusations in the way he did. You see, young Tony Jones is rather a spiteful youngster and, from the way I remember her, so's his mother—Jack's sister. You can understand the way they both played on the fellow's mind."

"Really poisoned it, you mean?"

"Not without cause, I suppose," remarked her husband.

*　　　*　　　*

As each week of July passed, the weather became hotter and hotter. How Janet longed for the relative coolness of the lakeside. Bev and the children were staying at the cottage during the hot season, the school term having come to a close at the end of June. Tom was travelling down to be with them at weekends; it was an arrangement many families had during the two hottest months of the year.

Janet soon learned that the best way to keep their city rooms cool was to fling open the windows quite early and let the morning breezes flow right through the apartment. Then before she and Norman left for their daily work, they closed every window tightly, thus retaining the fresh atmosphere. Even so, she often longed to lean out of the window during the evening but couldn't because of the fine wire mesh across each window frame, put there to keep out the mosquitoes. Likewise, every door that opened to the outside had the addition of a screen door in the summer, and these had to be kept carefully closed.

Janet soon became well aware of how troublesome mosquitoes could be. They made picnicking during the evening rather uncomfortable, even though aeroplanes flew low over the city and sprayed several square miles in an effort to get rid of the pests. Boats were used for fogging along the river banks, and both these operations were used to good effect any time a large open-air function was planned.

Norman had gone across to the church early one evening

to finish a few chores, and Janet was sitting beside the window, now open to the cool of the evening. It was still daylight, but she noticed a faint light go on in the sanctuary itself and presently the soft tones of the organ could be heard. She leaned back, listening.

Suddenly, she sat straight up. That was not Blair Andrews playing—it was Norman! She could never mistake her husband's music.

Quickly letting herself out of their apartment, she went across to the church, in by the side door and up into the choir stalls, where she could clearly see Norman's face. He was completely absorbed and she did not disturb him.

He was playing gently but soon the music took possession of him and, pulling out more stops and testing combinations, he soon felt the full power of the instrument. Great chords echoed around the empty hollowness of the building and then his fingers, coming alive again to their suppleness, began to break into arpeggios, running up and down the two consoles. Janet recognised a piece of Norman's own composition which he had written especially for their church's golden jubilee—a great hymn of thanksgiving. Then he slipped into something by Sullivan and finally on to the master of them all—Bach. The majestic chords of the great Toccata and Fugue boomed forth and the rippling accompaniment seemed to flow from the very tips of her husband's fingers.

Finally, he struck a triumphant Amen chord and sat back, completely spent. Janet came towards him, her face radiant. Only then did he notice her.

He put out his hand and she came to him, sitting beside him on the organ seat as she had done so often in the years past. He put his arm around her and held her close; no words could come, but she felt the trembling of his body. It was as if he had suddenly come alive after a very long sleep.

Eventually he spoke. "It's come back, darling, it's come back! I've felt it stir within me while I listened to Alex's records. The music I thought had gone from me for ever is still there. Strange, I've had no inclination to sit down at this organ in all the months I've worked here in the church. But tonight, it was open and, suddenly, I couldn't resist it."

"You've found your faith in mankind again, darling,"

Janet said gently. "And in finding that, everything else has stirred within you. God has been working . . ."

"Don't rush me, Jan," Norman warned. "It's not as easy as that, you know."

Wisely, Janet said no more, only leaned her head against his shoulder and silently offered a prayer of thanksgiving.

A slight sound made them look round quickly and there, walking towards them, his face drained of every hint of colour, his eyes staring as though right through them, was Blair Andrews.

"Norman," whispered Janet, "did you ask his permission to use the organ? You know how fussy he is about it."

"Goodness, no," whispered Norman back. "I never thought—it was open and I just sat down and played."

He slid off the organ stool and made his way out of the choir stalls, meeting the organist beside the pulpit.

"Blair, I hope you didn't mind my trying out your instrument. I should have asked you but . . ." Norman stopped abruptly for Blair was staring at him, obviously not hearing what he was saying. Janet had joined her husband and now laid a hand gently on the organist's arm.

"Blair, what is it? Are you ill?"

He turned to look at her although, it seemed, almost with unseeing eyes. Then, suddenly, he sank down on to the steps leading up into the pulpit and broke down into convulsive sobs, his whole body shaking, his long fingers nervously pushing through his fair hair.

Norman darted forward. "Man, what's the matter? Have you had a shock or something."

Slowly the man lifted his head, took off his glasses and wiped his short-sighted eyes. "Yes, that's what it is—I've had a shock, brought on by myself. I heard you play . . ."

"Go on," Norman prompted. "So you heard me play."

"That music, oh that music—it lives in you. And it was I—I who sought to do you harm, to drive you away from our city, away from this church."

Norman frowned. "Whatever do you mean, Blair? You've never done me any harm . . ."

Suddenly, Janet's womanly intuition came to the fore and she darted forward, grabbing Blair by the shoulder. "Tell us, Blair, tell us—is it about the missing money? Oh do say. . ."

97

D

Numbly the man nodded. "Yes, it's about the missing money." His voice rose again. "I took the money—I took it, hoping the suspicion would fall on your husband. *I'm* the guilty one," his voice broke. "God forgive me."

10

JANET AND Norman stared at Blair as he sat sobbing on the steps of the pulpit. It seemed they were living through a nightmare and any moment they would wake up and wonder where they were.

Norman was the first to speak. "Blair . . . I can hardly believe this. Why should you want to get rid of me—what have I ever done to make you wish to harm me? Why, we've hardly spoken to each other in all the time I've been here."

"No, I made sure we didn't," Blair's voice was muffled. "I couldn't risk having you near the organ . . ."

"But how did you know I played? No-one else did."

Blair lifted his head again and looked at Norman, his eyes still rather shifty. "I have a friend in England—I met him while he was here on vacation once—Mark Williams . . . you know him?"

"We studied together at the college of music."

"You didn't realise he had heard about the scandal at the school where you were teaching?" As Norman shook his head, Blair continued, "Well, he had. When he knew you were coming to this part of Canada, he wrote to me about you, singing your praises as a musician, and also mentioning your . . . your trouble at the school, saying what a pity it was. And in that letter he made a remark that I couldn't forget, even though I know he was merely joking. He wrote, 'You'd better watch it, Blair. Norman is one of the finest musicians I've met. You'll be losing your job at the church if he should happen to settle in your city and attend your church.'"

"And you were afraid that's what would happen, Blair?" Janet had found her voice at last.

Dumbly the man nodded. Then Norman spoke, and when he did so it was in his most bitter tone. "Professional jealousy, eh? Hardly the thing for a *Christian* musician, I should think!"

Janet caught her breath and her heart seemed to turn a somersault as the bright new world she had only just begun to glimpse came tumbling about her, like an echo from the past year. Her husband had been so near . . . what now?

Then, cutting across the stillness, they heard a polite cough, and Mr. McCall himself stepped out from the shadows of the corner.

"So, the mystery is solved at last," he remarked, almost pleasantly.

"You heard?" Norman queried.

"Yes, Norman, I've heard everything. Forgive me for eavesdropping. I was in my office when you began to play the organ and, thinking it was Blair, I came through to speak with him about the hymns for next Sunday. To my astonishment I saw it was you. I must admit," he turned slightly towards Blair, "I was so enthralled with the music I just stood there in the corner, listening. I couldn't move after that for the events which followed seemed to root me to the spot."

"So now you know what a hypocrite you've had as your organist," said Blair, it seemed almost with relief.

The minister did not answer the remark. Instead. he asked, "And why have you come out with the truth at this moment, Blair?"

The organist had remained sitting on the steps but now he jumped to his feet. "Why now, you ask? You heard the music—isn't that enough? I'd been told he was a brilliant musician but I never dreamed he was as good as this. Now I've heard him play—how can I dare let anything stop the outflow of that gift?"

"But, Blair, you're a fine organist yourself . . ." Norman began.

Blair turned and looked at him with an almost pitying smile. "Come now, Mr. Blaker. You know as well as I do there's no comparison. I'm all right technically, but with you—it's just *in* you," he broke off on another sob.

99

The minister laid his hand on Blair's arm. "Let's all go into the office where it's comfortable and talk this over. Norman . . . Janet . . ."

Norman shook his head, "No, Mr. McCall. This is something which you alone can help Blair with. It's far too personal for outsiders. Oh I know I'm involved. But when he feels like it, Blair can come and talk to me. My wife and I will just go along home now."

He took Janet's arm and silently they walked across to their apartment. Once inside, however, Norman sank into the armchair and pulled his wife on to his knee. She held him close, searching about in her mind for the right thing to say.

"Mr. McCall will sort things out, darling," was all she could manage, however.

A great sigh escaped Norman. "Yes, if anyone can help, it's the minister; what a fine man he is! But Blair—who would have thought he would have taken the money?"

"When could he have done it, Norman?"

"I was wondering that myself. I suppose it must have been when I dropped the keys outside the church office— you remember just after we had put the money away in the safe—and he brought them to us."

"Why yes, of course. I suppose he'd been looking for an opportunity of hurting you and, finding the keys, he saw his chance. I remember thinking at the time that he was unusually talkative and . . . oh, Norman . . . I've just realised . . . I was the one who mentioned that we had just put the money away. . . ."

Norman put a hand over her lips. "Now, don't let's have any self-reproach. That won't do any good now. If only I had known how he felt, I could have tried to be more friendly, although . . . no, I suppose I'd have just despised him for his jealousy."

"It sounded as though that's how you felt, anyway," Janet could not help the remark, nor the slightly bitter tone.

Norman frowned. "Yes, I know. Isn't it natural? It seems that everywhere I go, the so-called Christians let me down."

"Bev and Tom . . . Peg and Stan . . . Mr. McCall, for instance?" Janet's sarcasm was slight but so unexpected that her husband stared at her in astonishment. He sat silent for so long that eventually she got up and began to make some drinks. She bit her lip, striving to control her emotions, fearing she had said too much already. They exchanged very few words during the rest of the evening.

*   *   *

Janet had not even left for the office the next morning, when the door-bell rang and she found Blair on the step. Quietly she asked him in and they went up the stairs in silence.

Norman looked up in surprise as Blair came in. He did not rise, however, but just sat at the breakfast table, watching the organist.

"A cup of coffee, Blair?" Janet offered.

The organist shook his head. "No thanks, Mrs. Blaker. I want to talk to you both. To apologise seems almost futile, and I hardly know how to set about it . . . I don't really know what to say . . ."

Gently Janet pushed a chair forward and Blair sank into it gratefully. Then he continued. "I doubt if you'll understand but—well, Mr. McCall suggested I tell you what came out in our talk last night. You see, ever since my parents died, I've felt . . . well . . . unable to cope, somehow. They were both remarkable people, but they spoilt us both—Mary Jane and myself. When they were killed in a boating accident, it was so sudden . . . I had to take the responsibility for the home, to look after my sister —I felt lost. I was scared I'd lose her, too, so I made sure she had no men friends. I couldn't have faced life alone."

"Does a Christian have to face life alone?" asked Norman cynically.

Blair sighed so deeply that they were afraid he might break down again but his voice was controlled as he continued. "That's what Mr. McCall helped me to see last night. I'd heard it all, of course, many times but somehow I could never seem to lay hold of it . . ."

"But you understand at last, Blair?" Janet asked, almost breathlessly.

The organist nodded. "Dimly, but I've made a beginning. And just to prove it, I intend to go away and make a fresh start; I heard only recently of a vacancy at a small church out west. I've told my sister everything. It's tough on her, of course. but I believe she'll be happier without me. She has a girlfriend who's in need of a home so she'll probably ask her to stay with her for the time being. Then, who knows, she may even find someone to marry. I've often had the impression there was someone special she was interested in . . ."

"What about the music at the church?" Norman asked.

Blair turned to him, his thin lips twisted into a crooked smile. "That's up to you," he said softly. "I can't show my face at the church again. *You're* the organist now, Mr. Blaker; the choir is in your hands."

Janet gasped. "But, is that what Mr. McCall wants?"

"It's the only thing," Blair said ruefully. "Ironical, isn't it? My feeling of insecurity made me so desperate to keep my job at the church that I'd stoop to anything, even to harming another who threatened my position. But I've turned the tables on myself—almost thrust the job at you. I've only myself to blame."

Norman's face softened sympathetically. Janet loved him as he rose at last and placed his hand on Blair's shoulder. "Blair, I hardly know what to say myself, but remembering how the O.F.S.L. Club members treated me when suspicion first fell on me, all I can say is, 'God bless you.'" Then stooping down, he clasped the man's hand.

*　　　*　　　*

The news spread around the few church members who were still in the city for the summer. Odd little remarks were remembered, strange incidents, the organist's offhand manner . . . and people gossiped: "Of course, we should have realised . . . never did like that man . . . such a shame for the young English couple . . . fancy Norman playing the organ now. . . ." So it went on, in spite of the minister's request that the matter should be forgotten. He had made a brief statement at the end of the morning service to the effect that the mystery had been solved; Mr. Andrews had owned up, had left the city, and no further

102

action was being taken. All this Norman had willingly agreed to.

Janet's thoughts were often with Blair's sister, Mary Jane, and one evening she telephoned the girl.

"Mary Jane?" she spoke as cheerfully as she could. "This is Janet Blaker. Do you have anyone with you or would you care to come on over for supper?"

She heard a gasp at the other end of the wire. "Janet— why, I thought you wouldn't want anything to do with me. . . ."

"Whyever not? What's happened had nothing whatsoever to do with you. In any case, I imagine you're feeling pretty grim about everything. Norman and I are only too glad it's all cleared up. Don't worry, we won't interrogate you, or anything, if you come over. We just thought you'd need to be out a bit now."

"Well, as a matter of fact . . ." the girl's voice tailed off, she hesitated then went on, "someone else has just rung me and asked me out for the evening, so . . ."

"Oh. that's O.K., then," Janet said quickly. "I'll be in touch again and arrange for another time. Have a good evening. Goodbye for now."

She was grinning as she turned to face her husband. "Do you know, I do believe Mary Jane has a date! She sounded so confused. . . ."

"Oh come now," Norman chided her. "You're romanticising. . . . I mean, who would take her out? You never see her with anyone. . . ."

"Well, I don't know. I believe we'll see a change in Mary Jane. and she'll begin to come right out of her shell. But I wonder who's dated her?"

She was not to wonder for long. The following evening, Alex called to see them.

"Just dropped in to make arrangements for the last weekend in August when we're going out to the camp. You're both coming, I hope?"

"Goodness!" exclaimed Norman, "I'd completely forgotten about the camp. But I thought it was mainly for the youngsters?"

Alex grinned. "Oh come now, Norm, you're not so old yourself! True, it's really for the younger people but some of us older ones go along to help. Bev and Tom will be there; Tom's leading the camp and Bev is acting as camp mother; her parents are looking after the three kids for the weekend. Tom was saying he hoped you'd both come along."

"Norman, let's go," said Janet excitedly. "It'd make such a nice change. I feel I want to get away from the city for a bit."

Norman looked up at her where she sat on the arm of his chair, and took her hand in his. "Poor old Jan. It's sure been a tough year for you," he said softly. "All right, darling, we'll go. There's another man in the congregation who can fill in at the organ for that weekend—Mr. McCall introduced him to me last week. How do we travel, Alex, and what are the arrangements?"

"Well, I thought you'd like to come in my car. As a matter of fact . . . ." his voice dropped and he looked somewhat embarrassed, "I thought it might be a good idea to ask Mary Jane along—if you've no objection to travelling with her?"

Janet dare not look at Norman as, controlling her voice, she said, "Of course not; Mary Jane and I are good friends. Actually," she went on, choosing her words very carefully, "I asked her over for supper last night, but she had a previous engagement, so couldn't come."

Alex looked up sheepishly and very slowly the only flush Janet had ever seen in his cheeks rose. "Umm. I wonder who that was with?" he mused.

"You wouldn't know, I suppose?"

"Well . . . I thought she'd be feeling a bit fed up, so I took her out for a meal; she seemed to brighten up considerably by the end of the evening, too," and Alex's eyes took on a far-away expression; he had obviously enjoyed the evening.

Janet smiled to herself as she prepared coffee while Norman and Alex talked over the arrangements for the camping weekend. She had often wondered if this was where Alex's real interest lay, for on several occasions she had caught him looking at Mary Jane when he had thought no-one was noticing.

As Janet looked forward to the camp, she wondered within herself at her feeling of anticipation. It was more than mere excitement over the prospect of getting away

104

from the hot city for a few days; almost it seemed a premonition of a realisation of her dreams. Life, in fact, once again seemed to be beckoning her up to the heights of joy, but past experience had made her nervous of expecting too much.

The camp was situated on the shores of one of the many dozens of lakes within the Lake of the Woods area on the borders of Manitoba and Ontario. The drive to it, after the first hour or so of flat countryside, gradually became more beautiful as they went through mile after mile of almost dense forest. Mary Jane sat with Alex in the front of the car, and Janet and Norman watched them from behind with interest. There was little doubt that a comfortable companionship already existed between them. Janet noticed how animation brought the colour to Mary Jane's cheeks, making her look sweet and pretty.

Alex did not, however, neglect his friends because of the girl by his side. Once again, he proved an excellent guide. At one point, Janet pointed to a notice.

" 'Indian Reservation,' " she read aloud. "Surely they don't lump all the Indians together—I thought I had seen a few about the city."

"Yes, you have. The reservations are set aside for those Indians who want to be free to live their lives the way they've always done. They don't all choose to stay on the reservations, though. Some of them get jobs, although often they're rather lazy and unreliable."

"Quite a problem, eh?" Norman remarked.

"Well, it's the fault of the white man, really," Alex said magnanimously. "Those who came here taught the Indian that his ways were wrong and his religion not the right one. The trouble was, they didn't bother to teach him the right one, so now they've nothing."

"You think lots of the trouble between cowboy and Red Indian could have been avoided, then?" Norman asked, leaning forward.

Alex shrugged. "It's difficult to say. A lot's been done for them, but they need a lot more understanding. They work when they feel like it, then one day they won't turn up—they're away somewhere else."

The campers were to sleep in wooden shacks, on low camp beds. the girls at one end of the clearing and the

105

fellows at the other. Janet, with Mary Jane, was in charge of a hut with several younger girls in it.

Bev and Tom had arranged a well-varied programme of sports; swimming, boating, baseball, walks to different viewpoints. Carefully interwoven, however, were times of devotion, Bible-study and discussion. The programme had been so well thought out that, Janet noticed, the young people became keenly involved in every part of it.

Throughout the days, she saw little groups sitting together, sometimes with a Bible on their knee, deep in discussion. They would waylay Tom, asking him questions. Bev was usually surrounded by one or two girls, often in serious debate, although every now and then her gay laughter would ring out. 'That's why she gets along so well with them,' thought Janet. 'She's one with them, rather than like an older person talking down to them. She's full of fun as they are, so they feel they can talk to her and discuss their problems.' Her admiration for her friend grew.

Among the crowd of youngsters was Peter. He had returned from his trip west, turning up at his rooms one evening towards the end of the month. He seemed eager to join in with the camping arrangements, and was pleased when they arranged for him to travel down with some of the younger people.

It would all have seemed perfect to Janet, had it not been for Norman's strange mood. She had never known him quite so silent. When his moods were bad, there were usually bitter words on his lips. Now, however, she found it difficult to know what he was thinking, and as they had little time for private conversation she could do no more than pray that Blair's confession had not hindered the development for which she had been hoping. He took no verbal part in the discussions; merely stood by listening to Tom and watching the young people—Peter in particular.

It was the last evening of the weekend and a campfire had been arranged. Throughout the day, the pile of wood had grown steadily as everyone gathered what they could find. After a hot drink in the large hut which served as the mess, they donned warm clothing and made their way to the lakeside where the fire was to be lit.

The sun was setting behind the trees on the distant shore, sending brilliant crimson and gold streaks among the grey clouds and making patterns on the gently rippling water. Rocks, trees and promontories stood like dark etchings silhouetted against that brilliant canvas; soon right overhead a full moon shone and the stars sparkled in the clear sky.

Janet settled herself on one of the rugs which had been placed around the fire and watched as the young people gathered, quietly and reverently as if for a church service. It was, in fact, to be a devotional meeting and what better setting than where the Creator showed His glory in such splendour?

One by one the hymns and choruses rang out across the water, as the flames from the fire rose higher and higher until those nearest drew back a little from the heat. The soft firelight played upon faces glowing with the joy of fellowship and the thrill of the atmosphere.

Prayer was offered and then Tom spoke. It was only a short message but one full of meaning. " 'God so loved the world that He gave His only begotten Son that whosoever believeth' in Him should not perish but have everlasting life,' " he read. Then he went on to talk about that wonderful love which yearned that each of those young people present should give themselves to Him. He finished by asking if anyone would care to give a few words of testimony, and nearly every one of the younger members there spoke in turn. Stumbling sentences they were, but it was obvious that everyone had been greatly blessed during the few days they had spent together and they were completely sincere. Then Tom drew them closer to their Lord in prayer.

No sound came from those gathered around the fire after Tom had said "Amen"; the wood had now ceased to crackle, leaving merely a warm glow at the centre of the fire and the smell of woodsmoke; a bird called from across the lake, rustlings among the trees told of small wild creatures about their nocturnal ways. No-one seemed to want to move. Sitting near to Tom, Janet heard him quietly ask his wife, "Can you sing, Bev? 'The love of God'—you know it, don't you?"

Quietly Bev began :

> "The love of God is greater far
> Than tongue or pen can ever tell;

107

It goes beyond the highest star
And reaches to the lowest hell. . . ."

Bev's beautiful voice rang out in the stillness till everyone seemed caught up and at one with the message which
came not only from her lips, but from her heart :

"Oh love of God, how rich and pure !
How measureless and strong !
It shall for evermore endure,
The saints' and angels' song."

As the last chorus faded away the atmosphere, although
still quiet, seemed alive with expectancy. Then Janet felt
Norman stir beside her. Raising himself to a kneeling position, he spoke.

"The testimonies are over, I know, but before we leave
this wonderful spot, I want to add my few words. You all
know my story; it's been around the church enough. But
you probably don't know what has been going on inside
me. I came here to your country, shaken in my Christian
Faith, because I felt God had let me down. I had looked
for understanding from Christian friends, and they had
failed me. I became bitter—ask my wife. But here, in your
church, I met new friends who stood by me even though
suspicions heaped against me.

"Gradually, because of their love and sympathy, I have
grown to realise that the love of God reaches out to us in
our times of need, lifting us above our difficulties. We are
all human and we fail miserably, but God still loves us. I
felt my friends in England had failed me; I myself failed
because of my bitterness; but I know now that God has *not*
let me down. Rather, He has led me to this place and I
praise Him for it. Young people, whatever difficulties lie
ahead, never lose your grip of Him, as I did. Keep right on
believing and He'll bring you through."

Janet's heart felt as if it would burst for the joy welling
up within her. She knew how much it cost her husband to
speak in this way, but she knew, also, that every word was
sincerely meant. He had come through his long, dark
valley and would not look back.

There was a stir on the far edge of the circle of people around the fire. Suddenly, Peter leapt to his feet.

"Please . . ." he began in a choking voice, "I would like to say something—may I?"

"Sure, Peter," answered Tom. "There's no time limit on this service. Go right ahead."

"I can't let Mr. Blaker speak the way he has and not tell you . . ."

"Peter, be quiet," Norman's voice rang out with a sharpness which arrested everyone in the group.

11

PETER SQUARED his shoulders and looked Norman straight in the eyes. Everyone around the campfire seemed to be holding their breath sensing the tension between the boy and his ex-teacher.

"No, Mr. Blaker," Peter said firmly, "I will *not* be quiet any longer. I won't let these people go on thinking you ever failed in any way. You aren't the only one, Mr. Blaker. who's been roused by this weekend's fellowship. I, too, wanted to give a testimony just now, but I couldn't do so until I'd got right with God; and I can't do that while a good man takes the blame for something he would never have even considered doing."

"Peter!" began Norman again.

Janet pulled at her husband's sleeve. "Let him speak, Norman. It's his right," she said with sudden wisdom.

Reluctantly, Norman sank down beside the campfire and Janet waited breathlessly, torn with emotions. While her heart was happy because it seemed her husband's name was about to be cleared, she was apprehensive about the revelation Peter might make. Like Norman, she was extremely fond of the boy.

"You've heard what happened to Mr. Blaker in England," Peter began. "A large sum of money was missing from the Head's office—my father's office. Mr. Blaker was

109

seen coming away from that office on the afternoon it was taken; later the money was found in his pocket. As far as it could be understood, no-one else had been near the room. He did not deny the charge, pleaded guilty at the trial and went to prison." The boy paused and looked about the circle at those who had become his friends.

"While I've been out west, I've had time to think," he continued. "Gradually I began to feel I could keep the truth of what happened to myself no longer. This weekend has clinched it. I *must* tell you all—he did not take the money, he should never have gone to prison. I . . . I . . . want you to know . . ."

Again Norman made to stop him but Janet's hand was on his arm, and Tom motioned the boy to continue, waving aside Norman's protest.

"It was . . . it was . . . *I who took that money*! It was for *my* sake Mr. Blaker took the blame; it was to save *me* that he went to prison." His voice rose as he went on, until the words came out in a rush. "I don't understand why he thought no-one should know I was the culprit. I only know he did and I went free—free from blame, free from my father's scorn, free to continue my studies. I knew I had done wrong as soon as I had the money in my pocket, and I just don't know why I did it. I've never done anything like that before or since.

"It was my good fortune—no, it must have been by God's hand—that I ran into Mr. Blaker outside the school. He knew me so well, he could tell something was wrong, and I blurted out to him what I had done. He didn't criticise, although he was pretty stern. He made me hand over the money to him at once and took it back to the office, but heard my father inside so came away again without being able to return it. He was seen; the boy who spotted him told my father when the theft was reported, and you can imagine the rest."

Complete stillness and, suddenly, Peter sat down and groaned. The spirit that had been apparent among the O.F.S.L. Club members had, however, already begun to make its mark on the younger members of the church. The lad nearest to Peter put an arm about his shoulders and gripped him firmly.

110

Norman watched them, then catching Tom's eye, spoke quietly and steadily.

"Do not be harsh on Peter, I beg of you all. His life was not an easy one—we need not go into details. It was against my wishes that anyone should know this and I'm deeply grieved that it has come out. Maybe, however, it's better for Peter's sake that he should have told you. But, I must insist," and Norman was once again the schoolmaster, hammering out the words to make sure they went home, "this must not go any further—do you all understand? I put all you young people on your honour to keep what Peter has told you to yourselves. Especially those of you who know him at the university—let no rumour of this reach the staff there."

Now Tom spoke. "I'm sure everyone will respect your wishes, Norman. This is not the time for more words; we have all been deeply stirred but I thank God it may be because of this camp that a young man has been led to clear another man's name. We will pray that because of it he will be able to commit his life to the Father's service. I will now say the benediction and then we shall go to our beds."

The usual round of frivolity which accompanied the midnight hours at the camp was missing that night. Instead, the air was filled with a reverent stillness and the murmur of quiet voices as Tom sat talking with Peter beside the fire far into the night. Norman and Janet left the two together. As they said goodnight, Norman whispered to his wife, "I'll explain it all later on, darling. Just wait until I get out to the university and see how things are with Peter there."

Peter travelled back to the city from the camp with Tom and Bev, refusing Alex's offer of a seat in his car and not wanting the company of any of the younger people. He was flushed and embarrassed in front of Janet, and for once she found no words to say to him.

Stunned beyond measure that her husband had gone through so many trials because of this boy, she had to struggle with a feeling of bitterness. She was glad when the journey was over and she could busy herself about her household chores, striving not to think too deeply, praying for a spirit of forgiveness.

*   *   *

Norman took up his duties at the university at the beginning of September, immediately after the Labour Day weekend. He had offered no further explanation to his wife and, although Janet tried to appear as if everything was happy between them, they were both conscious of a restraint.

It was a relief when the O.F.S.L. Club's activities began again in earnest. Over the telephone one day Marion's cheerful voice came to Janet.

"Hi there, dearie," she called, "how about coming along out here and giving me a hand to get the weiner and corn roast ready for tomorrow night? Bill's busy building up the fire but there's a lot to be done with the food, so if you could spare the time, I'd be delighted to have you here."

"I'd love to, Marion." Janet's response was quick. "Perhaps you'd just tell me, though, what exactly a weiner and corn roast is?"

Marion laughed. "Why, it's just hot-dogs and corn-on-the cob. We usually start the club off for the season with a party like this. And as Bill and I have such a large garden, there's plenty of room to have the fire a good distance away from the house. We'll probably have a few marshmallows which can be roasted also, and some pop or coffee to wash it all down."

"Well, Norman has all sorts of things he wants to look into out at the university," Janet said, "so I'm on my own and I'd love to come over. Be with you in half an hour. Besides, it'll give me a chance to have a talk with my adopted 'Mum'," she finished laughingly.

She knew that a few of their closest friends had been told about Peter's revelation at the camp, although everyone had been careful not to let the recognised gossips get hold of the story. Mr. McCall had been having long talks with Peter and the lad was visibly becoming less embarrassed as the friendly folk of the church showed him sympathetic understanding. Janet was aware, however, that his natural nervousness was still there and seemed to increase with each week, until she would have felt sorry for him had it not been for her own rather bitter feelings.

Marion was a good listener and Janet unburdened her heart, telling her friend how difficult she had found it to forgive, and how she wondered why her husband had taken the blame in this way.

"Dearie," said Marion in her kindly way, "you told me once you would always believe in your husband. I'm sure he must have had very good reasons, and he'll tell you in his own good time. Don't fail him now, dear. You've been just marvellous the way you've stood by him. Keep it up and he'll love you the more for it."

Janet sighed. "Somehow," she said hesitantly, "we seem to have got away from each other during the last few weeks. Just when everything seems to be clearing up and my prayers for Norman have been answered, now I myself am filled with resentment. I've struggled and struggled, and can't seem to rid myself of it. I'm sorry for Peter, I suppose, but surely he should have been made to own up on the spot."

"I wonder what would have happened if he had," mused Marion.

Janet looked up sharply. "His father would probably have disowned him," she said without hesitation.

"Maybe that's the answer, then," Marion suggested.

Janet thought for a few moments. "There's more to it than that, I'm sure," she said.

The night of the party was clear and bright, and the O.F.S.L. Club members assembled in gay spirits. There was plenty of fun, lots of jolly singing and leg-pulling all round. Janet's heart began to warm as she noticed how different Norman was among these friends now. Instead of sitting on the edge of the crowd, merely watching, he made his own contribution to the conversation and frivolity. It seemed that it was she, now, who was on the fringe of things.

She wandered off to the bottom of the garden and looked back on the gay scene. Everyone was sitting around munching hot-dogs or gnawing corn-cobs. Janet herself had no hunger and seemed to want nothing but to be quiet. She noticed that Alex was sitting close beside Mary Jane, making sure she wanted for nothing, seeing to her every comfort. Janet was glad. The soft spot she had always felt for Alex was still there and she knew he was happy in Mary Jane's company.

She sank down on to the grass and looked up at the

113

stars, alone with her thoughts for a long time. But suddenly, someone was beside her. It was Beverley.

"Jan, dear, what's the matter? You're not joining in the fun. Are you all right?" her friend's voice was filled with anxiety.

Janet nodded wearily as she said, "I just can't seem to relax, that's all, Bev. I'm sorry. I didn't want to be a wet blanket but somehow I'm all out of gear. I don't know what's the matter with me."

"Come and have something to eat—maybe that'll cheer you up," Bev was practical for a moment.

"No—food doesn't seem to interest me. I'll be O.K., Bev. Don't worry about me. I don't want to spoil your fun."

Bev put her arm around her friend. "My fun will be better if you come along and join in. But first, tell me—is it because of what happened at the camp?" As Janet nodded, she continued, "Jan, then think of Norman's testimony; think how your prayers have been answered. Does it matter about the past? You've always been so sweet about everything. Don't change, Jan."

"It's reaction, I suppose," Janet sighed. Then she brightened. "All right, Bev. I'll try to cheer up, but please, don't offer me food; somehow I just don't feel like any. But I'll come back and join in the fun."

As the evening drew to a close, Mr. McCall stood to take the final devotions.

"I want us to concentrate our thoughts on the beatitudes," he began. "I'll read them with a few additional words here and there, as recorded in the Amplified Bible . . ."

Not very far away, the roar of traffic could be heard as it sped along the main road which ran from east to west through the city and out on to the Prairies. Here in the garden, however, it was peaceful and the minister's voice was clear to everyone.

He reached the third beatitude: "Blessed—happy . . . are the meek (the mild, patient, long-suffering), for they shall inherit the earth!" He paused and for a brief second raised his eyes until they rested on Norman; the next moment he was continuing with his reading. His thought was obvious and as Norman shook the minister's hand at

114

the close of the devotions, he murmured, "I only wish I had been more long-suffering."

"What you did, Norman," Mr. McCall assured him, "portrayed the true spirit of meekness. Do not fret. Your action will surely be blessed."

The words brought comfort to Janet and she kept turning them over in her mind during the next few weeks when September slipped into October and the days became cool.

*   *   *

As the season mellowed, so Norman himself seemed to take on a new dimension. Even at his best, while teaching the grammar schoolboys in England, she had never known him so filled with enthusiasm as now. Each evening he came home with eyes bright, plenty to tell her and nearly always with a smile on his lips. The only time he seemed quiet was when he noticed that she was not quite herself; then he would watch her anxiously until she forced a cheerful air.

On Sundays, Norman's spirit seemed to find release as he sat at the organ. The music that poured forth had such power that the most prosaic member of the congregation was moved. The choir liked the way he handled their practice and responded well. Gradually, Janet felt some of her bitterness slipping away as she rejoiced in the change in her husband.

"Things seem to be cleared up at the church now then, don't they?" asked Betty at the office one day.

Janet stared. Just how much had her work-mate heard? "You've been talking to your friend again, I suppose," she remarked.

Betty inclined her head, looking wise. " 'Twas that organist fellow that took the money, eh? Wanting to pin the blame on to your husband. Makes you wonder just why, though, doesn't it?"

Janet sighed. "You know, Betty, you should be sure you have all the facts before you start getting suspicious."

"Like why it was your husband went to prison in England? That still sounds fishy to me—the caretaker's wife didn't know about that one, although she'd heard that your husband's name had been cleared somehow. Likely you'll both be going back home soon, then?"

"Going back home?" Janet caught her breath. She hadn't given it a thought. Home! Back to Mum, Dad, her brother and sister; Norman's parents—how pleased they would be to know his name was cleared. Home! Her eyes became dreamy and she would have forgotten her companion had not Betty spoken again.

"Well, give us plenty of warning. We'll have to get someone else in your place in good time. And don't forget —I've a late holiday due to me this year."

Janet was so quiet during the evening that Norman eventually put down his newspaper, took her in his arms and, looking deeply into her eyes, asked, "Jan, what's on your mind? You haven't been yourself for weeks—ever since the camp. But tonight, you're all dreamy. What's happened?"

"Norman . . ." she began, then hesitated. Taking a deep breath, she went on quickly, "Now things have been cleared up . . . had you thought of going back . . . back . . . home?"

Her husband stared at her. "Back to England? Just when I've such a wonderful opportunity at the university? Jan, how can you even think of such a thing? Besides, the folks in England don't know the truth yet. Aren't you happy here? I thought you'd made so many friends and enjoyed the church activities so much you were content. What's wrong with you lately?"

She could not bear to see his eyes blazing in that way again. Swiftly she slid her arms round his neck. "Don't look at me like that, Norman. It's just that . . . well Betty said something about it today, and I only wondered. . . ."

"That girl!" Norman's face was grim. "She's been nothing but a worry to you ever since you went into that job. It's time you quit. There's no need for you to go on working now; I'm earning a good salary."

"But, Norman, we want to save up enough to get a better apartment, and buy some furniture of our own, and a car. . . ."

Norman looked at her in exasperation. "Just now you were talking about going back to England!" he exclaimed. "What *do* you want?"

116

Suddenly Janet crumpled into his arms. He drew her close, comforting her. "I'm sorry, darling. But it seems that ever since things became better, you've been unhappy. I thought you were praying that I'd find my faith in God again, that the music would come out in me again. And you know now what happened in England. . . ."

"But I don't know *why*, Norman," Janet lifted a tear-stained face to him.

"So that's it !" Then, very gently, he drew her down into their arm-chair and quietly he began to speak.

"Think of Mr. Sears, Jan. How do you remember him?"

"Oh, a thick-set man, balding, with bright eyes, rather a fierce expression when the boys had done anything wrong. . . ."

"What else—his temper, for instance?"

Janet laughed a little. "Oh yes, his temper. Shocking, wasn't it? It was because he flew into such a rage that the blame rested on you; he wouldn't let you explain, would he?"

"I didn't want to explain. But go on, what else?"

Janet thought for a few moments. "Wh , I don't know. I always used to excuse his temper. I thoug t perhaps his leg was troubling him. You know, people who lose a leg often say they get pain in the stump, and I thought that might have made him bad-tempered at times. He managed remarkably well with that wooden leg, didn't he?"

"Yes—the wooden leg. Ever hear how he lost his leg, Jan?"

She shook her head. "Some kind of boating accident, I believe, although I don't know the details."

Norman looked into her eyes. His words were punctuated with pauses as he said, "He—lost it—saving—my—life."

Janet stared at him. "Norman! You mean, when he save you from drowning—you told us about it that day you rescued Alex."

"That's right. That's why I was always particularly close to him. He'd never let me mention that wooden leg to anyone; forbade me to talk about it to any of our friends. He bore *me* no grudge, although he was bitter about it. He couldn't understand why God had let such a

117

thing happen to him when he was only trying to do a good turn."

"How did it happen?"

"His leg got caught in the screw of the outboard motor, as he was getting me safely into the boat. They rushed him to hospital with me; I came through all right, but they had to amputate his leg."

"Norman," Janet wanted to know, "what has this to do with letting him think you'd stolen the money?"

"Don't you see? When you've saved someone that way, and when you're the one who's been saved, there's a bond between you. You remember how he used to treat me—almost like his own son. It was mainly because of him I got such a good position at the school. It was because of his encouragement that I went to the college of music; it was his influence that got me the position of organist and choirmaster. I always longed to do something for him in return. I couldn't let him experience the bitter disappointment of knowing his only son had turned thief. You know how disappointed he was because he thought I had done the deed—can you imagine how he would have been with Peter?"

"Ruthless!" Janet agreed.

"He would have disowned him on the spot," remarked Norman grimly.

"So that's why you shielded him? Somehow, though, I feel there's more to it than that, isn't there?"

"A bit more. All I can say now is that I thought too much of the man, and of his son for that matter, to let one rather bad mistake ruin their lives."

"Norman—does Mr. Sears know you and Peter are in the same part of Canada?"

"No—apparently he remarked on it when Peter wanted to come but the lad told him that Canada was a big place and he probably wouldn't see me. As the Head didn't know just where I was, he didn't trouble further." Norman laughed suddenly. "He'd be furious if he knew."

"So one sin leads to another," remarked his wife. Norman raised his eyebrows quizzically, so she continued, "A boy steals, then has to lie to cover up the truth. . . ."

She was interrupted by a ring at the door-bell. She went down to answer it and, opening the door, stared at the man outside as if he were a ghost. Putting out her hand she clung to the door-post.

"Janet," the man's tones were distinctly English, "how are you, my dear? Sorry to give you such a shock, coming unexpectedly like this. But I must see Norman—at once." It was more of a command than a request and spoken in the loud, firm manner of the natural schoolteacher.

The voice had great carrying power and had reached the upstairs rooms. Janet, still speechless, turned as her husband came hurrying down the stairs. He, too, seemed bereft of speech, pausing half-way down the stairs and just gazing.

"Aren't you going to ask me in?" The man's voice was pleasant.

Janet stood aside for him as he limped over the door-step and followed them upstairs, holding the rail tightly while he pulled one stiff leg up step by step.

12

STILL UNABLE to speak, Janet indicated the armchair to their unexpected visitor and automatically went into the kitchen to put on the kettle and get out some cups and saucers.

The man looked about him. "Cosy little room this, Norman. Sorry to give you such a shock, turning up like this. I expect you're wondering what it's all about?"

Norman found his voice at last. "Yes, Mr. Sears, it is a surprise. The fact is, we were just talking about you and it was a bit uncanny the way you appeared at that moment."

"Talking about me, eh?" smiled Mr. Sears. "And not very pleasant talking, I shouldn't wonder!"

"On the contrary, Mr. Sears," Janet put in as she brought in a tray of cups. "Norman was telling me . . . well, he was speaking well of you, sir." she tailed off, suddenly realising their conversation should not be repeated to this man of all people.

Mr. Sears looked from one to the other intently.

"I'll come straight to the point, Norman . . . Janet," he began. "I've come all this way to apologise. I did you just about the gravest harm I could do you, Norman, and even a letter could not convey my regrets—I had to come in person; I had to come to apologise . . . and to offer you back your job at the school."

The gasp which came from Norman was echoed instantly by his wife. Blankly they looked at the man, unable to believe their ears.

"I know, I know," Mr. Sears almost laughed. "I'm the last man you'd ever believe could grovel in contrition. Maybe I am. But this was such a big wrong . . . well, what else could I do?" He rose and held out his hand to Norman. "I'm sorry, boy . . . what a trite phrase that is, to be sure . . . but if ever anyone *was* sorry, it's me. I don't know how I could have thought such a thing about you. And then to be so harsh, taking the case to court as well as influencing so many others against you . . . it was unforgivable. Truth is, it was such a shock, and the disappointment was so great—I had always thought so much of you . . . but what's the use of excusing myself? *Can* you forgive?"

Norman flung back his head and on his face was a glow almost of pride. He took the older man's hand again. "Of course, sir. I understood all along how you felt. Shall we say . . . forgiven *and* forgotten?"

Mr. Sears himself was silent now and Janet, noticing his shamefaced air, felt sorry for him. But the question which hung in the air between the three of them seemed to make a barrier, despite Norman's magnanimous words. It had to be voiced and it was Norman who spoke.

"I must know, sir, are you aware of the full truth now?"

Mr. Sears nodded and his sigh was so deep that Norman guided him back to the arm-chair, put his hand on the man's shoulder and looked him in the eyes.

"Who told you?"

"I had a letter—from Peter . . . my son—no, I refuse to call him my son any longer," and now Mr. Sear's voice held the old strident tones they knew so well. "He wrote and confessed everything—said he couldn't go on parading as a Christian and letting you be blamed for his guilt—I should think not, either!"

Norman signalled Janet to bring in the coffee and for a while neither spoke. Then, choosing each word with care, Norman began, "I knew you'd feel this way, Mr. Sears. That's partly why I let the blame fall on me. There was another reason, however. . . ."

"And what was that?"

Norman hesitated. "I can't say, tonight. As a matter of fact, I should receive news tomorrow which may confirm my thoughts about Peter. Then I shall be able to tell you everything. Mr. Sears, does Peter know you're here?"

Mr. Sears shook his head. "No, I've not communicated with him, and I don't intend to see him. . . ."

Norman raised his hand. "If you don't mind my saying so, sir, perhaps you should leave decisions like that until I've proved something to you. If I may suggest it, will you come back here tomorrow afternoon. . . I presume you're booked in at a hotel?" As the man nodded, Norman continued, "Well then, if you come back at about three, I'll probably have some news for you. *Then* you can decide whether or not you'll see your son."

Greatly mystified, Mr. Sears eventually agreed. When he had gone, Janet began to question, but her husband would tell her no more.

"Sorry, Jan," he said, "I don't want to say anything tonight. I've only ever confided my thoughts about Peter to one other person—Walter Turner, the maths teacher at the school. He was keeping an eye on Peter when I . . . when I was in prison. He and I have similar opinions about the boy. In a way, it was a wonderful blessing that Peter came here to this university, for I shall be able to get confirmation about our hopes for him. That is, if the staff there agree with me. By the way, can you manage to be here tomorrow afternoon, too? I thought you said something this morning about taking tomorrow off for some reason?"

Janet hesitated and busied herself with clearing the cups. "I have to go out in the morning. But yes, I can be here in the afternoon." She looked up suddenly and laughed. "Actually, I wouldn't miss it for anything; after all, I want to know just why you took that blame."

Norman smiled but said nothing.

* * *

Over lunch the next day, Norman remarked to his wife. "You're looking very pretty today, darling—in fact, I'd go so far as to say you're radiant. I haven't seen you look like that for ages. Is it because you're so excited to hear what I have to say to Mr. Sears this afternoon?"

Janet smiled secretly to herself. "You're not looking exactly glum yourself, Norman," she evaded his question. "Good news?"

Norman's dark eyes were bright. "Just about the best news I could have heard—but I'll say no more until Mr. Sears arrives."

The man was punctual, as always, and it was obvious he was bursting with curiosity, although he adopted a casual air in his effort not to show his feelings.

"Come now, Norman, what's it all about? Some great mystery, is it?"

Norman stood up and began to speak. "Mr. Sears, even my wife doesn't know what I am about to tell you. It's something I've suspected ever since Peter came under my tuition some six years back. I've discussed it with Walter Turner only, and he was of the same opinion. All we needed was confirmation by someone more qualified to judge. I decided to consult the science professor at this university. I got him to look at samples of Peter's work and have a chat with him. He was looking through the lad's books last night. Now he has given me the confirmation I wanted . . ." he paused.

"Well?" Mr. Sears raised a quizzical eyebrow.

"Your son Peter, Mr. Sears," and now Norman seemed to be driving home his words with hard emphasis. "Your son will not only make a *good* scientist, Mr. Sears. He will be *brilliant*. In fact, the words of the professor here were, 'That boy's a genius.'"

Janet gasped and Mr. Sears sat forward in his chair. his eyes never leaving Norman's face.

"Norman. . . ." Janet could not keep quiet. "*That's* why you took the blame? You didn't want anything to ruin Peter's career, as it would have done if he'd been found out. He's such a sensitive nature, he would never have got over a prison sentence and all the publicity."

Norman nodded and smiled gratefully at his wife. "Exactly, Jan. I guessed you'd understand once you knew.

But I didn't want to tell anyone my suspicions about Peter until I was sure, and I didn't want to raise his hopes too much, either. So I kept my thoughts to myself. That boy used to astonish me the way he grasped theories and went on to make experiments and work out possibilities. Do you know, Mr. Sears . . ." he continued looking levelly at the headmaster, "your son had got to the stage even before I . . . er . . . left the school, when he was almost teaching me. I knew he would go far and I suspected he was exceptional. Now the professor here wants to recommend him for a scholarship at an American university where they specialise in atomic experiments."

It was Mr. Sears's turn to gasp. "You mean that, Norman? You actually mean my boy's brilliant?" Norman nodded. "I never realised anything like this. . . . But why then, should he do such a thing as steal money?"

Norman stood up and shrugged. "A moment of weakness, shall we say? And maybe—if I may put it kindly—he didn't have very much pocket money?"

Mr. Sears lowered his eyes. "Umm. I didn't want him to have too much—thought he'd get into trouble with money to spare. Nevertheless," and again his voice was firm, "it was a despicable thing to do, and to let you carry the blame —no, I can't forgive him. I shall go back to England and tell the full story to all those who think badly of you. . . ."

Once again Norman bent over the man and looked intently into his eyes. "Mr. Sears. are you going to throw away all that I went through for that boy? I'm not begging sympathy, I'm merely making a point. Don't let it all be to no avail, I beg of you, sir. I won't deny it cost me plenty. I pray it won't be in vain."

For a long time, Mr. Sears was silent and the moments ticked by while Janet and Norman waited in suspense. Eventually, he lifted his eyes.

"All right, Norman, you win. I'll forgive him. But I am going to clear your name at the church. . . ."

"I'll let you do that," Norman smiled. "Although if you can do so without dragging Peter into it, so much the better."

"I'll find a way. But . . . what do we do now? When can I see Peter?" Mr. Sears spoke with characteristic determination, having made up his mind.

The young couple smiled and Norman turned to the window. "I guessed you'd make this decision, Mr. Sears, so I arranged to borrow a car to drive you out to the university at once." He looked at Janet. "Alex agreed to let me use his car," he explained. "I see he's left it ready outside the church. So, shall we go?"

Mr. Sears rose stiffly to his feet. "When you come back to England, Norman, I'll raise your salary and you can buy your own car."

"When I come back to England?" Norman raised his eyebrows.

"I told you—your old job is waiting for you, boy!"

There was a pause and then Norman spoke carefully. "That's very good of you, Mr. Sears. I expect Peter told you in his letter that I've just accepted a post at the university. I'd rather like to stay for one term at least. There's several new ideas I want to see into."

"Understandable," Mr. Sears seemed willing to agree to anything now. "Please yourself when you come; you'll be welcome whenever you decide to show yourself at the school again. And I know the choir at the church will welcome you with open arms. No doubt your pretty wife will be glad to be home again, eh?" he turned kindly to Janet.

She hesitated. "Well, in a way we've enjoyed life here, Mr. Sears. I'd really made up my mind to stay, but it's up to Norman. . . ."

"We'll think about it," Norman said briefly and led the way out to the car.

He had arranged with Peter to meet them in a quiet spot of the campus, having told him of his father's arrival. The boy was there, waiting, as they drew up and he came uncertainly to open the car door for his father.

The older man and his son stood for a long time looking at each other. Norman made no attempt to get out of the car and signalled Janet to remain there also. They both knew they had done all that was possible to heal the breach and that now everything rested between Peter and his father. So, they watched and silently prayed.

Then Mr. Sears began to smile as he held out his hand.

"I think we'd better just put the past behind us, eh, son?" they heard him say quietly.

Peter's flush was as deep as Janet had ever seen. He

gripped his father's hand as though he'd never let it go. "I won't ever let you down again, Dad," he said emphatically.

Norman had left the car engine running and now he quietly backed it away. There would be plenty for the headmaster and his son to talk over and Peter would make sure his father had transport back into the city. Quietly they drove off the campus and along beside the river where, some months back, they had been skiing in heavy snow. The car parked, they got out and strolled down to gaze at the water.

Although it was October, there was a warm spell—part of a glorious Indian Summer. On the opposite bank of the river the maple trees still held most of their leaves, foliage which had turned to an autumnal red; around them the poplars and birch were golden. A mystic beauty held the young couple almost in a trance; it seemed the whole earth was resting, waiting for something beautiful to happen. There was an air of expectancy, or was it urgency? Squirrels chased each other from tree to tree in search of a winter supply of nuts, rabbits scampered among the undergrowth and the last of the birds gathered ready for their long flight to the southern States. They knew it was but a lull before the onset of the long white winter, but nevertheless the air was sweet with pungent memories of a brilliant summer.

"Norman," Janet spoke at last, "will you take up Mr. Sears's offer and go back to England?"

He turned to smile down at his wife and gently put an arm around her.

"What would you like to do?" he asked kindly.

"No." Janet shook her head, "it really depends on you . . . and whether . . ." and now she lifted shining eyes to his and spoke softly, almost tenderly, ". . . whether you'd like our first child to be born here in Canada or back in England."

Norman gazed at her for a full moment while he took in the implication of her words, and as she nodded to his unspoken question, he gathered her to him and asked, "When, Jan?"

"In the spring," she told him. "The doctor confirmed it this morning."

The sun shone down on them from a cloudless sky and
125

all around the wild creatures continued to prepare for hibernation. Quietly they stood watching.

"I think we'll settle for a little Canadian," Norman said at last. "After that, we'll see. Oh, Jan darling, it's all we needed to make our happiness complete."

"And to enable us to inherit the earth?" she queried softly.

His eyes were eloquent and she smiled as she remembered the dark scowls of a year ago. Resolutely she put the memories behind her, content now and satisfied that her faith in her husband had been completely justified.